ACCLAIM FOR **Margaret Bullitt-Jonas**'s
Holy Hunger

"Margaret Bullitt-Jonas has produced a riveting story of recovery from food addiction. She's also created unforgettable portraits of her father and mother, and a thought-provoking account of the role of faith in healing. Because faith is at the center of the story, this isn't one of the current needy-victim memoirs but a complex narrative of a stormy passage to adulthood."   —Jill Ker Conway, author of *True North*

"[Margaret Bullitt-Jonas] conquered food addiction by feeding [her] spirit. . . . It's her faith, daily prayer and meditation that gave [her] the strength to resist temptation."
        —*The Boston Globe*

"Fearlessly honest. . . . Bullitt-Jonas refuses to play the blame game; instead, she infuses this intensely personal account of human frailty and addiction with empathy and compassion for all the principals involved in her story. A harrowing personal chronicle that reads like a novel."   —*Booklist*

"A memoir told with refreshing candor and charm, devoid of self-pity. Bullitt-Jonas is immediately likable . . . we rejoice when she claims her life for herself."   —*The Living Church*

"What Bullitt-Jonas does especially well is to tell her story in clear, expressive prose. Others who have struggled with overeating should find comfort in reading what this woman has gone through and how she combated her demons"
—*Rocky Mountain News*

"Bullitt-Jonas's impassioned story of discovery and recovery is a powerful invitation to allow ourselves to face unmet desire. Once met and embraced, the hungers of addiction can be recognized as guides who reveal that we are in a holy place, on the point of knowing ourselves to be the desire of God's heart."   —Martin L. Smith,
Superior of the Society of Saint John the Evangelist
and author of *The Word is Very Near You*

"[An] unusually well-written memoir of recovery.... With a steady hand, Bullitt-Jonas describes the years of whole pies and batches of pancakes, the fasting and compulsive exercise by which she tried to escape her pain, until she discovered that twelve-step programs helped her listen to herself. [*Holy Hunger* is] her account of her spiritual triumph."
—*Publishers Weekly*

"Bullitt-Jonas writes with an honesty and grace that nourish our hearts and deepen our capacity to understand and heal. Exquisitely written and so real, *Holy Hunger* is a new 'bible' to which I will return again and again for inspiration, quotes, and wisdom."   —Catherine Steiner-Adair,
Harvard Eating Disorders Center

"A moving and well-told narrative of universal hunger and hope."   —*Minneapolis Twin Cities Revue*

Margaret Bullitt-Jonas
Holy Hunger

Margaret Bullitt-Jonas was born in Cambridge, Massachusetts, and lives with her husband and young son in a suburb of Boston. She leads retreats in both the United States and Canada and has been involved with 12-step spirituality for eighteen years. She is an Episcopal priest who serves as Associate Rector of All Saints Parish, Brookline, and as a lecturer at Episcopal Divinity School.

Holy Hunger

A WOMAN'S JOURNEY FROM FOOD ADDICTION
TO SPIRITUAL FULFILLMENT

Margaret Bullitt-Jonas

Vintage Books

A DIVISION OF RANDOM HOUSE, INC.

NEW YORK

FIRST VINTAGE BOOKS EDITION, APRIL 2000

Copyright © 1998 by Margaret Bullitt-Jonas

All rights reserved under International and Pan-American Copyright
Conventions. Published in the United States of America by Vintage
Books, a division of Random House, Inc., New York, and simultaneously
in Canada by Random House of Canada Limited, Toronto. Originally
published in hardcover in the United States by Alfred A. Knopf,
a division of Random House, Inc., New York, in 1998.

Vintage and colophon are registered trademarks of Random House, Inc.

Owing to limitations of space, all acknowledgments for permission to
reprint previously published material may be found on page 255.

The Library of Congress has cataloged the Knopf edition as follows:

Bullitt-Jonas, Margaret.
Holy hunger : a memoir of desire / Margaret Bullitt-Jonas. —1st ed.
p. cm.
Includes bibliographical references.
ISBN 0-375-40094-X (hardcover)
1. Compulsive eaters—United States—Biography. 2. Compulsive
eating—United States—Religious aspects. 3. Eating disorders. I. Title.
RC552.C65B85 1999
616' .85Sdc21   98-87803
CIP

Vintage ISBN: 0-375-70087-0

Author photograph © Peter Vanderwarker

www.vintagebooks.com

Printed in the United States of America
10 9 8 7 6 5 4 3 2 1

For my parents

They did not stop their craving,
though the food was still in their
mouths.

PSALM 78:30

Contents

Acknowledgments

*T*he process of writing *Holy Hunger* confirms the wisdom that sharing a story, whether a rough draft or a tearful confession, can be redemptive. A story, a life, can be transformed as it is heard. I am grateful to the community that in different ways "listened" me, and this story, into being.

I give thanks for the late Henri J. M. Nouwen, who, a year before his death in 1996, spent three months of his sabbatical living with our family. When I told him that I wanted to write about desire, he urged me to reflect on what I'd learned from direct experience. Henri's suggestion helped set the book on its present course.

I am thankful for friends who read portions of the manuscript and offered thoughtful response: Gillian McMullen, Ruth Redington, Deborah Little, Lawrie Hurtt. For the support of the Freedom Writers group, Julia Slayton and Tansy Chapman. For the exquisite care with which Maria De Carvalho and Julia Gatta responded to the text, and for our lively conversations about the surprising ways of God.

I am grateful for the people who helped me navigate the period of my life that is covered in this book. For Jeffrey McIntyre, for his kindness, professional skill, and insight into addiction. For my friend Gillian McMullen, who cared enough to tell the truth. For Joan Bolker, who with apparently infinite patience coached me through the last stages of my dissertation.

For Al Kershaw, exuberant priest and prophet. For Barbara Pizer, whose compassionate listening helped me find coherence in my fragments of self and whose reading of the manuscript added clarity, grit, and nuance. And for my companions in recovery everywhere, whose desire for wholeness continues to give me courage, strength, and hope.

You are healers all.

Thanks to Elizabeth Valentine, whose touch helped keep body, mind, and spirit connected during the sometimes arduous process of writing.

To Rosemary Brennan, C.S.J., whose spiritual guidance offered me stability, perspective, and the relief of a good laugh when writing this book felt like running the rapids.

To the Society of St. John the Evangelist, especially Martin L. Smith, SSJE, and M. Thomas Shaw, SSJE, for the ways they inspire and strengthen so many seekers. To my dear friends in the SSJE Colleagues Group, for their companionship along the way. And for the hospitality offered at Emery House, where some of this book was written.

Thanks to my colleagues and friends at Episcopal Divinity School and to the Parish of All Saints, Brookline, especially its rector, David Killian, for their ongoing witness to the light.

To Belinda Berman-Real and Terry Real, who helped me find my agent, Beth Vesel, and to Beth, who believed in this book from the beginning.

To the professionals at Knopf whose skill and care contributed so much to this project: Debra Helfand, Virginia Tan, Claire Bradley Ong, Carol Carson, Stephen Amsterdam, Sophie Cottrell, Webb Younce, and especially my beloved editor, Jane Garrett, who welcomed this book, and its author, into print.

I am particularly grateful to Dorothy Austin, whose sensitive ear for language and whose psychological and spiritual savvy had a profound and gracious influence not only on the book but on its author as well. Her contribution is visible on every page.

Thanks go to my sisters and my brother, whose lives are interwoven with mine and whose friendship I cherish. To my stepdaughter, Chris Labich, and her creative, can-do spirit. To my son, Sam, whose ebullient energy gives me joy. To my husband and dearest friend, Robert Jonas, who shared the vision of what this book could mean to me and to others, and who was intimately involved in every aspect of this project, from fixing my computer to staying up late to read yet another revision. His presence means Home.

In the end, it is my mother who deserves the greatest thanks. The encouragement she offered from beginning to end speaks volumes about her integrity. I am grateful for her critique of the final drafts of the manuscript and for her generous permission to let this sometimes painful tale be told.

Holy Hunger

Lost and Found

When I was sixteen, I enrolled in Outward Bound and promptly got lost in the woods of northern Minnesota. Armed with a compass, a map, matches, tents, sleeping bags, and half a dozen sandwiches, we six girls made nearly every mistake in the book. First we discounted the map and the compass. Then we took what we thought would be a shortcut across a ridge. No such luck. It turned out to be a false trail, a trail to nowhere—at least nowhere we wanted to go. When it started to get dark, we decided not to pitch our tents, instead spreading out our sleeping bags under the stars. It didn't look like it would rain. And anyway, what if it did? By early evening it had started to pour. We were soaked, our sleeping bags wet through.

There we were, huddled in the dark in our sodden bags, when we heard some sounds not far off in the woods. Urgent, plaintive sounds. What in the world made a sound like that? Maybe a moose. A bellowing moose. We polled each other for information and came up short. Were moose aggressive creatures? Were they likely to attack? We didn't have a clue.

"Stay calm," we whispered to each other. "Don't make a sound. Don't attract its attention."

We found out later that the cries we heard were the shouts of the rescue party sent out to search for us.

Fortunately, I did know that when you're lost in the woods, it's best to stay put. For the next three days and nights, we drank the rainwater that we collected in our outspread ponchos. We tried to stay warm by clinging to each other through the long chilly nights. We kept up our spirits by telling our life stories. We divvied up our last chocolate bar and the leftover bits of stale sandwich, telling ourselves that we were explorers, that surely we'd survive. And we listened to the drone of a small airplane overhead. Sometimes we could see it and would run into the clearing to yell ourselves hoarse. On the fourth day, one of us, a former Girl Scout, remembered how to start a fire from wet wood. A thick plume of smoke coiled its way up into the sky. Before long we could hear the distant buzz of an airplane. Racing into the clearing, we shouted and waved our arms. At last, at long last, we saw the airplane tip its wing. Within an hour, the search party had arrived and we were on our way home.

For weeks thereafter I couldn't hear the sound of an airplane engine without a shudder. At once I would be brought back to the desperate, anxious longing to be found, to be seen, to be set free. How fragile our rescues seem in retrospect. What an extraordinary confluence of events needs to conspire for each of us, and all of us, to find our way home.

There are many ways of being lost. Even more ways of putting oneself in harm's way. In my case, I wandered into compulsive overeating and stayed there, trapped, not knowing how to find a way out. For years I was lost in a wasteland that could well have taken my life, without a clue as to how I'd gotten there, not knowing, much of the time, whether I even wanted to be found, whether I wanted anyone to catch sight of me and point out a path. It took me a lot longer than four days to get out. Addiction can go deeper than the Minnesota woods. As I look back over those years, grim with obsession and secrecy, I'm amazed at the contrast with my present life and the realization that it might not have turned out this way. I could have stayed lost forever.

But I did find a way out. And that is the story I want to tell. I hope it will be a map for some reader I haven't yet met. Maybe this story will give someone courage to take the next step. Maybe some people who have lost their way will find here the guideposts, the landmarks, that can help them discover their own path out.

When, by the grace of God, you've managed to save your life, you want to pass on what you've learned. I want to tell everyone who is lost: There are things you can do if your compass is missing. There are ways to collect rain until you've found your own spring. There are voices to which you should pay no attention, such as the voice encouraging shortcuts that go off to the wrong place. And there are voices to which you should cry out "Yes!" and "Here I am!" rather than mistaking them, as I did, for the voice of a moose.

CHAPTER I

Starving in the Snow

*L*ate at night, the supermarket is garish and dazzling in the cold glare of neon light. I walk in, trying to look as calm, competent, capable, as possible. I try to blend in, to be unobtrusive, to draw no attention to myself. I'm here on a raid, a heist, and I want no one to notice. I'd wear a hood over my head if I thought I could get away with it. Casually I pick up a plastic yellow basket, choose some yogurt and a loaf of bread. Then, very casually, as if I just happened to think of it, I take a look at the boxes of day-old bakery goods. I flip through them, looking for doughnuts. I act as if it doesn't matter much whether I find any or not. I'm the only one in this store who knows I'm looking for my "stuff." I'm here to get the goods. I don't have to use a weapon or threaten anyone. I don't have to hold anyone up: I have the money for my drug of choice, which is food. But I'm as hard-core as the guy on the street corner who stops passersby to demand money for his fix.

"Hey, girlie," he calls out to me in a tone at once wheedling and belligerent, "ya got a little something to help a guy?"

I pretend to be deaf. I look away, quickening my pace. I make no eye contact, acknowledge no connection between us—me, a well-dressed, well-educated young woman; he, an unshaven hustler with no known address. I conceal the truth, but the fact is this: we are compatriots under the skin. We inhabit the same dark land. What differentiates me from the addicts who roam the park and sleep on grates is that my drug is legal, I have the money to get it, and I can still pass as normal.

When I arrive in the supermarket, I sometimes spot a fat person with lonely eyes already picking over the bakery goods. As with the drunks and the junkies, I pretend we have nothing in common. I approach without saying a word, peering over the stranger's shoulder, impatient to get my hands on the boxes of day-old cookies and pies. I suppose I could buy fancy, name-brand cookies, and sometimes I do, but it's the leftovers that tend to attract me most—scraps, cheap goods that go down fast. I disguise my urgent, anxious greed; I keep my face calm, a mask of repose. I hope that anyone looking at me will assume it's only an accident that I—a person of average size, a thirty-year-old woman who looks perfectly normal—happen to be scavenging beside someone so fat. But I never even look around to see who might be watching. When the fat person steps away, I make my move. I finger the baked goods and make my selection as fast as I can, trying not to reveal my hurry. I'm intently focused on the task before me. I keep my head down, eyes forward. In the Star Market at 10:00 p.m., I meet no one's eyes if I can help it.

Every act of addiction is a criminal act, the most ferocious of criminal acts against the self. Like many crimes, addiction insists on stealth, secrecy, and isolation. And it ends in shame. The addict in the middle of a binge doesn't want to be seen by anyone, neither friend nor stranger, and most of all, not by the addict herself. All authentic human connection must be severed. As I put my basket on the checkout counter and open my purse, I'm elaborately deadpan with the clerk (You see? I came in for yogurt and bread. It's just a coincidence that I bought these lemon crullers; they happen to be boxed by the half-dozen, so that's why I picked up six).

Every con artist guards her secrets.

Then I calmly leave the store, clutching my stuff in a brown paper bag. I know better than to break into a run. A getaway must always be calm, unless you're under fire. Safe at last in the car, I sit huddled with the windows rolled up, eating one doughnut after another. If I could shoot up the crullers, I would. If I could mainline them straight into my brain, I'd do it in a heartbeat. Other addicts might try to swig their troubles away, but as for me, I'm going to take a big hit of sugar and shove it into my body. I'm going to blot out the pain any way that I can, as quickly as I can, as thoroughly as I can. I'm going to stuff down my fear, anger, and sorrow until I feel nothing at all, until I'm stupefied and numb.

Tomorrow, maybe, I won't eat anything to speak of. I'll go for a long run, maybe plan another diet. Maybe I'll stop doing this, stop having to stuff myself like this. Maybe tomorrow everything will be different. Maybe.

I've often wondered how I got so trapped. What half-truths did I consume as a child? What lies? How did my desires go so awry?

So much was unspeakable when I was growing up. To the outside world, my family presented every sign of happiness and success. My handsome father was a dashing, high-spirited professor of English at Harvard University, a popular lecturer among the students, the youngest faculty member ever invited to serve as master of a Harvard house. My mother was the beautiful, Radcliffe-educated daughter of a wealthy Midwestern newspaper family. A trustee of Radcliffe, she served on its admissions committee. She faithfully attended Christ Church every Sunday, kept an immaculate house, and, as wife of the Master of Quincy House, was responsible over the years for entertaining thousands of Harvard faculty, staff, and students.

As if repeating a refrain that is sung to comfort and to soothe, we four children told ourselves again and again that we were having a happy childhood.

But much of our lives could not be acknowledged or named, neither to ourselves nor to each other nor to anybody else. When I was ten years old, my best friend asked me why my mother always seemed so serious. I couldn't answer her. I'd never noticed it. My mother's almost perpetually somber mood was too familiar, too linked with who she was for me. Even more invisible, more unspeakable, than my mother's depression was my father's drinking. The acute panic before the beginning of classes that could be relieved only by Scotch; the lengthy cocktail hours that triggered a predictable slide into melancholy; the late evenings alone, sitting in front of a blank TV screen, talking to himself and nursing a drink—none of this could be noticed or named, much less discussed. A taboo arose among us, all the more powerful because it seemed to come from nowhere, and because it seemed as invisible and essential to life as the air we breathed. Don't say what you see, don't feel what you feel, don't speak, don't ask questions, don't rock the boat.

We are told by clinicians that children who grow up in alcoholic homes never witness or experience real feelings, but only the defenses against feelings. When parents, for whatever reason, can't bear their own desires and fears, they find it difficult to tolerate and respond to their children's feelings in a way that will help the children trust their own inner experience. Such children grow up mastering all kinds of strategies for ducking, dodging, and burying their feelings.

I know I certainly did. I became expert in the art of avoidance. I knew how to be a superintellect, able to rationalize, minimize, and argue myself out of a feeling at a moment's notice. I could be a superachiever too, so busy accomplishing, performing, and proving my worth that I never had to stop and feel my basic loneliness and sense of loss. Sometimes I avoided feelings by focusing on the "rules." I was a perfectionist bent on getting every detail "right," ready to pounce with condemnation on anyone—myself included—who got it "wrong." Sometimes I played the comic, the ever-cheerful, perpetually smiling mascot who made my family laugh. "Look how happy we are!" my grateful family seemed to cry. "No problems here!" Then there were the obsessions I could get wrapped up in as the years went by—smoking, eating, drinking, working, shopping, finding someone to yearn for obsessively, or someone to rescue. All these tactics left me numb, deadened to any vivid feeling, confused about what I really felt, really wanted. There must be an infinite number of ways to avoid the deepest feelings, the deepest longings of the heart.

So who knows what I felt, who knows what I was really longing for, when as a child I would secretly slip a piece of bread into my pocket after lunch. I certainly can't recall any inner voice explaining it to me. Who knows what I told myself? I had no idea what it was—a compulsion, a need, a desire, an unspoken something or other—that caused my small hand to dart out, reach for an extra slice of bread, then slip it quietly, unseen, into my pocket. A secret known only to myself, but not even to me.

Certainly I was not hungry for food. Perhaps it was human contact that I missed. Perhaps there moved within me a hidden yearning to speak my grief about my sad mother, a desire to express my confusion about my volatile and sometimes frightening father, a longing to share a child's anger, wonder, sadness, and joy with another human being. But I could find no one to hear me. None of these longings could even be named. I could not have said what it was that I wanted. All I knew was that I was starving.

And that was the game that I'd play in my room after lunch: I was a wild horse alone in a blizzard, starving in the snow. Back and forth across my bed I cantered and trotted, walked and staggered, slowly dying of starvation, my head bent down, my windswept mane heavy with snow. I was lost in the storm. I was starving and alone. And then—Aha! I found a piece of bread! I nuzzled it. I licked it. Slowly I nibbled at it. The blizzard still roared around me, but now I had a bit of nourishment. I would see how long I could make it last. Maybe I would live after all.

Quincy House was built for adults, no doubt about it, nine stories of brick, concrete, and glass rising on the outskirts of Harvard Square, just a stone's throw from the Charles River. We moved into the penthouse on the top floors of Quincy House right after it was built in 1959. I was almost eight years old. To me, everything about the place was impressive. I was proud to live there. My father must be important, being in charge of all this, so it followed that I was important too. Besides, no one else in my third-grade class had an elevator.

Still, I was somewhat daunted by our new quarters; clearly the penthouse had not been designed with children in mind. A long hallway ran half the length of the eighth floor. It was lined with my father's collection of eighteenth-century prints and opened onto a formal dining room and living room. Beyond the parquet floors and Oriental rugs stretched a gravel-covered terrace with a trellised arch down the center. Who could say how many guests would gather here over the years, indoors and out, their hands reaching for countless delicacies laid out on countless trays, innumerable streams of cocktails easing their way down countless throats, the distant sounds of laughter and impassioned conversation floating down the long hall to the children on the other side of the house? My siblings and I learned, when company came, to smile politely, pass a tray, perhaps, and then disappear quickly behind the door that divided the public side of the house from the private living area.

We retreated to the playroom, the library, the master bedroom, or our own bedrooms downstairs on the seventh floor, out of the way of the grown-up world.

I always got the feeling that children didn't quite belong in Quincy House. The front-door buzzer was too high for us to reach, too high, in fact, for the average adult, so that an extra stone step had to be placed on the ground beneath it. Looking back now, it seems to me that something about the whole place was too high for the average adult, no less the average child, and that none of us could quite live up to it. So many of us got lost there, adults and children alike, as if we had not paid enough attention to the map, or the woods were overgrown, the trees too high, the path too dark to see.

The first one of our household to go was the smallest. Early one morning shortly after we moved into Quincy House, I saw our dog fall off the roof. Corky was a Welsh corgi, a short little dog with wiry brown hair and a stub of a tail. He had the run of the terrace, eight floors up. Somehow, in all the bustle and distraction of the move, no one had paid much attention to the fact that the chain-link fence encircling the terrace wasn't finished yet. Corky liked to slip through the hole in the fence and run out along the terrace ledge. Obviously there was a risk that he might fall, but where else could he run? We lived in the city and had no yard. Besides, my father said, the fence would be finished soon enough. Corky was a nimble fellow. He could fend for himself for a while. My parents had more important things to attend to than this one little dog. Unpacking and moving in was only the beginning. My father had lectures to prepare, classes to teach, exams to write, papers to read, hundreds of students to oversee. My mother had a large household to manage; a new staff to hire, train, and supervise; and soon there would be hordes of guests to feed and entertain.

I was standing right beside the ledge when Corky fell. We'd gotten out of bed before dawn to watch an eclipse. A few students had been invited to join our family on the terrace. Corky was running back and forth along the ledge, excited by all the people gathered at this early hour. I saw him take a step backward, as if he meant simply to turn around. I saw the surprise in his eyes when he found no footing. Then I saw him drop over the edge and disappear.

I didn't have the courage to go look for his body, so my father and older sister took the elevator downstairs together. Later they told me that Corky had bent a parking meter in his fall and made a messy landing in the driveway. He was buried in a construction pit behind Quincy House. The library was built over him, as if his broken body had sprouted books.

Our next dog, another Welsh corgi, never went out on the ledge. By the time he arrived the terrace fence was finished, and he stayed safely inside its bounds. Corky the Second, as we called him, didn't fall off the roof. Instead, he went mad. At least, that's what we children were told: He "went mad" and he had to be "put to sleep."

It began innocently enough. Corky the Second was nosing around our playroom one day when he picked up a safety pin in his mouth. Afraid that he would prick his tongue, I reached impulsively into the puppy's mouth to extract the pin. The dog was startled, and he nipped my fingers. It wasn't much of a bite, but I ran off to tell my parents.

That might have been the end of it, but several days later, my older sister got into a fight with my father. Who can say what she'd done to upset him, or whether he was drunk at the time. All she remembers is racing down the hall as fast as she could, down the stairs, into her bedroom, my angry father running after her, Corky the Second barking anxiously at their flying heels. The dog was my older sister's staunchest ally, her dearest friend. My sister fed him every day and brushed his wiry hair, and at night the two of them would curl up together in her bed. Not surprisingly, the dog leaped at once to my sister's defense.

By now my father was furious at my sister and increasingly irritated by the barking at his feet. His anger shifted to the dog, and he chased the puppy under my sister's bed. Although my sister begged him to leave her dog alone, nothing could stop my father when he was in that mood. Getting down on his hands and knees, he peered under the bed. The dog was cowering against the far wall. My father yanked off one of his shoes and, reaching as far back as he could, began slapping his shoe into the darkness, searching for haunches, head, anything to hit. Corky the Second snarled and bared his teeth. When the pounding shoe came too close, he sank his teeth into my father's hand.

My father sprang back, nursing the injury. "That's a mean dog," he yelled. "A mean dog. We'll have to get rid of it. It bit Margaret and now it's bitten me. That dog should be killed."

"You can't do that!" my sister cried. "That's not fair! He was frightened, that's all. He's not mean. He's a good dog. He's *my* dog. You can't kill him."

But my father was adamant, triumphant. He'd won. The mean one, the mad one, would be sent away and killed. My father would see to it.

My sister went to our mother to plead her case. Mother tried to console her, but there was nothing that she could do. Her husband wasn't about to change his mind. Going along with his wishes seemed the only way to keep the peace.

"Then I'll run away!" my sister said. "I'll leave this family forever if you kill my dog!"

Her threats and pleas were no use. There was nothing my sister could say to change the decision, nothing she could do. Within the week, our mother scooped up Corky the Second, put him in the car, and drove him off to the vet. The vet was surprised when she asked him to "put the dog to sleep," but he didn't offer much resistance. That was the end of Corky the Second.

We never got another dog after that.

My older sister did run away, as she'd promised, but where could she go? She was only ten. She took the elevator downstairs, walked down DeWolfe Street and across Memorial Drive. There, hidden under the footbridge that spans the Charles River, she sat, as she remembers it, for several hours, timing her defection by her watch. Perhaps it wasn't really that long. To her it must have felt like forever.

She didn't really want to run away, she tells me now; she just wanted to give everyone a good scare. She wanted them to be sorry for what they'd done to her dog, sorry for how they'd treated her. She sat in the shadows under the bridge for what seemed like ages, imagining her mother's grief, her father's guilty face, her two parents worried and upset that she'd disappeared, suddenly aware of how much they loved her, how poorly she'd been treated. She imagined the search parties they would send out, the boats that would scour the river, the people who would come on foot.

After a while she got tired of waiting to be found. She walked home.

What a shock to discover that everything was the same as before. No one had noticed she had gone.

The image of my father and his pounding shoe melts imperceptibly in my mind. My father grows stouter before my eyes; he is aging, balding, suddenly dressed in a suit and tie. As if in a shifting dream, the dog cowering under the bed fades away too, the scene in the bedroom dissolves, the room grows larger, the walls fall back, and I am in an amphitheater. A crowd of men and women ranged in rows listens intently to a man, who is no longer my father but an even more frightening personage who sits at a desk and pounds his fist, pounds his shoe, shouting angry words in an unknown tongue. I can't make out the meaning of the words, but their tone is unmistakable. Protest. Threat. Revenge.

I don't remember if I watched the TV coverage of Nikita Khrushchev visiting the General Assembly of the United Nations in 1960, if I saw the pictures in the newspaper the next day, or if I only heard my parents' worried talk. And yet the image is seared into my mind, because it captures in one moment, coalesced in a nightmarish joining, the menace that secretly paced and prowled within my family and the menace that brazenly stalked the world.

Of course I knew nothing much about politics at the time, nothing about the strategic and political struggles that had been developing in the decades after World War II. But the image of the Soviet premier roaring and pounding before the nations of the world made a strong impression on me. What was the meaning of this moment, of this man? Was he a comic figure, a buffoon, an unpredictable, bombastic zealot whom I could afford to mock? Years later, I saw a picture of Khrushchev, a preposterous portrait really, in an advertisement for shoes. It was the famous shot of him raging, shoe in hand, ready to strike. Above his glowering face someone had written, "These shoes are killing me."

I always find it unnerving that our consumer culture can trivialize anything, that it can take our most potent memories of collective fear and inject them into the marketplace, using them as incentives to buy. But maybe anything can seem funny in hindsight, once the danger has passed. I'm not sure. I do know, though, that back in the early sixties, I saw no humor in Khrushchev's tirade. On the contrary, I saw in it a reflection of the same peril, writ large, that I dimly perceived in my life at home.

It was peril, perhaps, that gave me my first glimpse of what I might do with my life. Surely my task was to stand up to injustice, make peace, bring reconciliation. After all, I was born on October 24, United Nations Day—a fact that seemed to me charged with significance. I drew a time line of my life when I was eleven or twelve, adding, in addition to such personal information as "born in 1951" and "move to Quincy House, 1959," the notation "Dag Hammarskjold dies, 1961." I'm not sure I knew at the time what the life of the second secretary-general of the United Nations meant to me, why it was so important that his life intersected with mine, why I loved so much to stare at the photograph of Hammarskjold and my grandfather, a newspaper publisher, striding together up the steps of the Swedish Institute in Minneapolis. But I do know that I wanted to make peace. I too wanted all the bickering nation-states—of my family, of the world—to find some way to communicate with each other. I wanted to hold my own clan together. I just didn't know how. But with adolescent earnestness, I knew I would try.

The Cuban missile crisis took place in October 1962, the year my older sister and I were sent away, along with a cousin, for a year in a Swiss boarding school. I was in sixth grade, a girl of ten going on eleven. News of the naval blockade began filling the newspapers and airwaves just weeks after we arrived, shortly before my birthday. The world held its breath. Already desperately homesick, I was now panic-stricken by the rumors of impending war. As the days dragged by, we garnered what news we could from the radio, waiting in suspense to learn if and when the world would end. I'd thrown up the first night that I'd arrived at the school, and now I had to throw up again, whether from flu or sheer anxiety I do not know. Between trips to the bathroom, I lay on my bed and imagined falling bombs. When my older sister sneaked into my room to visit me—students were forbidden to visit anyone whose bedroom was on a different floor—I asked her whether perhaps the bomb had already dropped, and no one had told us, no one had wanted us to know.

"Maybe I'm the first person to be poisoned by radiation," I suggested, looking at her anxiously. "What do you think?"

"I'm sure the bomb hasn't dropped yet," she reassured me. "Someone would have told us."

But really, how could you know for sure? I had learned by then that grown-ups didn't always tell you the important stuff. No one in my family said a word about my father's drinking, my mother's depression, or the anxiety and loneliness that infected their four children. We got by with silence and pleasantries. As far as I was concerned, it was entirely possible that the bomb had dropped already and that, for reasons known only to themselves, the adults had decided not to mention it. Maybe they wanted to protect children from troubling facts, or wanted to be polite.

It was my paternal grandmother's idea to send me off to school in Switzerland. My parents agreed. My father would be on sabbatical in England with the rest of the family, doing research in Oxford. My older sister and I would study French in Switzerland, just as my grandmother had when she was a child. It was years before I learned that my grandmother had been as miserable in her Swiss boarding school as I was in mine. So I wonder why she encouraged two of her beloved grandchildren to be sent to Switzerland. Was it an attempt to replay or repair what had happened to her? Maybe she thought that if she could comfort us, she could salvage her own childhood in some way.

In any case, DeeDee rented rooms nearby in Lausanne, while my sister and I endured our long exile, debating the relative merits of running away, putting up a fight, or gritting our teeth and sticking it out. Every month or so, we would join DeeDee for an elaborate dinner in a local restaurant. She always sent us back to school with large paper bags full of peanut butter and Swiss chocolate. Maybe she thought, maybe *I* thought, that food would fill the gaps, sweeten the bitter pill.

I remember DeeDee with great affection, the way she'd burst into a room. "Let me take a look at you!" she'd say, gathering me up in her arms and pressing me to her soft bosom, planting loud kisses on my neck. What pleasure I took that DeeDee so delighted in me. Patiently she'd explain the rules of a game called Sir Hingkum Funnyduster, slapping down the cards with glee. When we visited her home in Maine, she'd stir up pots of her legendary "chocolate sauce that hardens," watching in triumph as the thick syrup solidified around a mound of ice cream. DeeDee showered us with presents— handmade afghans for our beds, cookies, sometimes a pair of earrings. And she welcomed everything, even our most outlandish crafts projects. I remember wrapping a Styrofoam ball in thick pink yarn, braiding eight legs, and sticking on two googly eyes. *Voila!* An octopus, which DeeDee adored. I remember the paint-by-number pictures she bought for me, and how carefully I colored in the barnyard scene of a horse (brown body, black mane), barn (shades of red), and sky (shades of blue).

How many lonely evenings I must have spent sitting on my bed in Switzerland, unscrewing the lid of the jar of peanut butter she'd given me, spooning it out or sucking it off my fingers; filling up on DeeDee's candy; wondering if she knew how much I missed her, missed my family, how much I wished this food would fill the hole in my heart.

In addition to a smattering of French, I took one other thing home with me from Switzerland: a vow, taken during the Cuban missile crisis, to learn everything I could about the Soviet Union, this mysterious enemy that filled us with such fear. Who was this adversary of ours? What could I find out about this enigmatic, hostile country whose very existence threatened Americans to the core? In seventh grade I devoured a paperback with a lurid red cover, written by FBI director J. Edgar Hoover, about the evils of the Soviet Union. I read a tract about the "naked rise of communism." I pored over *Nicholas and Alexandra*, wondering about the life of the tsar, the daughter who disappeared. I wondered why so many adults seemed able to divide the world so neatly into good and bad, right and wrong. What made "them" so wrong and "us" so right? I puzzled over what connections I might make, what bridges I might build, between these opposing sides. I pondered the fact that a distant relative of mine on my father's side, a cousin at some complicated degree of remove, had served as the first American ambassador to the Soviet Union after the 1917 revolution. I learned that my mother had studied Russian in college. Studying all things Russian became a way for me to express my longing for communication, integration, reconciliation, in a family and a world so fraught with hostility and division.

But my dream of eventually taking on a healer's role in the big world of adults was accompanied by an undertow of panic. I was desperately afraid of bombs. I'd already seen a dog fall from Quincy House. Who knew what else might fall? I spent much of my early adolescence worrying about bombs. The Cold War was at its height. Again and again I would stand on the Quincy House terrace, looking out over the expanse of Cambridge and Boston—the blue tower of Lowell House, the Charles River, the big Coca-Cola sign that flashed night and day, the distant skyscrapers—and see all of it, every last building, person, car, and tree, spread out in smoking ruins before my eyes.

Mushroom clouds and terror filled my dreams. If the bomb dropped, what would I do? Where would I go? Would there be room for me in a fallout shelter? Would I be left outside to die, horribly injured and alone, my skin falling off? Would I be locked inside a shelter, gasping for air, crammed elbow to elbow with strangers?

No one knew when the bomb might fall. It could come at any moment—in the middle of the night, perhaps, when everything was quiet, when everyone in the universe was asleep except for me, and I alone was awake and vigilant, the only one not fooled by the silence, the only one expecting its coming just then.

I knew plenty about silence already: the hush that fell over the dining table when my father had had too much to drink and was launching into a tirade or an off-color joke; the unspoken tension between my parents; the tacit family agreement that we keep up appearances, make everything look normal. I knew about the sudden eruption of my father's anger when he was drunk, the scared flurry to protect myself from his vicious words.

Although I could never have expressed it, I must have sensed that something was wrong. Still, I never worried explicitly about my father, my parents' marriage, or the future of this family. I couldn't bring myself to imagine a danger that was so close to home, already inside its walls. Instead I imagined bombs—an enemy outside, a threat from beyond. Whatever rage I felt, whatever longing I secretly harbored to blow the family charade sky-high, was poured into these imaginary bombs. As was my fear of such an explosion, my desperate desire to protect my family from my anger or from any other harm. I wanted to keep them safe and to guard the fragile life we now enjoyed. Perhaps I already suspected that this uneasy peace couldn't last much longer, that beneath the family facade, all hell was breaking loose.

Beyond the generally placid order of our days, beyond the steady rounds of homework and school, piano lessons and visits with friends, family breakfasts in the morning, the clink of glasses in the evening, the regular rise and fall of the elevator, I knew that danger was nearby, even "imminent"—a word whose meaning I had lately learned from the public service announcements on TV that told us what to do in the event of disaster.

I was vigilant, on alert, a radar screen ready to pick up the slightest hint of trouble. You never knew when the bomb might drop. It could happen in the middle of a meal, when everything looked normal, when everyone was talking, passing plates, even laughing. I alone had the sense to eat quickly, protein first, so that after we'd rushed to the fallout shelter I'd survive a little longer.

Food was already a comfort to me, a key prop in my inner drama, a source of solace and strength when I felt cut off from the people around me. Or so I thought.

My family moved out of Quincy House the year I entered tenth grade at a boarding school in Maryland. It was the year I learned to binge. I remember the secret thrill of a handful of coins, feeling them jingle in my pocket as I walked oh-so-casually to the vending machine at the foot of the stairs, inserting dimes into the slot, pulling the lever, waiting for the satisfying thump of a candy bar falling into my hand. The thrill of tearing off the paper wrapper and taking the first bite, and the next, the next.

I was fourteen when I left Quincy House and my family— for boarding school. Somewhere between Boston and Baltimore, I managed to lose my grip. I felt as if everything were slipping away from me, as if I had no ground to stand on, the world having tipped over on its side. Our life in Quincy House was over, a closed chapter. It was as if all of us had suddenly fallen off, had slipped inexorably over the edge of the balcony, like our first little dog. Unlike Corky, however, we landed not in a single pile, but in different places, scattered across wide distances.

I didn't know it then, but the Harvard administration had asked my father to take a leave of absence. He was on the brink of a nervous breakdown, sometimes irrational, often drunk. Over the summer he began training for a post with the Peace Corps. He expected my mother to join him in the fall, but to everyone's surprise—including hers—she found herself unable to board the plane to Bolivia.

My older sister called me long-distance at my boarding school.

"I bet our parents will get divorced," she declared. I don't remember offering any objection, any reassurance. It was too late for that. I knew she was right. The bomb was out of the chute, already falling, on its way down. I don't remember telling anyone at school about the imminence of its fall. Why broadcast the news? Its impact would be felt by me alone, I figured, so why speak of it to roommates or anyone else?

Eventually my mother flew down to Maryland to tell me that she and my father were indeed going their separate ways. She wouldn't have thought it appropriate to tell her child just why it was that she and my father had "grown apart," as she tactfully put it. Even so, it was clear that the marriage was over.

The bomb fell. It had finally fallen, and my world was blown to bits. I was devastated. But not really surprised. I'd been on alert for years.

My mother asked me if I had any questions. I didn't know what to say. I didn't know what to ask. I had no words. I didn't even know what my questions were.

When she left, I ate. By now I'd discovered that sugar could make me sleepy, dull the edge of any feeling, take away any pain—at least for a while. I took myself off to the candy machine, put my hand on the lever, pulled it again and again. The sweets dropped like tiny bombs into my hands, doing their own secret damage. I wept alone, in the company of peanut bars and chocolate chip cookies. In public, I kept on smiling, kept on studying, kept on making the honor roll.

I began studying Russian as soon as I got to high school. I needed to learn to communicate with the enemy. Like many a schoolgirl, I quickly fell in love. The loops and curls of this alien alphabet thrilled me. So did the guttural vowels, the deep murmur in the throat, the mouthfuls of sibilants. The aesthetics of Russian—the way it rolled off the tongue and sounded so lush to the ear—pleased me no end. What's more, I liked the challenge of cracking its code. I liked being able to decipher paragraphs that to the uninitiated eye were only gibberish on the page. I liked being able to write diaries in a language so secret, no one could possibly steal a peek.

There was power to be had in penetrating the secrets of the Russian language, a sense of mastery and control. More control, certainly, than I felt in my own family, where, by the time I got to high school, communication between my parents had entirely broken down. They might as well have been speaking in mutually unintelligible tongues, so opaque had they become to each other, so estranged. Even before my mother told me of the impending divorce, I was beginning to suspect that I'd failed miserably in my self-assigned role as secretary-general of my family. Still, the longing lived on in me, the yearning to create a space where everyone could speak, to open communication, to transform enemies into friends. I wanted to keep it all together—the world, my family, my life. And yet that task seemed increasingly impossible. More and more often I numbed myself, stifling and choking off all my longings, all my feelings, with food.

In 1969, I graduated from high school and set out for college. I went as far away as I could, all the way to the West Coast. For me, Radcliffe was out. I wouldn't consider any college on the East Coast. I wanted to put it all behind me, leave my family in the dust, head out to sunnier climes. Off I went to Stanford to study Russian. Before long I claimed Dostoevsky, Tolstoy, and Gogol as my own, reading their works and those of the other great Russian masters with a passion that fed my soul.

But it wasn't only hard work that I was up to. I did more than study. There were so many issues to negotiate, so many paths to choose among, so many decisions to make, about marijuana, alcohol, sex. Within months of arriving on campus, I was breathing in tear gas and watching other students hurl stones at the library. I searched for my own perspective on the Vietnam war, my own way of protesting evil and standing up for life.

I had left Harvard behind me, my family behind, all of them behind me, three thousand miles away. Everything was different now—the blue California sky, the arching palm trees, the vast landscape of the Pacific coast. I was meeting new people, making new friends. Although I continued to be a serious student, I wanted to make my own choices, free of my family's influence or constraint.

For one thing, I stopped going to church. I'd worshiped in the Episcopal church all my life. In boarding school I so loved the chapel services that I spent two years helping to organize them. But when I got to college, I left all that behind. It wasn't a dramatic or even an especially conscious decision. It just seemed that conventional Christianity had lost its meaning. Its rituals no longer spoke to me. Its values and beliefs no longer seemed particularly relevant or interesting; they no longer connected me with anything transcendent.

Instead, I studied yoga and learned to meditate. I poured into literature my passion to understand the ultimate questions of life, studying Dostoevsky and Dante, Melville and Tolstoy. Except for the evening when Joan Baez appeared in the Stanford chapel to talk about her trip to Hanoi, I don't think I once set foot in church while I was at college.

I explored the new identities of my generation. I wore bell-bottoms and batik. I danced to the Grateful Dead and the Rolling Stones. I lived in a house devoted to nonviolent social change, and discussed Betty Friedan and Simone de Beauvoir in a women's consciousness-raising group. I threw myself into leafleting and walking picket lines to support Cesar Chavez and his struggle to empower farmworkers. I joined in sit-ins and other demonstrations against the war in Southeast Asia.

Despite all this, some part of me hadn't changed at all. Some stubborn, primordial part of myself was untouched by all these changes. I was still preoccupied with food. I still worried how I'd get through the day without extra helpings at mealtime, without a few secret trips to the corner store, the dining hall, the nearest candy machine. Too often I ate in secret, looking to food for solace and companionship. Of course, I joked about it with my women friends, trying to make light of this obsession that so many of us seemed to share. And I tried to hide it from my boyfriends. I didn't gain an extravagant amount of weight, because I alternated periods of bingeing with periods of eating nothing at all. During my freshman year, I fasted for a total of thirty days, usually for five days at a stretch; on one occasion I ate nothing for ten days. Sometimes I fasted—or so I told myself— for moral and political reasons, as part of a public protest against the war in Vietnam. Sometimes I fasted with a spiritual purpose, to cleanse my body and refresh my soul. Always I fasted with the hope that afterward I'd be able to keep my eating under control.

But the more I experimented with food, using food to express and to manage my emotions, the more obsessed I became. I spent a lot of time worrying about food and a small cluster of questions: What should I eat? How much should I eat? Should I stop eating? *Can* I stop eating? Should I eat in front of other people? Should I eat alone? How can I get through a day without losing control of my eating?

The very thought of giving up sugar panicked me. Whatever longings and desires might have been stirring beneath my craving for food, I swallowed them. I didn't know what they were, and I didn't want to find out. No one knew the trouble I was in. I binged only in secret. In public, I was the model student—compliant, aspiring, successful.

After my freshman year, I took a year's leave of absence from college and flew off to Newfoundland to teach kindergarten in a village outport on the northern coast. When I came back to Stanford, I went on studying Russian and graduated with honors. But I was restless and way out to sea. I didn't have a clue how to proceed, how to make sense of the conflicting voices at war in my head. I wanted to be of service, to do good in an often violent and fearful world, but I seemed to be locked in an internal conflict of my own, with no truce in sight.

I wanted my life to make a difference, but how? Should I become a lawyer? A social activist? After college, I spent a year working as a VISTA volunteer at a public interest law office in Philadelphia, but I didn't have a logical, lawyerly mind, and I had no taste for combat. It was literature I loved, the play of words and sounds, the search for meaning. Why not study more than Russian, open up the horizon to a larger context, a wider field of vision? I decided to begin a doctoral program in comparative literature. I wanted to see how the great books connected with the world, how they might lead to social change. Were there books that had the power to create a new heaven, a new earth? Were there words of such accuracy and beauty that reading them could change everything? Was there something I could read, something I could study, that could change *my* life?

I looked into many different programs and received several scholarship offers. But with a dim sense of destiny, as if some unfinished business from the past were calling out to me, luring me home, insisting on my return, I decided in the summer of 1975 to pack my bags and go back to Harvard. My father had pulled himself together enough to resume teaching and now lived with his second wife just a few miles from campus. My mother had remarried too, and continued to live in Cambridge. My brother and two sisters had all fled the scene, heading out to faraway places. I alone seemed to feel a need to go back, back to the world of my father, to my family's world. I wasn't sure what I'd find; I wasn't even entirely sure what I was looking for. But I knew there was something there I had to face.

I would put off facing it for years. Instead, I began eating compulsively as I never had before. The secret pilgrimages from my apartment to the grocery store began in those years, the raids on the Star Market at ten o'clock at night, the tormented obsession with doughnuts and candy. My life was increasingly consumed by overeating and by the struggle to make myself stop. I bought diet books, studying them as assiduously as I studied Old Church Slavonic. I riffled through magazines, looking for information on the latest diet fad. I stared at the models: thin, skinny, skeletal. I drafted painstaking charts with a downward-sloping line: my plan for weight loss. If I lost two pounds a week, by such and such a date I would reach my supposedly "ideal" weight. I bought an expensive doctor's scale and weighed myself religiously every day, carefully marking the good or bad news on my chart. I bought little magnets and stuck inspirational messages on the refrigerator door. I made pledges and promises that I would stop overeating. I took vows. I gave myself deadlines. I signed up for Weight Watchers. I enrolled in a hospital program for people with eating disorders. I agonized about eating with a therapist.

Trying to stop the violent bouts of overeating was no idle pastime for me, no subject for trivial chitchat. At some level I already knew that what I was doing with food was a matter of life or death. I felt confused and desperate, like an animal caught in a trap. I was doing everything I could think of to keep these mysterious cravings at bay, and yet over and over again they would wash over me. Like waves overwhelming a small boat, the sudden, urgent drive to eat would come crashing down on me. Frantically I'd start bailing with my bucket, bailing with my bare hands, but the waves would be too much for me, the boat would rapidly swamp, and suddenly I'd find myself holed up in my car somewhere, or hiding in my kitchen with the curtains drawn and the phone turned off, gulping down pudding or bread or bowls of cereal as fast as a drowning man swallows water.

On one diet plan that allowed unlimited quantities of vegetables, I ate so many pounds of raw carrots that my skin turned orange. The doctor burst out laughing when I showed her my yellow palms.

"I've only seen skin like that on toddlers who've just discovered squash."

I tried to laugh along too. But I knew better. I was in deep trouble. I couldn't stop overeating, though I tried everything I could think of to hide the damage, to look good. I bought fancy jogging shoes and expensive, color-coordinated outfits to go with them. I ran seven miles a day at dawn, rain or shine, in blizzards or ozone-laden heat waves, it didn't matter. I ran six-kilometer and ten-kilometer races. I collected T-shirts from each race, stuffing them into my bureau drawers. I ran the Boston Marathon. I ran the New York Marathon. I'd run ten miles in the wake of a binge, even though my ankles were swollen, my stomach full.

I tried clinging to my willpower until my knuckles were white. It didn't work. I ate.

Eating in secret made a liar out of me, a consummate fake. In the company of others, I acted normal. I ate a normal meal. By myself, I could put away a loaf of bread and a bar of cheese. Or a stack or two of pancakes with strawberry jam, along with handfuls of peanuts and apricots. Hardly anyone ever witnessed my binges, but if someone did, I just pretended I was invisible. I was invisible when I ate. The larger my body became, the more I hid myself inside it. For me, food was like a child's magic ring: If I walk down the street eating a Snickers bar, you won't be able to see me. This candy bar will protect me. You can't see me if I'm eating.

And how I dreaded to be seen. When I lost weight on one of the diet programs, my collar bones began to show. I was scared. I stood up and told my diet group that I thought my bones looked angry. They laughed. What I was telling them didn't make sense. They didn't understand that if my bones were starting to show, my feelings might start showing through as well.

That night, when I got home from my group, I started eating. I ate that night and all the next day. I ate my way around the clock, from morning to night, until the sun went down, until it got dark and nobody could see me. It wasn't long before my bones disappeared.

What was happening to me? How had I come to this? What seeds were now bearing such bitter fruit? Like every child, I'd learned very early what could and couldn't be expressed at home. Every family has its mother tongue, its way of shaping the boundary between what can be spoken and what can never be named. Every family has its own map of what may be known, which territory is permissible and safe to walk on, which places are dangerous. Every family has its edges. Trouble is, the map doesn't always show where they are, and sometimes people fall off. Not to mention dogs.

The language that was spoken in my house when I was growing up was the language of achievement: excellence, accomplishment, performance. In different ways, both of my parents urged the pursuit of perfection. The most desirable goal in life was to compete, to get to the top, to be the best—this was the message that my father drove home to us. Winning his approval was a game of trying to earn infinitely receding plums of praise. The prize always dangled tantalizingly out of reach.

"Three A's and one A-minus," he would muse, studying my report card. "Those A's are fine, but an A-minus is a rather ambiguous grade. . . ."

His voice would trail off, and he would skewer me with his blue eyes. Maybe I would do better next time. If I did manage to bring in a report card with perfect marks, with nothing on it but A's, he would look it over carefully, then turn to me with a face full of innocent concern and ask, "Don't you think you're turning into something of a workhorse?"

Infuriated, confused, I would turn away, wondering if I'd been tricked, wondering what I could do so that I could finally receive my father's approval. The goal he had set before us was to be first-rate, but at the last minute he always changed the rules. None of us could ever measure up, however hard we tried. We had to win, and it was impossible to win.

Clinging to the hope that one day we might finally bask in our father's love and approval, we children strove for excellence in our respective fields—neurosurgery, comparative literature, ballet, geophysics. In an unspoken pact, the four of us avoided competing directly against each other by choosing areas of expertise that did not overlap. As it turned out, my brother and I both ended up playing the piano, but we worked it out so that I played only classical music and he played only jazz; I was able to sight-read, and he was able to improvise. We did what we could to protect each other. If there was room for only one person in the winner's circle, then at least we could try to make several circles.

And so the four of us got to work, accumulating everything we could—grades, prizes, fellowships, grants, publications, recitals. In a society that rewards personal accomplishment, we fit right in. If the highway to happiness in America is defined by the drive for individual achievement, we had the pedal pressed to the floor.

I remember the rueful smile of one of my Harvard professors as he showed me an envelope someone had addressed to him. The letter had been sent to "The Department of Competitive Literature." The misnomer was in fact accurate enough. Competitiveness hung like invisible motes in the air that all of us breathed. Daily we sucked it in, and willy-nilly we let it do its imperceptible work upon our souls.

Certainly there was heady excitement if you were the one who came out ahead. After I opened the envelope that contained the grades for my first semester of graduate work, I held it in my fist and made a triumphant circuit on foot around the perimeter of Harvard Yard. Surely Joshua's march around the city of Jericho was no more jubilant than my own victorious march around those ivy-covered walls. Clutched tightly in my hand was final proof that I was worthy, final proof that I was good enough. I'd done it. I'd made it. I'd entered my father's boxing ring and I'd won the round.

But this brief moment of satisfaction swiftly passed. Dependent as I was on external sources of affirmation, I found no abiding resting place in one semester's set of grades. My quest for academic achievement was largely driven by the longing for my father's love, but somehow all the A's in the world seemed powerless to win his affection or to fill my lonely heart. My father demanded nothing less than perfection, and it seemed to me that at any moment my deepest fear would be exposed and confirmed: the fear that at some essential, irrevocable level, I didn't measure up; the fear that he withheld his love because I didn't deserve to have it in the first place.

I never dared to stop and feel my sadness, fear, and rage, my utter helplessness and frustration. Experiencing my feelings was difficult enough; expressing them was even harder, since voicing emotion was not encouraged in my family. I whirled instead in a feverish cycle of striving and accomplishment. Maybe *this* time my father would be pleased. Maybe *this* time he'd be satisfied with what I'd done, satisfied with *me*. Like a snake biting its own tail, I twisted around in an endless loop of craving and dissatisfaction. You can never get enough of what you don't really want. I grabbed for good grades and I grabbed for food. And was perpetually hungry. I couldn't bear to feel within myself the constant, palpable, physical speech of my body, its thirsting and yearning for a love that seemed forever out of reach.

I knew, above all, that in my father's presence it wasn't safe to have feelings. It certainly wasn't safe to be sad.

"Aren't we down in the dumps," he might comment mockingly if my frozen smile slipped off my face and the underlying sadness peeked through. "Let's have a bout of real self-pity, shall we?" Jeeringly he'd thrust his thumb into his mouth and begin to suck.

It wasn't safe to feel lonely, disappointed, or anything much, and it definitely wasn't safe to express these feelings. Only a breezy, intelligent good cheer would do. In my father's company, woe betide you if you were feeling vulnerable or uncertain, or if you expressed a feeling without covering it over with a little dose of self-mockery. Having a conversation with my father was sometimes like being a young untrained soldier, bewildered, unarmed, totally unprepared for the battle that lay ahead. If I were lined up in the cross-hairs of my father's wit, I might as well have been a child caught in a war zone, looking desperately for a bunker, a barrier, someplace to hide, so that I might have at least some protection from the torrent of ammunition that would shoot from his mouth, almost always reaching its mark.

And so I began to live with anxiety: to breathe it, sleep with it, eat with it. I learned to guard my feelings, conceal my hurt. I learned the art of camouflage. All my energy was turned outward toward the impossible: the demand to appear perfect. Inside, I felt increasingly isolated, alienated, and alone. I felt as if I were living a double life.

Today, more than ten years after my father's death from lung cancer, I often wonder what loneliness and anxiety he hid from himself and any onlooker. Once, when I was at the crest of a wave of academic applause and recognition, I saw something like wonder and sorrow in his eyes. In a rare moment of intimacy, he told me that *he*'d never been so warmly received at Harvard; *he*'d never enjoyed that kind of acclaim. I glimpsed his envy of my success, and I sensed the sadness of a man who had lived his life under the tyranny of perpetually trying to prove his worth to the outside world. Although outwardly successful, a tenured professor of eighteenth-century English literature, all his life he toiled in the shadow of the internationally acclaimed Harvard scholar who'd been his mentor in graduate school. No matter what he did, in the eyes of his peers he'd never be more than second-best—and in his own eyes, that was as good as failure: an A-minus, a rather ambiguous grade. For all his combative feistiness and charm, for all his intelligence, perseverance, and wit, my father's self-doubt and self-rejection sometimes seemed to know no bounds.

In another rare moment, my father confessed his conviction that his whole career was based on a lie: he'd cheated on a test in seventh grade.

In my years at Harvard, I lived inside a whirlwind of anxious cravings: to get good grades, to prove my worth to the university, and above all, behind it all, to earn my father's love. Even when I began to suspect that there was no winning in this game, that the whole enterprise was futile, that my father wasn't able to love me any more than he loved himself, I could still hear inside me the pleadings of a small child: "Look at me, Daddy. Look at what I've done. Isn't it good? Aren't *I* good? Do you love me now, Daddy?"

None of these yearnings were speakable. To voice such feelings in my family would have been absurd, childish, an alien tongue. That kind of talk was shameful, a breach of etiquette that surely we had the good manners, the good sense, to avoid. Only other people, we told ourselves—people more crude than we were, more self-indulgent, more sentimental— spoke in such a direct way of the longings of the heart. Only other people had such feelings, such needs. If I merely sighed in my father's presence, if I took in a long deep breath and let it go, his face would tighten with anxiety and he'd remind me sharply, "You're giving in. Don't give in." Once, when I actually dared to weep as we sat together at the kitchen table, he leaned forward and offered me the only consolation that he knew: "You can go cry alone in the bathroom if you want to."

I can think of two good reasons why my father chose the eighteenth century as his academic focus. First, here was a period of clean, bright light, rational thought, straight lines; here was the orderliness of the Age of Enlightenment. And here too was the fun of the picaresque novel, the zing of irony and banter, the "satirical merriment" of Samuel Johnson.

Here was the realm of the rakish hero, whose wit and devil-may-care exploits always seemed far more charming to me on paper than they were in the person of my father.

In any case, the struggle to prove worthy of my father's love was beginning to take its toll. Behind the competent, cheerful, cooperative exterior, behind the perfect facade, a self-destructive chaos was breaking loose within me. My father chose alcohol. My drug was food. Peanuts, pudding, brownies, chocolate, bread—you name it, I took it. I swallowed it in secret, sometimes in a thrill of defiance, sometimes with the anguish of guilt, always, in the end, with despair.

CHAPTER 2

Angels, Ghosts, and Knives

I learned to read in my mother's lap. One of my earliest memories is of sitting with her in a lawn chair on the porch, a cool spring breeze blowing through our hair, as I read aloud a story about a bunny in search of a home. My older sister, who was hovering nearby, insisted that I was much too young to be reading. She said I'd only memorized the lines after hearing them read to me so many times. But I paid no attention to her. I was safe. I was enclosed in my mother's lap, resting in the happiness of her body's warmth. I ignored the interruption, snuggled back against my mother's blouse, and kept on reading and turning pages, repeating the question that the little rabbit posed to one animal after another, "Are you my mother? Are you my mother?" until the true mother is found at last.

That tale of a little bunny in perpetual and patient search for her lost mother was perhaps the most absorbing one I knew. The only story that could match its power was found in the brand-new picture book that my mother placed in my hands when I was four. *Play With Me* instantly became one of my most cherished childhood possessions. It was my talisman, my catechism, my Rosetta Stone; it was the story in whose light I could read my own story, the story that unlocked the hieroglyphs of my mother's relationship with me. I would hug the book to my chest: it was a sign of my mother's love. And more than that, it was my story, it was her story, it was our story.

In the first picture, a little girl is walking through a field toward a tree and a clump of grass. The sun is shining and the girl is happy. Her eyes are expectant and full of hope. She's alone but she's not lonely: at any minute she'll meet some playmates, make some friends. "The sun was up," reads the text, "and there was dew on the grass and I went to the meadow to play."

The following pictures show the girl repeatedly reaching out, in word and gesture, to befriend one little creature after another. "Will you play with me?" the little girl asks a grasshopper, and then, in turn, a frog, a turtle, a chipmunk, as she stretches out her hand to touch or catch each one.

But each creature quickly flees. The turtle plops into the water, the chipmunk runs up the tree, the blue jay flies away. When even the snake runs away, disappearing down its hole, the little girl finally realizes that "None of them, none of them, would play with me." Idly, she picks a milkweed, blows away its seeds, and, with a face of exquisite, wordless sadness, sits down on a rock by the pond to watch a bug make trails on the water.

What happens next was always a moment for me of breathless suspense. As the nameless little girl continues to sit on the rock without moving a muscle, "without making a sound," the grasshopper comes back and sits beside her, and then the frog, the turtle, and all the other little creatures—chipmunk, blue jay, rabbit, snake—until, wonder of wonders, as she sits very still, "without making a sound (so they wouldn't get scared and run away)," out from the bushes comes a fawn. "He came so near I could have touched him," says the girl, "but I didn't move and I didn't speak." She holds her breath and the fawn comes still nearer. At last her patience and stillness are rewarded. She is granted her heart's desire: the fawn comes up and licks her cheek. "Oh, now I was happy," the book concludes, "as happy could be! For all of them—ALL OF THEM—were playing with me." In the last picture, we see her waltzing home alone, arms upstretched with joy, the radiant sun beaming serenely down.

To me, the book was comforting: the child finally finds some friends. She can return home singing. But the book was vaguely troubling too, and I didn't know why. Only much later did I realize that the girl's contact with her playmates comes at a literally breathtaking cost. The little girl yearning for friendship and connection is finally able to "play" with her companions only when she's sitting perfectly still, silent, without so much as a word, practically holding her breath. It's only when the little girl is hushed and motionless that the animals dare to venture out to her, and even then she can't respond to them in any way. She can't move, can't speak, can't touch these longed-for friends. She can only receive a distant, silent kiss. Presumably, when the little girl finally stretches or stands up, the animals will scatter back into the woods.

Like her, I experienced myself as being near an elusive presence with whom I longed to make contact, with whom I yearned to share my active, vital self and all the pleasures of play. My mother was like the fawn in the forest, an infinitely precious, shy, and enigmatic creature who'd peek out and draw close only if I was very, very still. Too sudden a gesture, too raucous a laugh, too desolate a wail, too quick a movement, and Mother would surely take inward flight.

It would be years before I realized that my mother was not only the fawn in the story, she was also the little girl. In giving me this book, my mother was offering me a portrait of patience, a tale of a child's attentiveness to the natural world, a story of friendship with animals, and a depiction of one child's willingness to learn a different way of communicating. It was one of dozens of books that my mother gave me when I was little, nothing special to her, just another fine book for children. But to me this story was unique. In its pages I found a portrait of my mother, a glimpse into her own childhood, when she too had taught herself the art of sitting still.

Only recently did I learn of something that happened to her when she was three years old—an experience she considers formative, a pivotal moment in her growing up. In 1929, during the early days of the Depression, my mother contracted scarlet fever. A quarantine was instantly imposed. Her sister was hustled away for the duration of her illness, and her parents departed for a long-planned trip to Arizona. My mother was left behind, in a huge and empty house, in the custody of a hired nurse whom she did not know at all. One of her earliest memories is of looking out the bathroom window at her mother and father down below as they climbed into their car and drove away. The nurse urged her to call out a goodbye, but my mother refused. She wouldn't say good-bye. She wouldn't even wave. She stood at the window without moving a muscle, without saying a word.

What did this moment mean to her? Did her silence stem from anger? Was it protest that her mute body expressed? Or was it hopelessness that left her unable to speak, unable to move? Had the decisive moment arrived when she first realized that she must conceal, even shut down, the deepest longings of her heart? Had she suddenly understood that she was being abandoned, that there was nothing she could do to bring her parents back? Was this the moment when my mother began learning the language of solitude, stillness, silence?

When I was little, I haunted my mother like a ghost. I watched her. I adored her from afar. I remember sitting on her bed and studying her as she combed her hair. In her long white nightgown, with her black hair let down her back, she was an angel to me, the most beautiful woman in the world. Sometimes she was a princess gazing out from her high tower, and I was the suitor destined to coax her down and set her free, so we could run off together and play. Other times she was under a spell, bewitched, enchanted, and my mission was to awaken her and bring her back to life.

"Little merry sunshine," she would call me. "My Rock of Gibraltar." I basked in these terms of endearment, I savored them, but sometimes my cheek muscles ached from smiling. I sensed that for her own well-being, my mother needed me to be a certain kind of person: cheerful, chipper, steady, calm. I did my best to be what she needed me to be. I wanted to make her happy.

In one way or another, I orbited around my mother like a planet around the sun: here was my source of light and life. I circled her like a spacecraft revolving around the earth and sending messages back to the command center.

Reel me in, I signaled in code. Help me land. Take me home.

I wrote my mother notes. When she left with my father for a dinner party, I sneaked out of my room after bedtime, tiptoed down the hall, and left urgent messages on her pillow, begging her to come back soon. Once I hid behind her bureau when I heard my older sister and the baby-sitter coming. I curled up tight and held my breath, but they caught me anyway, and I was sent back to my own room. I so yearned for my mother's presence that I scarcely knew how to express my desires.

I also wrote notes to God. When I was about six, I wrote God a letter, folded it up, and threw it out my bedroom window so that it would get to heaven. The letter landed in the front yard, where my mother picked it up. For years she kept it in a drawer of her file cabinet. It said, "God, please help me be good."

I can't help wondering now whether the message was intended as much for my mother as it was for God. As a child, I felt as if something was pulling her away from me; as if, even when she was looking at me, her face was inwardly turned toward someone or something else. Even as a child, I knew that she was devoted to God, so perhaps it was God that absorbed her inward eye. I had no way of knowing. If I wanted to receive my mother's attention and love, was it God with whom I must contend? Was I competing with God for my mother's attention? Maybe if I spoke to God directly, and if I was very, very good, I could make God love me. And if God loved me, then my mother would have to love me too. Maybe then she'd venture a little way out of her inner forest, come sit somewhere close to me.

I tried my best to keep quiet as a child, but some deep part of myself urged me to move. My favorite early-childhood game was Horsie, played on hands and knees. Far and away the best stall was the space under my mother's desk. It was large enough for a small horse-child to turn around in, and from the security of its walls I could look out serenely at the world beyond. All of us children coveted that stall, my mother's stable, and my younger sister and I often squabbled over whose turn it was to get it. The loser had to settle for a corral under the card table.

As I grew up, horses continued to be my passion. I devoured all the usual books: *The Black Stallion*, *Misty of Chincoteague*, *King of the Wind*. I collected tiny china horses and lined them up on my bookshelf. I hung a picture of horses on my wall. I drew pictures of horses—wild horses, running horses, horses with pounding hooves and manes that blew back in the wind.

When we were young, all four of us enjoyed inventing and performing plays, with our parents as audience. Each of us had strong opinions about the roles we were willing to take. My older sister had to direct the play and be its hero. My younger sister insisted on being the beautiful princess or fairy. My younger brother (who, as the youngest, never got a full vote of his own) had to play whatever part was left over. As for me, I always wanted to be an animal—a bear, maybe, or a lion. Best of all was when the script called for a horse.

Whenever the family went on long car rides, I sat by the window and imagined an invisible horse running alongside the car. Sometimes I was riding her, and sometimes she was me. Either way, she was always large and strong, beautiful and free. She could jump without effort over any obstacle—an overpass, a hedge—then land gracefully and continue running. Her hooves pounded the earth. No one could see her but me. She was mine. I gloried in her energy and power.

On several family vacations and during my years in boarding school, I seized every opportunity to ride: to feel the exhilaration of sitting on a horse's back, my legs pressed against its sides, its powerful body moving beneath me. Galloping fast on a horse with the wind in my face made me sing with joy.

It seems to me now that my passion for horses was one of the ways that I kept myself alive. In a family so muted by depression and anxiety, so constrained by perfection, so riddled with addiction, I found in my love for horses a place to pour out my passion, a way to nourish and keep alive everything in me that was instinctual, spontaneous, and vibrant. By loving a horse's sheer bodiliness, perhaps I could dare to love my own. Even now, I am thrilled by the sight of a horse running in a field. I see a creature who is both purposeful and playful. I see the beauty of a creature who is full of desires and free to delight in the sheer gift of being alive.

As a child, I had no idea what my mother was up against. Saddled by the multiple demands of running the master's residence in Quincy House, supervising the kitchen staff, volunteering on numerous charitable boards, raising four small children, and providing support for a husband whose professional life was increasingly marked by strain and anxiety and whose private life was increasingly blurred by too many beers and too much Scotch, my mother struggled to maintain order. She gave my father a safe haven, a soothing oasis for his restless spirit. She covered for his alcohol-induced lapses of manners and memory. She made amends for him, offered explanations and apologies on his behalf. And she gave us children a sense of structure and predictability. Each day began with formal breakfast in the dining room at 7:45 in the morning and ended with "inspection" in the library at 7:30 at night, when we lined up to present to her our clean teeth and washed hands.

Hers was a very public life of providing hospitality week after week to innumerable Harvard faculty, students, and visiting luminaries. A lot of effort went into presenting the proper appearance: a clean house, fine refreshments, a gracious welcome, pleasant conversation. I don't know who, if anyone, my mother talked to about her own inner life. Certainly my father was too deeply absorbed in his own ambitions and fears to give her his undivided attention. I don't know if there was anyone else—except maybe God—with whom she was able to share her worries and hopes, her longings and desires. Perhaps she dismissed such intimacy as an unnecessary luxury, even selfishness: there were so many people who needed her right then. Her own needs would have to wait. In any case, my mother was always a very private person, and I suspect that no one—maybe not even she herself—knew the extent of her isolation. I doubt that she knew how much it filled her children with loneliness.

What I *did* know, as a child, was that I couldn't find her, couldn't touch her, couldn't feel her touch me. She was absent, elusive, gone. I knew she loved me. Even so, when she was with me she was not fully there. It was as if something essential in her was shielded from me, guarded, hidden under lock and key.

Like Hansel and Gretel, I began searching for the crumbs that would finally lead me home. I turned into a kind of spy, a sleuth, a detective sent on a secret assignment to investigate my mother's desk. Furtively I peeked at her papers. As fast as I could, I deciphered the notes on her Phillips Brooks calendar. I peered sideways into the sheet of glass that covered the surface of her desk, studying its hidden swirls and patterns. I was a bloodhound sniffing for a trail. I was Dick Tracy with a magnifying glass pressed to my eye. Maybe I'd find a clue about a possible crime: we'd received reports of a missing person. Maybe here in these papers, among the personal effects of my mother's busy life, where she kept records of meals served, guests entertained, and appointments scheduled and kept, I'd find a clue to who she really was. Maybe here, in these furtive searches, by secretly handling these papers that I was forbidden to touch or to disturb, I'd uncover what she really felt, what she really cared about, what she really wanted, worried about, hoped for, and loved. Maybe here I'd find my mother.

I used to worry that my mother was a saint. I had plenty of evidence to support this suspicion. For one thing, I could see that she was not like me. She didn't seem to have the same messy, volatile, sometimes unexpected feelings that I did. She was always composed. She was self-contained. I never saw her cry. I rarely saw her get openly angry. Under duress, she might sometimes admit to being "cross," and then we children trembled, wondering what enormities of anger were pulsing beneath that careful word. Still, she almost always maintained a surface of unruffled calm.

When I was young, I concluded that true saints have no desires. The person who was truly spiritual was empty of feeling, indifferent to the body, and free of desire. My mother showed us how to do this. At mealtimes, for instance, the spiritual person ate just a little bit, and very neatly. Spiritual persons never noticed their own hunger; instead, they kept themselves alert so as to anticipate what the people around them might need. The goal was to guess correctly what the other diners wanted without their having to say a word. If you passed someone the salad or the bread before he or she had to ask for it, my mother would beam her approval. As children, we perceived that our own hungers were suspect. The noblest thing was not to have any needs and to spend one's life anticipating and fulfilling the needs of everyone else.

My mother was obviously a good person, unfailingly generous, enormously kind. When the cat chewed off the eyes of my beloved Foxie, she sewed them carefully back on. When I needed to vomit in the middle of the night, she was always there, patiently holding the saucepan, spreading out the towel. She never complained, she never asked for help, she always seemed to do what was selfless, what was right.

The clincher to documenting my mother's sainthood was how passionately she loved God. She read books on Christian mysticism and prayer. She borrowed or bought every biography of Teresa of Avila that she could find. In Quincy House, she tells me, she used to carry books about Saint Teresa wherever she went, even as she moved from room to room. Faith was her anchor, her mainstay. She saw to it that the children were fed and neatly dressed on Sunday mornings and took us to the local Episcopal church every week, while my father put up his feet and read the Sunday papers.

I was in awe. I compared myself to her, and all I could see was my own selfishness, my neediness, my profusion of desires, my welter of failures and mistakes. There seemed to be too much of me. I was too unbridled, too unkempt. I had too many feelings, too many needs; there were too many things I wanted to talk about. Once I had an awful dream in which I had seven fingers on one hand.

My mother's saintliness made me anxious. It's not necessarily good news to a child to learn that her mother is a saint. After all, if your mother has a direct pipeline to God and you don't, then what she says carries the seal of ultimate truth. You may disagree with her, you may see things differently, but like it or not, in the end (perhaps at the end of time, but surely, inevitably, at *some* point), you'll have to admit that your ideas, your behavior, perhaps even your inmost self, were never good enough.

When my mother spoke of spiritual things, she had a way of gathering in her breath and pulling in her energies, as if just speaking of these things gave her the power to go on with life. Her voice would take on a dramatic hush. She'd speak with a tone of quiet authority and conviction that permitted no doubt. She knew about hidden things, wonderful things, things that only very, very special people could possibly understand. If we listened quietly, she might teach us something.

In these moments I could tell that my mother was offering us what was most precious to her. She was tenderly unwrapping a box covered in brown packing paper. Gently lifting the box's lid and breathing ever so quietly, she was carefully unfolding the delicate white tissue paper inside. She was reaching in to show us her well-kept treasure, and here is what was lying inside—she would lift it up for us to see—here was the pearl of great price.

I could feel her reverence, her sense of amazement and awe. I could see that she was giving us the finest, the most wonderful gift she had. I loved this moment of longed-for disclosure, this precious instant when a door in her was open and she let us catch a glimpse of what she held most dear.

But at the same time, whenever my mother gave me a spiritual lesson, something in me froze. I'd learned, like the little girl in *Play With Me*, that in these fragile moments I must remain very still. I knew that I had to receive this gift intact, entire. I knew that I must accept this gift without question, comment, or challenge, with no emotion but the same amazement and awe that my mother felt. I sensed that there was no room here for my own experience of God, for my own ways of naming and holding the pearl of great price. When my mother opened her world to me, I had to step into it completely and leave everything of my own behind. When she invited me into her world, I had trouble staying connected with my own.

If I did ask my mother a question or express in any way an emotion other than awe, something like deep pain would flash briefly across her face. Hastily she'd press the pearl back into its tissue, back into its box. Quickly she'd fold up the box and slide it away into a hidden corner of herself. There, she seemed to say, that's enough of that, let's not go into that any further. And again I'd find myself outside a closed door, wondering with guilt and anxiety what I'd done wrong, how I'd hurt her.

Because I was so hungry for my mother, I tended over the years—and long into adulthood—to accept her way of framing our relationship. I let her be my spiritual teacher. I gratefully took in everything she told me about the spiritual life, even if it meant that my own world was eclipsed and swallowed up in the process. When she spoke, I disappeared, but at least I could see where she was. Sometimes, after a conversation about spiritual practice, I had to shake myself awake. Where had I gone? What had happened to me? Why had I closed down? The cost of these conversations was connection with my own spiritual truth, but at least I got to be close to my mother.

The only time that I ever saw my mother get really angry was the first—and only—time that I invited my college boyfriend home for Christmas. My mother and stepfather were hosting all four children for the holidays. No one had bothered to talk ahead of time about the rules and expectations of the stepfamily; we were still operating under the basic principle of "Don't ask, don't tell." My mother had never asked me whether Bob and I were—to put it politely—"romantically involved," and I had certainly never volunteered any information on the subject.

And so, late one afternoon shortly before Christmas, as the rest of the family was downstairs getting ready for supper, Bob and I made the mortal mistake of lying down on a bed side by side to read the newspaper. I hadn't intended to provoke my mother, at least not consciously. As I tearfully pointed out later that evening, Bob and I were lying on top of the sheets, the door was open, and we were both fully dressed. But my younger sister happened to walk in on us. She took one long look, turned around, and disappeared out the door. I thought nothing of it.

At supper, we took our places at the table and helped ourselves to pot roast, mashed potatoes, and peas. Then we folded our hands and bent our heads for the blessing.

"Almighty God," my mother began as usual. "Bless this food to our use and us to your service." So far, so good. But then there was the flicker of a hesitation, which stretched out into an actual, full-fledged pause. The bodies around the table tightened. We were on alert. Something was coming.

My mother took a breath and then continued to pray, speaking very carefully. "God forgive our human frailties. Amen."

She lifted her head, unfolded her hands, offered someone the bread basket, and, picking up her fork, began a dinner-table conversation. But an energy as nervous, jumpy, and invisible as electricity had been released around the table. Something was up. But what? Who had done something wrong? To whom was my mother's prayer addressed?

I cringed. I was sure that she was speaking to me. I had put a great heap of mashed potatoes on my plate. She must have spotted it. I took a few bites of peas, and then, when it seemed to me that she was looking away, I pushed the potatoes to the side of my plate, pressing them into as small a pile as I could.

In later debriefings with my siblings, I learned that my older sister had assumed that the remark was directed at her because she'd done nothing to help with supper; she'd neither set the table nor helped with the cooking. My brother was also guilt-stricken: despite our mother's attempt earlier that evening to persuade him to go caroling with the neighbors, he'd adamantly refused. So all three of us sat in secret squirmy guilt at the dinner table, trying to pretend that nothing was wrong. Conversation went on as usual.

I stole a look around. Bob was cheerfully talking and eating his food, unaware of the bomb that had dropped. Nothing as big as a hydrogen bomb, to be sure, but something with enough explosive power to send shock waves through anyone who knew the language of this family.

As I looked around the table, only my younger sister seemed to be eating calmly, with a look of satisfaction on her face. In fact, the more I looked at her, the more she seemed positively smug, the proverbial cat who swallowed the canary.

Suddenly I understood what had happened. She had squealed on me. I glared at my radiant little sister, stared back down at my plate, and tried to still the blood that was rushing past my ears. This was going to be a bad one.

The family got through the courteous, strained, and relentlessly pleasant meal. After supper was over, we broke away from the table in relief and began carrying dishes to the sink. I was about to give my younger sister a piece of my mind when I suddenly realized that my mother had vanished somewhere with Bob. I found them in the library. My mother's face was tight. Her lips were white. I'd never seen her so angry.

"You violated the trust that we placed in you," she was saying to Bob. "We invited you into our home, and we expected you to respect the family's rules. But you violated that trust. You refused to respect this family or honor its rules."

Catching sight of me, my mother turned to direct the full force of her anger toward me. "Margaret, I'm shocked," she said, every word distinct. "You know perfectly well what the family can and cannot accept in this house. Your behavior was outrageous."

I jumped in and began babbling my defense, such as it was: we'd been fully clothed, we'd left the door open, nothing had happened, et cetera, et cetera. I was trying with all my might to look composed. I dearly wanted to rise to the occasion, to be rational, logical, and mature. I wanted to show my mother how grown up I was, how well I could handle the situation, how forthrightly I could stand up to her and clarify this innocent misunderstanding. But despite my best efforts, all I could do was to cry. In the face of her open anger, I got scared. In the heat of the moment, I couldn't find my own inner fire. I wilted like a plant in a tropical sun.

After what seemed like a desperately long interchange, we all managed to calm down. My mother's lips returned to their normal color. I was able to dry my tears. Bob apologized profusely, and despite his offer to leave at once, my mother didn't send him off to a hotel. We got through the rest of his Christmas visit without incident.

Years passed before my mother and I ever talked about the episode again. For a long time it simply disappeared into the family silence, like water vanishing down a hole. According to family custom, anger was to be neither expressed nor discussed. A flare-up within her or between us was a lapse, a breach to be overlooked and set aside as swiftly as possible. We didn't do feelings in my house, and whenever they leaked out—as inevitably they would, in one form or another—we did our best to ignore them and move on as quickly as possible, without looking back.

As far as I was concerned, I didn't even know what I felt about the incident—humiliated, angry, or vaguely amused. But it confirmed my longtime suspicion that my mother sometimes concealed strong feelings in her holiness, or encoded them in her public prayers. It also showed me how deeply her anger frightened me when it was expressed openly. I didn't know how to meet it without anxiety, or how to stand my ground. The more her anger filled the room, the less air I found to breathe. I ran away. I fled. There was no way for both of us to be together when either one was angry. When her anger was invisible, she disappeared; when her anger was visible, I disappeared. Like any strong feeling in our hide-and-seek house, anger had the power to make somebody vanish. If you concealed it, you were no longer visible; if you showed it, everyone around you disappeared. It was as if our family had invented a bizarre new law of physics: No two people with strong feelings, or conflicting feelings, can occupy the same space at the same time.

Growing up, I had no clue about how to express my anger, or how to listen without panic to the anger of someone else. What I did learn, only too well, was the art of self-attack. I was proficient when it came to turning anger inward, cultivating depression, and nursing self-doubt. I've since come to understand that when a parent only rarely expresses anger, or repeatedly denies feeling angry, in times of conflict his or her children are forced to resort to shadowboxing. If a parent purports to be too mild, too pure, too holy to feel anger, the children are obliged to find another target for their rage and frustration. And when it comes to shadowboxing, there's finally only one person close enough to take the hits, and that's yourself. When I struggled with my mother, my anger inevitably turned into shadowboxing, and I'd end up taking it out on myself. How could I express my anger to such a saintly mother? It was like having an argument with God. It wasn't until I was well into adulthood that the possibility crossed my mind that God might actually welcome my anger, might actually rejoice at my willingness to tell the truth.

When I was growing up, it seemed to me that my mother and father were a study in contrasts. From my mother, I took in the message that good people had no desires or needs of their own. My father, on the other hand, was obviously a man filled with desires. He drank beer, he drank Scotch, he went scuba diving into shipwrecks, he headed his sailboat straight into stormy weather. I admired him tremendously, yet sometimes I found him scary. The drunken laugh, the boozy caress, the mocking words that could pierce the heart—all these led me to hide, to lay low, to keep my feelings to myself. The choice seemed clear: either eliminate my desires and become as saintly as my mother, or welcome my desires and become as chaotic as my father.

The first path seemed to me the better choice; the trouble was, I couldn't seem to make my desires disappear. I tried to eat only tiny, saintly portions of food, but a ravenous hunger opened up within me. I tried to need nothing, want nothing, and feel nothing, but I couldn't seem to stop the surges of anger or grief or sexual desire from breaking through. I lived a high-powered intellectual life as a graduate student at Harvard, I won prizes, I earned fine grades, but my body was beginning to rebel from its exile. Deep sleep escaped me. Food became a lure and a trap. I stayed up late night after night, feeding the hunger within me by stuffing down enormous quantities of fats and sweets. I'd awaken in the morning angry at what I'd done and filled with confusion and remorse. I wondered if, by imitating my mother, I'd turned into my father. I couldn't seem to put together in any coherent way what I'd learned from my parents about desire. The path of ignoring and suppressing desire had led me straight to a dead-end, where I found myself caught in the grip of desires I could neither understand nor control.

My mother generally expressed her anger in understatement, in hints. My father's anger, on the other hand, took the form of out-and-out combat. I always got clobbered. I remember his boast that he knew nine different ways of killing a man with his bare hands. My father's father had been the amateur boxing champion of Kentucky while he was a student at the University of Virginia, and he arranged for his son to be trained by some of the best retired fighters in the country. By the time my father was an undergraduate at Harvard, he was considered one of the finest amateur boxers of his generation.

According to his colleagues in the English department: "During his college years, he was repeatedly a runner-up for the National Lightweight championships, never reaching first place only because, in his laughing and carefree way, he refused to go into training or to stop smoking until three or four days before the boxing finals began." In his senior year, my father taught his fellow students "how to defend themselves against thugs advancing on them with jiffy-knives. Henry Lamar, the boxing coach, said that [he] was one of the greatest experts he knew in the art of defending oneself against 'dirty fighting.'" After graduating from Harvard, my father joined the army. He taught athletics and personal combat to recruits, spending nine months in occupied Korea.

By the time I was born, my father had long since given up boxing and was established at Harvard as a teacher and administrator, but he still retained an aggressive, combative, chip-on-the-shoulder attitude. Descended from a long line of lawyers, my father was a master of words: eloquent words, articulate words, words that could make you laugh, words that could bite and sting. In the hand-to-hand combat of verbal skirmish, my father had no intention of being a lightweight. He never really left the ring. He loved a good argument, loved to make a point, loved above all to win. Like any scrapper, he knew that the best defense is a good offense. My older sister, who in many ways was a match for him in temperament and cast of mind, relished their friendly disputes about philosophy and politics, but as the years went by and alcoholism took its toll, my father increasingly used his wit to wound and his words to deliver body blows.

"Slabs of meat," he'd muse, gazing with a mixture of fascination and contempt at women sunbathing on a beach. Women's bodies and women's minds became the objects of his scorn. When my younger sister, emotionally and physically spent after years of grueling training at the Royal Ballet School in London and the National Ballet School in Toronto, gained weight in college and came home to visit my father and his second wife, he directed some pointed barbs at her across the dinner table. Unsatisfied with their effect, he demanded that she stand up and turn around slowly, so we all could see her shame. With burning cheeks, she stood silently before his dancing eyes.

I hope now, with all my heart, that at this point I spoke up in protest on her behalf. Perhaps I did, but I can't remember. Shock has erased the memory of what happened next. It's likely that I simply sat immobilized, in stricken silence. If I did dare to object, I can guess what my father said in reply, for I'd heard it before any number of times: "What's wrong with you? Don't you have any sense of humor? Can't you take a joke?"

Only once did I see my father at a loss for words. For some reason, he decided to join us at church one Sunday. I remember glancing up at him and being startled to realize from his muttering and fumbling that he couldn't recite the Lord's Prayer. In that moment I understood that the language of worship was for him a foreign tongue.

Still, words were the tools of my father's trade, sharpened and polished to hold the attention of the hundreds of students who attended his lecture courses in Sanders Theater. And they were weapons when he needed them, jiffy-knives capable of cutting their targets to ribbons. Even my older sister, his beloved debating opponent, was not exempt: when she announced to the family her desire to become a surgeon, my father scoffed, "I wouldn't let you operate on my hangnail."

In the face of such "dirty fighting," my own words seemed paltry and inconsequential. They were too weak to draw retaliatory blood, and I didn't really want them to. They were too weak to stop the assaults and too weak to stop the bleeding. My words could do nothing.

I learned the power of language from my father. The power of words to create and to destroy. The power of words to weave poetry and story. The power of words to kill the spirit. Compared to his words, my own seemed feeble, so I learned to keep quiet. I learned to settle for grimacing, for rolling my eyes, for silently walking away.

I learned, in the end, to eat.

If my father was the master of words, my mother was the master of silence. An unusually thoughtful and articulate person in her own right, my mother nonetheless took silence as her area of expertise, her practice, her art. The more my father bullied his way through the world, the more my mother found another way to speak. Often her silence was eloquent. And certainly it was forceful. She tells me now that my father never spoke harshly to her. She and she alone was spared my father's verbal assaults, as if she lived within a charmed and cloistered circle of one. But in truth she reigned in silence, and it was this art that she wanted to teach her children—the subtleties of communication accomplished by signs. From her we learned to be as sensitive as radar: to take note of the slightest of gestures, the tiniest of hints; to register the significance of a glance, a single nod of the head.

It always seemed to me that what was powerful in my mother's world was not what was seen but what was unseen. To her, the visible world existed only as an indication of invisible, unspoken depths and densities. Only the unspoken had power and reality. Everything of truth went unsaid. If it was spoken aloud, if it was seen, if it was standing right there before us, it wasn't real, it wasn't true, it was unworthy of notice.

Perhaps it was too painful for her, or for any of us, to see clearly what was right before our eyes—a father and husband increasingly consumed by drink, a man we all loved turning mean from liquor. It's not that we chose not to see what was happening. We simply didn't see it, couldn't see it. It's as if we were in the midst of a hurricane—the wind blowing hard, the rain pelting down, and everything topsy-turvy. We couldn't see what was happening, much less make any sense of it. Trying to speak to the situation seemed about as useful as putting up a hand to stop the wind.

If ever I did venture to break the silence and put words to what I felt, my mother fled from me just as I fled from her that Christmas vacation when she expressed her anger to me. We were mirror images of each other: Whenever I tried to express my anger, she turned in upon herself. She collapsed. She folded herself up into an envelope and mailed herself off to a faraway country. Even if I didn't use words, if I merely gestured toward my anger, if I gave it the politest of nods, Mother would vanish. She would still be with me in the room—we'd still be talking with each other as before—but I'd see from her eyes that she was gone.

Not surprisingly, I watched the television show *The Incredible Hulk* with more than passing interest. Whenever the character played by Bill Bixby began to feel angry, his eyes flashed and his body began to swell. With a mixture of horror, envy, and arousal, I'd stare as his muscles bulged and the fabric of his clothes tightened, drew taut, and finally split apart. Anger transformed him into an enormous monster, roaring with rage. As I remember it, he tore up trees and threw cars around; people ran away from him. Yup, I thought, that was me, that's what my anger would do if I let it loose. It would kill.

Of course, I didn't need to turn on the television to witness the potentially destructive effects of anger. All I had to do was to watch my father. But the story that I couldn't bear to watch, the one that was not on TV, the one that was not being played out in my father's life, was my own story. I couldn't bear to stare into the screen of my own life and to connect with the anger, the murderous rage, that threatened at any moment to erupt within me. I tried to make the picture disappear. I couldn't bear to look. I scrambled to change the channel. I kept trying to turn the volume down. Why? Because the sound of my own anger and sorrow would have been deafening. It would have unleashed—who knows what? Something so terrible that it couldn't be endured. A nuclear disaster, perhaps, or some kind of torrent or volcano that would have swept away everything in its path, everything that was familiar, everything I knew.

And so I was stuck, consumed by an anger that I couldn't express. I didn't know what to do with it—how to discharge it, how to contain it, how to live with it. I certainly didn't want to commit murder. So I tried to make the anger go away. Bite by bite, gulp by gulp, I swallowed it. I ate it. I consumed it whole.

My body swelled, but at least I wasn't throwing trees and cars around. If you didn't count the devastation that such eating was having on me, you could have argued that at least I wasn't killing anyone, but it wouldn't have been the truth. I was consumed by rage. In fact, I was dying from it. And I didn't even know it.

Children tend to draw large figures, often without nuance or detail. As children, we sometimes pit images of our parents against each other in order to make sense of who they are, and of who we are too. These figures are undoubtedly caricatures, because we're just beginning to draw the lines. We're not yet psychologically adept. We see things as either/or, black or white, with little shading. It's how we make our first maps of the world, how we find our first footing and give ourselves a place to stand.

When I was a child, I'm not sure I could have drawn my father without exaggerated, vivid shapes of excess, thick dark lines, bright, emphatic colors, and a great balloon, filled with words, coming from his mouth and looming over his head.

By contrast, I think I would have sketched my mother's portrait by suggestion and subtle shades, in hints drawn with gentle strokes of the crayon. She stands tall in my imaginary picture, a towering silence.

My father's caricature shows him plunging forward with an angry, in-your-face presence. My mother is silently standing her ground, or perhaps moving back.

In this imaginary picture, I am fending off my father and reaching for my mother.

I carried the universe of my childhood deep within me until well into adulthood. I couldn't reconcile the two worlds of my mother and my father.

When it came to expressing my truth, communicating who I was, I didn't know how to speak or how to be silent.

My father welcomed words, but he used his words to pierce or stifle everyone else's. My mother would have nothing of argument. She was above argument and offered no counter-argument. The only words she used were the pleasant ones, the happy ones. Everything else was left unsaid.

I felt isolated, trapped. If only there were words that could connect us—good, strong words, as solid and trustworthy as a stout rope someone might throw down to you if you had fallen into a pit. Hand over hand you could pull yourself up to safe ground, each word as sure and true as the next knot on the rope, until your feet touched earth again and you could drop the rope to embrace the person who had saved your life.

If only there were silences like that, silences in which we felt not just the distance between us, not just our separateness from one another, but also our connectedness, our desire to meet. Silences that invited each person to be fully present, not to hide anymore, not to close down.

But I could find no such words, no such silence. In my family, words estranged us. Words made us strangers. We used words as artillery or camouflage. And our silences were equally explosive.

So I ate.

CHAPTER 3

Body Language

*H*ere are some things you won't find in this book: stories describing the sensual, aesthetic pleasures of delicious food. You won't find any lingering accounts of flavor or aroma. You won't read any titillating descriptions of oral sensations, such as how one sort of food melts on your tongue, or how another crunches against your teeth. Compulsive eating is thoroughly nonsensual. For me, anyway, bingeing involved no savoring, no pausing to take pleasure—almost, in fact, no tasting at all. Except for a brief flash of flavor in the first bite or two, the food went down so fast I hardly bothered to notice how it tasted, much less to appreciate how it looked or smelled.

It's as much a mistake to assume that compulsive eaters love food or love to eat as it is to assume that sexually promiscuous persons love the partners that they seduce and discard. In my years of compulsive eating, I never loved food. I craved it, I needed it, I felt greedy for it, I used it, but I never loved it. I would have loved to have loved it. I would have loved to know what it was I really wanted, what it was I really felt. But since I had no clue what, if anything, I really loved, and since it surely wasn't food, I never paused to give thanks for the plants and animals whose bodies I consumed. I never considered with gratefulness the human labor that had gone into growing, harvesting, or preparing the food that was in my hands. I never paused to contemplate what I was about to eat; to notice its texture and temperature, color and shape. I never tasted the food with full attention, never swallowed it with delight. I certainly never understood how the act of eating—even solitary eating—might deepen my connection with other human beings, with the natural world, or with God.

Overeating had very little to do with providing fuel for my body, with giving myself pleasure, or with opening my heart to love. It had everything to do with desperately trying to communicate after ordinary methods had repeatedly failed.

Overeating is a language with its own grammar and vocabulary.

If I was unable to express my anger to my parents, at least I could express it to myself. I could grab, I could bite, I could gnaw, I could force as much food into myself as I wanted to, even when my body begged for rest. I could take the anger out on myself. And I could imagine my father or mother reading my body like a text.

"See how angry I am at you?" I was silently saying to them. "It's written all over my body."

A binge often began with an angry mind, but by the end of the binge, the anger would be comfortably cloaked and soothed. Carbohydrates left me in a stupor, my body as smooth and thick as the snow in Robert Frost's "Desert Places," "with no expression, nothing to express." I was motionless. I was numb. The anger, for now, was gone, the angry bones hidden. I was a sheer and vacant surface, a blank piece of paper with no message for anyone.

If it was loneliness and grief that I couldn't bear, I could always snuggle up to food. I could always fill up the emptiness, plug up the hole. Food would never abandon me. Food would never leave me behind or shut me out. Food would always be there in as large a quantity as I wanted, whenever I wanted it, for as long as I wanted. Food was my friend. Eating when I was sad was a way of comforting myself: "I, at least, will never leave you. I am here for you. You can have what you want. Take it. Eat it. Stuff it. It's yours. Have as much as you want."

But the language of compulsive overeating is tragically jumbled and ineffective, as multitoned and multivoiced as Cerberus, the dog who stands at the threshold of hell in Greek mythology, each of its three heads barking independently. A person who stands at the brink of addictive behavior is listening intently to conflicting inner voices: voices that urge her on and hold her back; voices that goad and that counsel caution; beguiling voices that lure, beckoning with promises; and savvy voices that warn her of traps. Which one should she listen to? Which is worthy of her trust? The voices that swirl in the addict's mind can be as bewildering and incomprehensible as the languages that suddenly multiplied at the Tower of Babel. Every addict thinks and speaks in tongues. Forked tongues. The message is always garbled.

It would begin with a small, seductive voice that made promises it couldn't keep. "Here, I'll take care of you," it would murmur in my ear. "I see you're feeling a little down. Let's just comfort ourselves with a bite to eat, shall we?"

"Oh no, not again," another inner voice would object in alarm. "I'm not going to eat right now."

"But why not?" the first voice would wheedle insistently. "It's just this once. You feel so sad. Let's do something to make you feel better."

"But I can't. I shouldn't. I'm not hungry. I'm sad. I want to cry."

"Hey, you don't have to feel that sadness. Don't give in to it. Leave it alone. Come with me. Let's go see what's in the pantry. Just a little something to eat, that's all you need."

"No. Go away. I really don't want to eat right now."

"It's OK. Just a bite, that's all. Who's gonna know?"

"But I shouldn't. I promised myself I wouldn't do it again."

"Never mind about that. You can be good another time. Have a little something, just a little bite, maybe a cracker or two. It's no big deal."

The argument would escalate rapidly, inexorably, until my mind was filled with the din. In effect, I'd be distracted from the grief, and the voice of sorrow would be silenced. The clamorous debate would absorb my attention, eclipse my awareness, extinguish every other concern, smother every nuance of feeling, until absolutely nothing mattered to me but the single question: Should I eat right now or not?

Once that question was looming before me, I could never get away from it. I couldn't shake it, couldn't turn my attention to anything else. It was a question that demanded an immediate answer. And once that fearful question was posed, once the competing inner voices had funneled all their energy into that urgent and utterly absorbing question—To eat or not to eat?— I always came up with the same answer.

Practically clapping my hands over my ears to stop the racket, I succumbed to the voice that promised quick relief. I yielded to the temptation to eat. Maybe I'd start with just a cracker, but before long I'd be eating my way through a loaf of bread or a pan of brownies. Stuffed to the teeth, crammed full of food, I'd turn for solace to the little voice that had promised to take care of me, but by then it would have disappeared back into the shadows from which it came. Nobody would be there. I'd be alone, suddenly remorseful and confused, my hands and mouth still sticky with sugar, my heart choking on stifled grief.

In the same moment that I was trying to soothe myself with food, I was also abandoning myself. Like a desperate mother who deserts her children because she can't handle their demands, I was walking out of my house and never looking back. All that I was giving myself was food, when what I really hungered for was embodied love. It wasn't doughnuts or brownies or cheese that I needed, it was companionship, the compassionate attention that could help me explore my feelings, give voice to my anger, release my tears. But I was too shy to ask for such help, too proud, and too ashamed. With every bite, I was saying to myself, "Look, you don't need to ask anyone for help. I'll take care of you. Here's something to eat." But I was also saying to myself, "I can't listen to you now. I can't bear to hear your sadness. Be quiet." In the confused language of overeating, I was simultaneously comforting and ignoring myself.

The messages that the addict sends to other people are as confused as the messages that she sends herself. With every defiant bite or slug or hit, the addict declares to the outside world, to her parents, to her friends, "I don't need you. I can handle my feelings by myself. Go away. Get lost. I can take care of this alone. And you know what else? I know how to get to you: I'm going to deprive you of *me*." But with every bite or slug or hit, the addict is also willy-nilly declaring to everyone around her, "I can't cope with this! I can't handle my life! I need help!" Every act of addiction is a plea for help that is retracted in the very moment that it's uttered, a cry for relationship that is throttled before it can be fully expressed.

The addict may ache with loneliness, but every act of addiction, large or small, tangles the threads of human relationship. Eventually those threads start to break. The longer the addict depends on eating, drinking, or any other kind of acting out as a way of communicating with herself and with the outside world, the more isolated and confused she becomes, torn loose from the fabric of human community.

The more I stuffed myself with food, the more I kept myself hungry. The more I forced my body to enact the suffering that I couldn't speak, the more difficult it became for me to express—or even to know—what it was that really troubled me, what it was I really wanted.

It would be years before I'd find a language that could make sense of this confusion of tongues, this cyclone of voices that wracked my body. It would be years before I could do anything as "reasonable" as weeping with others when I was sad, expressing my rage when I was angry, or even looking at a pie without gobbling it down in a single sitting.

In those years of overeating, I was trapped in a web of warring desires. It wasn't that I wanted too much, but that I wanted disparate things. What did I really want? I didn't know. I wanted everything. I wanted opposite things. If you'd offered me a questionnaire designed to probe what I was longing for, I'd have marked a yes in every box.

I wanted to make a speech as pointed and pungent as anything uttered in the eighteenth century, and I wanted to make my father listen to it in silence. He'd be spellbound, awestruck, as a smile of amazement and respect spread slowly across his face.

And I wouldn't have dared to utter a word. I knew I was defeated. I knew I was unprepared.

I wanted my father to light up when he saw me. I wanted to run into him on the street one day, maybe somewhere near Widener Library, and to hear him exclaim, "How good it is to see you! You're a chip off the old block! Let's go sit down somewhere and have a cup of coffee together." He'd put his arm around me and we'd walk together, we'd laugh and talk, enjoying each other's company without any strain or fear.

And I could barely imagine such a possibility, so deep ran my fear of disappointment, so raw was my dread of again being criticized or attacked.

I wanted my father to scribble something on a piece of paper, fold it up, and pass it to me with a mischievous grin. I'd open up the note to find these words written in bold black ink:

"I love you, Margaret. Daddy." For a long moment we'd smile at each other, and then we'd hug. That little scrap of paper would mean more to me than any degree I could ever receive. It would be worth more to me than any of the diplomas that hung on my wall.

And I wanted nothing of the kind. I wanted no unexpected notes from my father, no surprises, no possibility that I'd be caught up short, again found wanting.

I wanted to weep in my mother's arms. I wanted her to take my face gently between her two hands and to look me steadily in the eyes. I wanted her to say to me, "I love you. I am here. I'm not afraid of your feelings. It's OK to cry. I feel it too. I know how hard it is. I am with you. There's nothing you can't tell me or share with me." I wanted her to say all this, to convey all this, in a way that made me know it, and believe it, and feel it, and trust it.

And I wanted to run away from such intimacy. I wanted no such self-exposure, no such vulnerability. I wanted to protect myself from the possibility that she'd disappear, or flinch, or—worst of all—go dutifully through the motions of caring without actually being present emotionally, as if she were only playing the part of a mother. I wanted to avoid the possibility of her eyes meeting mine and going blank, of her face becoming reserved and uncomprehending.

I wanted to live inside every inch of my body. I wanted to feel its motion, enjoy its rest, be completely at home inside my skin. I wanted to accept and welcome and listen to my body as I would a cherished friend. I wanted to be free from the grab in the stomach, the clutch in the throat, the tightness in the chest, the unshed tears that gave me a headache.

And I wanted to be rid of my body. I wanted to ignore it, avoid it, escape it. I wanted nothing to do with it. I wanted to punish my body for its needs.

I wanted to disclose my sorrow and my anger. And I wanted no one—not even myself—to know the depths of what I felt.

I wanted to be awake. Present, vital, alive. And I wanted to be asleep. Entirely numb.

I wanted my life to be unpredictable and fresh. I wanted to face life as it is, to be open to mystery and surprise. And I wanted everything to stay the same. I wanted to be in complete control.

I wanted to live in the truth. And, if I got scared or over-whelmed, I wanted to live a lie.

I wanted to be real. And I wanted to be perfect.

The fact is, I had no idea what I wanted. I didn't know how to make sense of these conflicts, how to live with the contradic-tions. Like the winds in Gogol's fictional St. Petersburg, my desires were blowing in every direction at once.

I played out the dilemma with food. If the part of me that was willing to feel my feelings had the upper hand, I ate with moderation and enjoyed the meal, tasting every mouthful. If the part of me that wanted to escape my feelings took over, I ate randomly and mindlessly, as much and as quickly as I could, without tasting a thing.

One day I'd be able to trust the desire to be open to life, and I'd eat lightly and with joy. The next day I'd be gripped by the desire to stay in control and keep life's mystery at bay, and I'd binge.

On days when I was willing to face each moment as it came, I'd eat when I was hungry, stop when I was full. Other days, when I wanted only to escape from life, to hide out and avoid, I'd reach for the sugar, grab a bag of chips.

I dimly knew that some of my desires led me to fullness of life while others led me to a barren desert place. But I had no way of aligning myself for any length of time with the desires that gave life. Like a Ping-Pong ball, I ricocheted between conflicting impulses and needs. Whenever the battle grew too intense, I succumbed to the urge to eat.

"This *must* be what I want," I'd tell myself as I reached for more food. "Look how much of it I'm taking."

Addiction divides the self. The mind becomes a tyrant and the body becomes its prisoner, the target of its assault. It's not the body that wants another handful of peanuts or an extra slice of bread. The body watches in wonder and sorrow. What can it do? All the signals of bodily satisfaction have been sent to the brain. The stomach is pleasantly full. The belly already presses firmly against the belt. All is well in the body. There is food enough. Hunger is gone.

But an anxious, greedy craving still prowls restlessly in the mind. Addiction has its own voice. To the body it says, "I don't care what you tell me. I don't care what you want. I'm going to keep on eating. I want those extra bites. I can override you. Your voice doesn't count. You can't stop me. I'm in charge."

Addiction silences the voice of the body. Addiction refuses to hear the body, to listen to its natural appetites. Addiction renders the body mute, so that its wisdom can't be expressed or heard. Addiction distorts and shuts off the inner communication that makes any person a harmonious whole. It closes down the space that allows inner speech.

So I eat. I eat. I eat past the point of being physically full. I eat until I'm stuffed. I eat until I hurt. I eat until I feel nothing, until I'm numb, until I'm weary of eating and can eat nothing more.

A triumphant, angry mind, gripped by addiction, and a sorrowing, suffering body.

From the outside, I appear to be a single person, one organism, a unity, a whole. But within, there is civil war. The wounded and the dying lie stretched out over the battlefield. The victors gloat over them, but already, even now, they feel the first pangs of the guilt that will soon overtake them. Already they try in vain to run, to duck, to flee, but of course flight is futile: they are trapped within the very body that they have tried to kill.

The only way to blunt the sharp tang of remorse is to eat again, as much as possible, as soon as possible. To numb the body again, to kill it again, to put it to sleep again with sugar, starch, and fat, until the dead and the dying again litter the battlefield, and the victors again declare their triumph. The whole cycle repeats itself again and again, as relentless as a cog spinning in a vast war machine, beyond human arbitration or control.

Toward the end of my graduate career at Harvard, the obsession with food began to run my life. For several years I'd been living alone in a small house near Cambridge with no regular companionship except for several complicated and frustrating relationships with men, a few close women friends, and a solitary cat. I was like a runaway eighteen-wheeler going downhill at sixty miles an hour, careening off the road. My academic work was stalling out, on its way to screeching to a halt. Although I enjoyed my work as a teaching assistant, I couldn't seem to pull together a prospectus for my dissertation. I'd spend days fine-tuning a single paragraph, tinkering with one sentence or another, while leaping up repeatedly from my chair to down a few more slices of bread. A paralysis of inertia and self-doubt was beginning to creep into my heart. I was increasingly tempted to dawdle, to procrastinate. Desperate for a change, I found a part-time job as a residential coordinator at a state mental hospital near Boston, where I began to work with a group of twelve men living with chronic schizophrenia.

During this period I also began to organize a family intervention into my father's alcoholism. In a family that had long operated by denial and avoidance, by silence, secrecy, and isolation, this was a rare venture indeed: an attempt to gather together as a family and to tell the truth as each one of us perceived it. We would attempt the heretofore impossible: to share strong feelings and to stay together in one room. We would try together, once and for all, by word and gesture, to communicate with my father, to convey to him our concern about his drinking, and to express the pain that it was causing us. We would set before him what each of us would do if he refused to seek professional help.

I wonder now if I was recapitulating in those months my early admiration for Dag Hammarskjold, my persistent childhood longing to break down the barriers that divided the people I loved from one other and from me. If only we could connect at last, find a way to listen to each other, find a way to love. As I worked to plan the intervention, I suppose I was on a kind of rescue mission to find my father, my real father, the one who'd somehow been kidnapped by the man with the pounding shoe, the one who'd been slowly transformed by booze into a man I scarcely recognized. Would the intervention work? Would it make any difference? In our own high-stakes drama, our own family showdown, not only my father's life but all our lives were on the line. Would anything come of it? I had no idea. But I had to try.

Shortly after Christmas in 1981, my father's first and second families gathered in the office of Jeffrey McIntyre, who was then working as an alcoholism counselor at Mount Auburn Hospital in Cambridge. Everyone was there—my mother, my older sister, my brother, and me, as well as my stepmother and her two young sons. Everyone except my younger sister. To her it seemed that such "tough love" could only be cruel. For weeks we had begged her to join us and not to sabotage our efforts, but she was unwilling to budge. My father shouldn't go into treatment, she said; he should come instead to stay in the religious community to which she belonged and receive help there.

My father was the last person to arrive at the meeting. When he walked in, I was amazed to see that he was all dressed up. He was wearing a suit, a white shirt, and a tie. Furthermore, he was clean-shaven. His beard was gone. His cheeks were bare. It was as if he'd guessed that he was about to face a turning of the tide, a sea change, and had decided to dress for the occasion. But what occasion was it? Was he a catechumen dressed in white, preparing for new life in baptism? Or was he a prisoner who puts on his best clothes to face the jury or the firing squad? Was he a kamikaze pilot dressed carefully to perform a final ceremonial ritual before carrying out a suicidal bombing run, his last and fatal dive? Was it life or death that my father was facing as he stepped into that room? Perhaps it was both. And which one he chose would be up to him.

My father had another surprise for us. He agreed at once to the terms of the meeting. Its focus was to be not on him but on us. He'd be given time to speak, but only at the end, when he decided whether or not to enter a residential detox center for a month-long program of treatment.

We went around the circle one by one, each of us presenting, as coherently as we could, our memories of the ways our father's drinking had wounded or frightened us. For a long time, my father leaned back in his chair, now and then smiling and taking notes, playing with the tape recorder, puffing on a cigarette, twiddling his glasses. His face radiated a kind of forced and jolly irony, as if he were amused by the spectacle before him.

My stepmother and her two children spoke first. One by one the stories began to pour out: embarrassing stories, humiliating stories, stories of drunken outbursts, night sweats, misjudgments, fights.

It seemed to me that my father began to really listen only when it was my mother's turn to speak. She was so nervous that her mouth was trembling, but she spoke with clarity and precision.

"I am glad to be here," she said carefully, "because of our children."

My heart leaped at that lovely phrase: *our children*. How sweet those words can sound to the child of divorce.

"And I am glad to be here," my mother went on, "because I once loved you and because there is something in you that I love still."

"What?" my father interrupted, leaning forward eagerly as if he'd suddenly gone deaf and needed to hear that sentence again. I wondered if he was hungry for these words.

"It's true," my mother said. "There is something in you that I love still. But you've changed. Alcohol has blunted you. You are not the person you used to be."

I looked at my mother, astonished. I'd never seen her speak with such simplicity and power. I'd never seen her so forthright with my father. I'd never seen such authority in her, the basic human authority of speaking one's truth without hedging or holding back.

My father was no longer taking notes. He listened in silence as my mother spoke. She'd decided, she said, to focus her remarks on the last year of their marriage. Quietly she recounted one incident after another. I'd never heard most of these stories before, and for the first time I saw clearly the pain hidden within those outwardly glossy years at Quincy House. My father listened sadly. He made no argument and offered no excuse. When my mother had finished, he confessed that there were other drunken incidents during that year that she hadn't mentioned and that she didn't even know about.

Next it was my brother's turn to speak, then my older sister's. Trembling, I too read through my list of memories.

More stories were laid bare, stories of how, in the face of our father's drinking, we children cringed or wept or raged, or simply gave up hope.

When all of us had had a chance to speak, we adjusted ourselves in our chairs, took a deep breath, and waited for my father's reply.

"I've listened to each one of you," he said slowly, as he pressed out the stub of a cigarette with his thumb. "Some of you I trust more than others. Some of you are here, I think, because you're trying to manipulate me. You're trying to control me. And not only are you trying to make me do what you want me to do, you're using some of the younger ones here for your own purposes." His eyes flashed angrily toward my stepmother.

"To the rest of you, I want to say this." His eyes were milder now, but his jaw was set. "I appreciate your concern, but my drinking is none of your business. What I do and do not drink is entirely up to me."

He stopped. There was a frustrated and anguished silence as we took this in. And then we picked up the conversation. We kept going. We tried again. More pleas, pressure, urgent discussion.

My father was adamant. He'd made up his mind and that was that.

Suddenly the telephone rang, and I gave a start from nervous tension. McIntyre picked up the receiver. My younger sister was calling from Michigan. She wanted to speak to our father. McIntyre handed him the phone, and while my father held it to his ear for several long minutes, the rest of us exchanged glances.

"Don't be a jerk," I muttered under my breath to my absent younger sister. "Don't be a jerk or I'll kill you."

When my father hung up, he shook his head in confusion. She'd changed her mind, he told us. He was no longer invited to stay with her after all. She now agreed that he should go into treatment.

The timing of that call still astounds me. Coincidence, luck, grace—who knows? The call came just when we needed it most. I breathed a sigh of relief. The conversation gained fresh momentum, and at last my father announced a new decision. He'd try an experiment, he said. He'd quit drinking for six months.

My stepmother objected: No, that wasn't enough. He couldn't do that and expect to return home.

My father made a counterproposal: All right, he was willing to see an alcoholism counselor once a week.

McIntyre adroitly agreed that this could be arranged, he knew a good one, but—turning now to look toward my stepmother and me, who were firmly shaking our heads—he needed to check with the family first.

No, my stepmother and I insisted, that would not be enough.

"Why not take advantage of the resources that are here to help you!" I pleaded with him, urgently.

There was further discussion. Finally, my father announced that he'd let us know the following day what he would do. He'd give us his decision in twenty-four hours. Was that acceptable?

The assembled families nodded their agreement.

"So," my father said, turning with a smile to McIntyre, "I'll call you tomorrow."

I felt a sudden rush of anxiety. I knew that this meeting was our last chance. "If we aren't going to meet again as a group," I blurted out, "then I want to be sure I've said everything I have to say. May I add something here?"

McIntyre nodded.

I took a breath. I gathered my courage. I turned to my father.

"If you don't go into treatment," I said slowly, "then I don't want to see you again."

My father stopped and looked at me. Now I'd said everything I had to say. I'd played my last card.

"Well," he said. "I guess I can't let everything go down the drain, can I? No." He was thinking it over, turning it over in his mind. "OK, I will go into treatment. In fact, if I'm going to go, I think I'd better go right away. Today. I'll go this very afternoon."

I was amazed—both at what I'd dared to say and at how he had responded. For the first time in my life, I'd mustered up everything that was in me, speaking words that sprang from one of the deepest desires of my heart, the desire for authentic relationship. For the first time, I'd placed my commitment to speaking the truth above my fear of offending or displeasing someone I dearly loved. For the first time, I'd listened long and clearly to what I most deeply wanted, so that I was able at last to put my whole self on the line.

Even if my father had ignored my ultimatum, if he'd responded with a glare or a shrug, I still believe that my words would have had an effect—on my own soul, if on nothing else. Every word of truth that is spoken in love carries a resonance and makes an impact—perhaps on the world at large, perhaps not, but certainly on the speaker herself. With every truthful word we speak, the capacity for truth enlarges within us, and more truth becomes possible among us.

After my father announced his decision, there was an outpouring of relief in that tension-filled room. My brother and I stood up to give him a hug while McIntyre stepped outside to make the arrangements. I returned to my seat and we waited in awkward silence. No one dared to move until it was clear that my father really had a place to go.

Sure enough, that very evening, my older sister, my brother, and I made our way through a heavy snowstorm to deliver our father to a residential treatment center north of Boston. I was so tired, I could barely talk. We dropped him off in the front hall. As he went off to look for a bathroom, I saw a brisk and friendly woman lead him away by the elbow.

"You'll do yours in a cup!" she said cheerfully.

"Have another boyfriend?" an orderly teased her.

I felt happy and relieved. At last my father was safe. At last he was in a doctor's care.

The intervention was an act of hope, and it bore rich fruit. I had devoted many months to organizing and preparing for the confrontation, months of meeting with Jeffrey McIntyre and of learning everything I could about alcoholism and how the disease affects those close to the drinker, months of patient phone calls with my siblings and long conversations with my mother and my stepmother, as I labored to persuade everyone close to my father to join me and my stepmother in this effort. The sheer fact that almost everyone in the family had shown up seemed miraculous. The long years of confusion and denial seemed to be coming to an end. We'd taken our first steps as a family to speaking the truth to one another.

The preparation for the intervention was an important step in the gradual process of the family's healing. Time and again, as we shared our memories over the phone, one sibling would end up saying to another, "That happened to you too? You noticed that too? You felt that way too?" For each of us, I think, there was astonishment and relief in the discovery that we weren't alone, we weren't crazy, we weren't the only ones who felt mixed up, sad, and angry while growing up in this family. As the twelve-step program puts it, "You're only as sick as your secrets." We'd begun to share our secrets with one another at last.

The intervention also gave me a glimpse into the potential healing power of shared words and silence. I felt that it was my ultimatum that had finally goaded my father into action, but I knew that the power of my words at that particular moment depended entirely on the presence of everyone else in that room and on the power of their speech. The intervention gave me my first direct experience of the transformative power of gatherings in which people commit themselves to speaking the truth, however awkward and painful it may be, and to seeking healing for themselves and those they love.

As I look back on it now, I can see that an intervention is not so different from a religious ritual. Both are carefully orchestrated events (with McIntyre's guidance, we had each prepared our personal statements ahead of time, and we had decided beforehand on the best order in which to speak). But both kinds of gatherings are, in the end, utterly spontaneous and beyond anyone's control. In both cases, the participants hope to create an atmosphere, a context, a space, in which fixed and rigid patterns of relationship can break open, so that something new can happen, something new can be born. When an intervention or a religious rite works, everyone who participates in it has been changed. No one is the same going out as he or she was coming in. All the participants have received a healing of some kind, whether or not they know it at the time. Everyone has been touched by the fire of truth.

As for the outcome of this particular intervention, my father was galvanized to spend thirty days in a treatment program. Unfortunately, no one was able to break through his refusal to admit that he was dependent on alcohol. Despite the pleas of the treatment center staff that he stay on for a second thirty days, my father returned to Harvard to begin the next semester of teaching. He stayed sober for about twelve months, thanks to the sheer force of his own strong will. I had one precious year in which to know my father sober. Then drinking reclaimed him. When my father was dying of lung cancer several years later, he persuaded his friends to smuggle beer and whisky into the hospital. After that one year of sobriety, I hardly ever heard my father's voice without the accompanying clink of ice cubes, hardly ever drew close without picking up the smell of malt and hops.

What had become fully known to me during the intervention was the life-threatening, lethal power of addiction. I saw it, I spoke up against it, I stood up to it in my father's life. But although I could speak directly, without compromise, to the life-and-death fork in the road that my father had now reached, I was not yet ready to face the same choice set before me in my own life. I knew that my father had work to do. The unspoken text, the hidden text, the text that I could not address, and certainly not with the conviction with which I faced my father, was the story of my own addiction. My own silence—not as saintly as my mother's—was crippling my life, was sucking the very air and speech out of me, was drowning me.

I was completely unprepared for the aftermath of the intervention. It stirred feelings in me that I had no clue how to handle. When my father entered treatment, the relief and joy that I felt were intense but extremely short-lived. Right behind them flowed enormous grief and anger, and a sense of loss such as I had never known before. What had I lost in the intervention? I'd lost the illusion of having had a happy childhood. I'd lost the pretense that I had a father and mother with whom I could share my real self. I'd lost the mirage of belonging to a healthy family that encouraged honest communication and genuine contact. I felt orphaned, bereft.

My shock was as acute as if I'd suddenly discovered that the building in which I'd lived my whole life was only a facade. It was like discovering that only a paper shell had been surrounding me and protecting me all these years. Now it had collapsed and blown away, and I was left behind, staring with dismay into an empty space.

Suddenly I felt very alone.

Healing begins with the end of illusion, but the fire of truth burns even as it heals. I ran from its pain. The work of mourning was too much for me. I couldn't bear the grief and rage. I couldn't face my emptiness. In the months after the intervention, I ate as I never had before, in binges so frenzied that I was frightened. After spending a year focused on my father's addiction, on what he was doing with alcohol and what I could do to get him help, I found to my alarm that my own addiction was taking on a virulent life of its own.

Journal entries:

January 10, 1982:   I'm plugged up with food. My legs are swollen. They ache when I walk. My cheeks are fat. My stomach bulges. I hate my body. I'm ashamed of what I've done to it so quickly, so ruthlessly. There is such despair within the greed.

I went to a wedding. The bride and I whispered furtively over the remains of the wedding cake, the grand chocolate cake made so lovingly by her sister. The two of us grazed quickly through the leftovers, rushing from plate to plate, hurriedly grabbing clumps of cake and stuffing them into our mouths, while the wedding guests headed out the door, oblivious and cheerful.

Even as I stuffed myself, I knew it was hopeless. The cake would never fill me. Even if I loosened my belt and ate again until I bulged, still I'd be yearning for more. There is such despair in knowing this, even as I continue to eat.

I am bloated, burping, uncomfortable. I skirt the grief.

January 24, 1982:   I tried to kill the day. A good job of it. I slept until almost 10:00 a.m., ate whenever I could, and watched TV with as dull a mind as possible. It works. You go blank. You get stupid.

I considered setting fire to the house, starting with a bonfire in my living room. That, or throwing everything I possess into the snow, all of it scattered like the wreckage of a plane. An Air Florida jet went down in the Potomac River. How many died? I forget. Investigators say they died from the crash, not from drowning or freezing in the water. I wonder if that's true. I can imagine what that might be like, slowly freezing, growing numb.

A weekend of isolation and despair. What shall I do? Shall I go to bed? Or, before sleeping, shall I first go into the kitchen and put slices of bread in the toaster, cut some hunks of cheese, and watch TV standing up, until finally I'm too bloated to eat any more, too groggy to watch any more TV?

I don't know what I want. I want to die. I want to be alive and happy. One or the other. But more than anything I want only this: to feel no more pain.

February 10, 1982:   I don't know what's happening to me. Out-of-control eating began inconspicuously on Thursday night, when I couldn't bear the sensation of yielding to sleep. It escalated the next day after I saw a former boyfriend and felt aroused, sexy, hungry, yearning. We've stopped seeing each other. Our relationship never worked. We always ended up hurting each other. But I still miss him sometimes. This time, we flirted a little and then we said good-bye. Afterward I didn't know what to do with myself, didn't want to feel a thing. It was too painful. I started to eat. The gorging took on its own dull rhythm, as if I'd suddenly jumped onto a conveyer belt and was now forced to act according to some mechanical pulse that is alien to my own.

My abdomen is as tight as a drum. I've gained eleven pounds in four days, and I'm still eating. Last night it was a whole batch of pancakes. Suicide food. And then, three or four hours later, another batch. What do I want? I want to hide. I want to be invisible, to pull down the shades and disappear.

I'm afraid of eating lightly and of being my real self. Why? Because, for one thing, if I feel my needs, who knows what will happen? I won't be in control. Won't be perfect. I'll make mistakes that people see. Maybe life feels flat, even hellish, on the days that I binge, but at least I can predict what will happen.

It's safer not to feel anything. My needs and passions seem enormous. If I allow myself to find out what I'm feeling, what if I end up needing the world? What if I need everything? It's too scary. How can I dare to want? How can I endure the wait before a need is filled? What if it's never filled? What if I never get what I'm longing for? Yes, it's safer to suppress my hungers with food. To stay aloof from life. To feel nothing. Want nothing.

March 8, 1982: I've been undermining myself for the past five days. It's like involuntary travel to another planet, like being abruptly transported to a familiar, hostile world that I despise. I hate going there. At first, everything was fine. I was dozing late at night in front of the TV set. Then suddenly I was calmly deciding to eat instead of go to sleep. Not openly self-hating, just calm. Coolly matter-of-fact. A murder in cold blood.

Afterward, I slept fitfully, my stomach aching.

I remember a day just last week when I lived some-where else, some other place than this. It was a simple pleasure to walk, to feel my body move. I was filled with health and vitality. Everything that I perceived was clear and vivid. I felt awakened, alert. I felt the simple joy of physical well-being, the delicious sense of inhabiting my own body.

It would be a new way to live, to do the gentle, pa-tient, probing work of finding my feelings. But how could I stand them? How could I bear to be awake? I'm afraid of life. It's not death that frightens me most, it's life. So I substitute this half-life. Numb, blurred, I cruise along, always on the surface. Always in a hurry. Always in hiding.

Part of me doesn't want to live. I won't literally kill myself, but a figurative death is fine. I want to get out of this life. I'm in a life I can't live, in an unlivable life.

March 23, 1982: This can't go on. Yesterday was worse than it's ever been. Near despair, I ate cheese and half a grapefruit in the morning. Before a friend came over for lunch, I went to the bakery and bought an apricot pie and two cookies. I ate the pie very fast, standing at the kitchen counter. I ate a light lunch with my friend— how discreet I am in public, how normal, how appar-ently sane. After she left, I went out and bought more food: a coconut custard pie, a loaf of bread, and a box of English muffins. I ate them all.

March 25, 1982: I'm groggy with sleep. Stuffed with binge foods. From one bakery I bought a loaf of cheese bread and a small roll; from another, two brownies and a loathsome banana cream pie. I peeled the whipped top-ping away with my fork and flipped it into the sink. Finally, late at night, I cooked and ate a whole box of wheat pilaf. The dimensions of a binge are increasing. It's scary. I don't dare look at my body.

Last week I awoke with an orgasm for the first time in ages. In my current state of dissociation and emptiness, it was no more moving than a sneeze, a mechanical release of tension with no particular pleasure, liveliness, womanliness, or joy. Just a body, releasing physical tension. Profoundly anti-erotic.

I'm trying to find my way back to myself, to let myself again be embodied, to work mind, heart, and body back into integration, into one home together. Compulsive overeating makes everything fly apart.

My task as a residential coordinator was to help twelve men living with chronic schizophrenia to make the transition from long-term residence in a mental institution to living in a halfway house. I saw a reflection in these men of my own pains to stay connected with the world. In their struggle to maintain some semblance of coherence, their effort to preserve some continuity of self, I was reminded of my own difficulty in remembering who I was. Their enormous loneliness seemed to mirror my own. I felt for these men a compassion and a kindness that I found difficult to extend to myself. With the rest of the staff, I shared the pleasure of trying to be of service, trying to help others to find a way home, even if I myself was so thoroughly lost.

One night I ate supper at the hospital and attended an evening house meeting. Ted,* a client whom I particularly liked, was full of medication that night: Thorazine, Stelazine, lithium. He twitched incessantly.

---

* To protect their privacy, the names of clients and staff have been changed.

"I had my hair cut today," he told me, smiling nervously. "It used to come down to here," he said, showing me with the side of a jumpy hand.

"I like it short," I said.

He looked relieved.

Richard, a new client, commented, "After all, Ted, you're not Jesus Christ." But this hearty remark suddenly veered off into doubt. "Are you?"

Ted was instantly angry and anxious. "Don't joke like that, Richard. It's not funny. I'm not Jesus and you know it."

At the meeting, the patients took turns explaining what they'd done that day. When Richard's turn came, there was only silence.

"Are you having trouble remembering what you did today?" a staff member asked.

Blank face.

"Can someone help him out?"

"I'll help," volunteered Joseph, another client. "Today he went to day treatment program."

"Day treatment program," echoed Richard, watching Joseph's face.

"He went to the museum."

"Museum," repeated Richard blankly.

"He went to a meeting."

"Meeting."

"He went to Kentucky Fried Chicken for lunch."

Suddenly Richard's face broke into a smile. He remembered. He was back. That piece of his life had been redeemed from oblivion.

"Kentucky Fried Chicken," he repeated slowly, with delight.

Sometimes we need other people to help connect us with ourselves, to remind us of who we are. With coaching from his friends, the memory of food finally brought Richard back. As for me, for the most part I was too isolated to have a circle of friends like that, friends who could help me remember who I was. And food functioned not to bring me back to myself but to erase any traces of that self, to erode any contact with my real feelings and identity.

Later that night, alone at home, I quietly ate my way through a large bowl of tapioca and a jar of mixed nuts.

I knew I was abandoning myself, but I vowed that tomorrow would be different. Tomorrow I'd be myself again.

Late one night in March 1982, three months after the intervention, I received a call at home from Joseph.

"Guess what?" he said breathlessly. "Alice committed suicide last night."

Alice was not one of the clients. She was one of the staff members. After I hung up the phone, I paced the living room. I wrote myself a note:

What makes life worth living? *Is* life worth living? What you have now is *not* worth living. It's merely hiding out. Don't decide whether or not life is worth living until you actually *are* living. Decide *then*.

Later that night I woke up weeping. If Alice had intended to send a message by her death, what was it? To whom was it addressed? Was it anger? Sorrow? Despair? Faithful Roman Catholic that she was, had she believed that she would go to hell? Or had she felt that she was there already, cut off from life, from love, from God? Had I let her down? Was there something that I could have done?

I imagined her despair, and I wept for her. And for myself.

The staff decided to pay their respects during the calling hours at the funeral home rather than attend the church service. The drive took more than two hours. We talked the whole way, reviewing the events of the past few weeks and the evidence that Alice's sudden death was indeed a suicide. Of course we couldn't be sure of exactly what had happened. None of us had known Alice very well, but we all agreed that she'd seemed unhappy. We recalled several conversations about her schizophrenic mother and confusing family, her threats of suicide, her decision over the weekend to resign. We had heard a rumor that a note had been found with her body. As far as we knew, the contents of the note had been disclosed to no one but her family and her closest friend. It seemed that Alice had been found unconscious in her apartment on Tuesday night. From what we could gather, she died that night in a hospital from a drug overdose.

The funeral home was typical: neutral colors, clean surfaces, vases full of flowers, a chapel alcove, soothing music in the background. Impersonal, unchanging, timeless. A somber crowd was waiting in line at the door. We took our places, single file, at the back. Once there, I realized that I'd been hoping for something quite different: people sitting close together, talking with each other, feeling free to cry. This seemed too formal and contained.

A Catholic priest led us through a brief service. I wept a little as the homily began, but suddenly I felt a flash of surprise and anger. As far as I could tell, the priest's remarks were brazenly disguising the truth.

"Alice's life was short," he observed mildly. "Who can say why God wanted it to end when it did? Alice loved life. Her parents passed on to her a zest for life, and they gave her a lot of love."

Jane, a fellow staff member, was obviously upset, even seething. I put my arms around her.

"He has to say something to help the parents keep on going," I whispered to her. "It wouldn't help anyone if he blamed them."

"Thank you," she whispered back to me. "I see what you mean."

Still, if Alice's last message to her family and to the world had been one of anger and despair, that message was being taken away from her. I knew it wouldn't have helped Alice's parents cope with her apparent suicide if the priest had blamed them for her death. Assigning blame would be absurd. The decision to take her life, if that is what she did, was Alice's decision to make and hers alone. But to deny the truth of her feelings, to insist on obscuring the desperation of her felt situation, to drag in the name of God as a way of buttressing the lie—all this made me dizzy with anger and anxiety.

Alice's body was dressed in pink chiffon. That was part of the strangeness of it: I'd never seen her wear such a thing. There was a rosary in her folded hands. Her face was turned toward us. Her eyes were closed, and one side of her mouth drooped, as if she were frowning.

I began to cry as I shook hands with Alice's mother. I introduced myself. The mother was near tears too. She began to explain how her daughter had died: Alice had gone on a hiking trip last week, she'd fallen, she'd gotten a blood clot, she'd had a pulmonary embolism.

Alice's mother introduced me to her husband. I murmured something about having gotten to know Alice over the past year, how we'd worked together on many shifts. And then her father launched into the same story of how she'd died.

His last words were decisive. They closed off any argument.

"There was an autopsy to confirm this," he said.

"There *was*?" I couldn't help blurting out in surprise.

"Oh yes," he assured me severely.

I was caught between astonishment and courtesy, between amazement at what I perceived to be an obvious lie and the duty to be polite.

Next I shook hands with Alice's two sisters. One of them smiled brightly at me. "Now Alice is in heaven," the sister twinkled. "Now she can make us happy. That's what she always wanted to do, to make us happy. I talked to her today. You should talk to her too."

Her smile spread across her face like a Japanese fan, concealing everything behind it. I resisted the impulse to stare. I felt as if I were in the presence of a mannequin. I adjusted my own mask. I pulled my lips into an answering half-smile and tried to look understanding.

The sister introduced me to her husband. Once more I was walked through the story of how Alice had died.

By now I felt crazy. Trying to keep my voice from shaking, I ventured the question, "So that's what you think happened?"

"Yes." She grinned. And then there was a momentary crack in the facade. For one brief instant, questions poured out. "Do you know where Alice used to go hiking?" she asked me. "Do you think she really went hiking? Who do you think would know?"

But I'd grown too used to faking my way through. I was too familiar with falsehood, too used to playing along with the lie. Caught off guard by this invitation to say a word that was actually true, I equivocated. Looked away. Shrugged vaguely. Murmured something polite.

Then I fled the room. I was frightened. When we participate too long in the game of lies, their pull can become too strong to resist. I lacked the inner strength to stand up and tell the truth, even when someone asked me to. Who was I, I wondered, to tell her what I thought I knew?

. . .

If Alice had intended her suicide to be a statement addressed to her parents, it was a message that went unrecorded. If she'd meant to cry out that she could no longer bear her family's lies, its system of denial, its unreality, its unspoken pain, apparently they never heard that cry.

And I didn't help her tell her truth.

What was really going on? Was there any way of knowing? All I knew was that I'd entered the funeral home with a knot of feelings. I had no idea which feelings were most loyal to Alice, however fervently I longed to side with her, whatever her truth was. I didn't know what Alice would have wanted me to do. Would she have considered it an act of treason for me to accept what her mother and father and sisters were saying? An act of cowardice? An act of kindness?

I didn't know. I was lost in a confusion of feelings. Not knowing what to say, I fell back on manners, on custom, on what was expected, on what I'd been taught was polite. Inside, I wondered, I questioned myself: What should I do? What is the truth here? What is *my* truth?

As I looked down at the dead body of my friend, my mind flitted to images of my own dead body. If I were found dead, if I overate so ferociously and so systematically that I finally put myself to death, what would my family think? What would they tell themselves? What would my friends think? What would I *want* them to think?

Now, as I look back at Alice's death, it seems to me that she must have been trapped in a life that felt unlivable. I will never know for sure. But what I do know is that on the day of her funeral, I too was caught in an unlivable life of my own. Whatever else Alice's apparent suicide meant to her family, coworkers, and friends, however they interpreted the meaning of her life and death, Alice had given me a gift: the gift of seeing my own life and the choices before me more clearly. Staring down at her mute body, I couldn't help but ask myself, Do I want to live or die?

This painful question resonated inside me in the weeks that followed. Was there a message in Alice's life and death that could give me new energy to go forward, new courage to speak my truth? Was there something I could say to myself, something I could hear, that could make a difference? Or would I have to settle for dying in this life, arriving at the end of my days only to discover that I'd never lived? Would I have to settle for strangling and choking off the desires of my heart? Or would I dare at last to let the message of my life be openly expressed?

Struggling as I was with my own life-and-death issues, I found Alice's memorial service profoundly unsettling. I sensed that it could be, if I only let it, a time to address seriously my own questions about life; a time, as all tragedies are, for clearing away the brush that obscures what matters most; a time for truth-telling, for reevaluating what I held most dear. Profound loss offered me a time-out, a moment suspended in time, for the deepest interrogation of the heart. I was beginning to learn that loss could reveal what I loved most.

And if it was *I* who was lost, if I knew in my bones that I'd lost my way, then I needed to do the work that it takes to be found. I needed to stop pretending that I had the trail all figured out, to admit to myself and to others that I didn't have a clue where I was. I needed to stop flailing my arms and stumbling around in the dark, to sit down, to wait, to listen for the voices of the search party, to watch patiently for the sources of light, and then step by step to follow where the light might lead. I needed to chart a course that I had not taken, to reassess where home was, to take a new look at where I'd started from and where I intended to go.

At the memorial service, I saw Alice's mother lean again

and again over her daughter's body, touching it, pressing her face to it. I had to turn away at the sight of such grief; it was more than I could bear. My anger at her family eased just a bit. I could see they were suffering. I could see they were doing the best they could. Still, I was horrified by her family's persistent misreading of Alice's last message, their implacable determination to deny the fact of her pain. It was as if a stone had been hurled furiously into a pond, and the pond's surface had rippled only for a moment before once again turning a smooth face to the sky.

After the service was over, I whispered to one of my fellow staff members, "If I commit suicide, I'll tattoo a message on my body. People will read the message on my body, if my dead body alone is not communication enough. I will make my message clear."

"Well," he shrugged, "they could always just close the lid of the coffin."

As the days and weeks wore on, I tried to put the pieces together. I wondered whether I was like Alice. I couldn't help noticing that the role Alice had played in her family was not unlike my own. I couldn't help seeing that her story could well be mine, that even its ending could be mine too, if I so chose: The daughter whose job it is to make everyone happy is secretly filled with anger and despair. She can't make her family happy. Her efforts have failed. Her assigned role is impossible. She herself isn't happy, but she can neither face nor express the depth of her anger and pain. No one in the family can listen to her. No one in the family can understand what she's saying. This is meant to be a happy family. There's no room here for any other truth. The daughter is desperate. In the end, she kills herself. Her resolutely smiling family dresses her body in pink chiffon.

If Alice was unable to convince her family of her pain by speaking of it, by weeping, even by threatening to kill herself, what else could she do? Suicide may have seemed the only way out. Maybe if she killed herself her family would understand the extremity of her suffering. After all, suicide is a form of communication, even if a final one. But the one who commits suicide never has the last word. The message can be missed. "There was no suicide," the survivors can stubbornly insist. Or they can claim that the victim's level of pain did not warrant suicide: "There was no such pain."

Maybe, I thought to myself, maybe the only way to have the last word is to outlive everyone. Or maybe we can struggle to have the *best* word: to make the meaning of our life so eloquently clear that no one is confused, no one feels a need, after our life has ended, to battle over what we wanted our life to mean. In the end, each one of us faces this simple question: What is the message—the "word"—that we want our lives to express?

All through March of 1982 I tried to control my grief, anger, emptiness, loneliness, fear—all those primitive, overwhelming feelings—with food. Alice's death had sharpened the choices before me, and my grief over her death mingled with the store of grief that I'd accumulated over my family. But I hesitated at the doorway that leads into feeling. I'd pace back and forth, wrestling with my fear, and then I'd turn away, and eat and eat and eat. Filled with disgust and self-hatred, I'd battle my way back to the edge of my feelings. Again I'd stand at the doorway, again I'd be overwhelmed with fear, again I'd eat, in a flight from rage, from grief, from discovering what I truly wanted.

I'd been in therapy for years. I wonder now how helpful any insight-oriented therapy can be—however gifted the therapist—if a client is in the throes of active addiction. For me, at least, insight alone never seemed enough to stop the deadly plunge into food. Still, I clung to my therapist's words when she observed that eventually I would have the strength to keep myself company. One day, she said, I'd be able to feel my way through the emptiness and pain. I listened hard. I hoped what she said was true.

In the meantime, I swallowed everything, food and feelings alike. The more I ate, the less I felt and the faster my mind raced. Caught in a traffic jam one morning, I noticed that I was assiduously translating my thoughts into French, German, and Russian, the three languages I'd studied as an ambitious and obedient graduate student at Harvard. As if a thought repeated and refined at length in three different languages, spun out elaborately in three different ways, was worth more attention than one raw feeling.

A friend commented that I was leaping from the brain to the belly and avoiding the heart. From ideas and concepts—the life of the mind—I'd jump to my stomach, embark on a binge, never pausing in between to feel a thing.

The disembodied intellect skitters along the surface from one point to another. It flies, it speeds. Feelings take shape slowly. I made sure I kept thinking, kept moving along fast. Perhaps my feelings would never catch up.

I didn't know it then, of course, but these would be the final weeks of crisis. I was hiding myself as completely as I could, a runaway trying to cover her tracks. I wanted no one to find me. I was nowhere to be found: as far as possible, all feelings were dodged, all traces of self erased. Compulsive eating is one of the most effective ways to efface yourself. Like a dutiful child who tries to be neither seen nor heard, I disappeared.

My younger sister once told me about the time she used the guest bathroom in Quincy House. We weren't supposed to go in there, much less dirty its shiny surfaces or touch its tiny scented soaps. So my sister cleaned up carefully after herself, removing every speck of dirt, every drop of water. Our mother later admired her work, offering my sister her highest praise: "It looks as if no one were here!"

As I look back over my journal, recalling the encounters, the conversations, the observations recorded there, many of them now seem like signs along the road, pointers that eventually brought me to a place where I could begin to confront how confused I was, how badly lost. As I look back now, I remember moments that signaled a fork in the road, moments that marked the choices as clearly as the dotted lines on a map provide orientation and direction to someone trying to find a way out of the woods.

Early in April, I wrote the following in my journal:

Shut down and gloomy. I binged last night, after two days of eating well. I loitered in the Star Market, debating. I toured the frozen-food section, the shelves of cookies, the racks of baked goods. I studied the breads. I argued with myself. I considered and discarded alternatives. Finally I yielded to impulse and bought another coconut pie, and then two Snickers candy bars to tide me over on the car ride home.

Later that day I called my friend Gillian.

"I don't feel close to you anymore," she told me. "In fact, I feel like shaking you. I don't know what you feel. It's as if you were covered with Styrofoam. I want you to feel *terrible*. Because then you'd be *here*. You'd be *present*. It's as if you're going around in circles. I want you to stop and sit down and feel what you feel. I don't like what's happening to you. I love you, and I can't stand this. You can't just let your relationships deteriorate."

Just as my father had struggled to receive the message of the intervention, I groped to understand what she was telling me.

"I know this sounds stupid, Gillian," I faltered, "but I'm having a hard time taking in what you're saying. Are you saying that I have a choice: either pain and a life of relationships, or no pain and no relationships?"

"Yes," she said. "That's right."

I phoned Jeffrey McIntyre, this time not about my father's life but about my own. I needed to know from him: What could I do? How was I going to find a way out? What were the next steps for me to take? Knowing what he knew, could he offer me some hope? Could he point the way? *Was* there any hope for me?

"Sometimes you need to be hopeless before you find true hope," he told me. "You need to give up trying external solutions, whether it's eating, gambling, working, drinking, whatever. You need to realize that they won't help. Grieving takes a long time. It takes a long time to work through the sadness over what you never had."

"What can I do?" I asked him. "Can you give me a list of three things I can do?"

"Well, I'll try. You might begin by joining a group for adult children of alcoholics. There's one that begins here in just a few weeks. For many people it offers a place for learning about how addiction, our own and that of others, continues to affect us, and how we can begin to heal."

"OK," I said. "I'm willing to consider doing that. What else do you recommend?"

"You can know that the struggle is a noble one, that it's worth doing. You can know that *you* are worth it."

I was silent for a moment as I tried to absorb his words. For some reason, the first thing to be destroyed when you are actively addicted is your own self-esteem. The first thing to go is your capacity to feel loved and worth loving.

"OK," I said after a pause. "I'll think about that. Anything else?"

"You can learn to meditate or to pray. You can learn to dig deep, to get down to it."

"How? What kind of meditation? When I was in college, I tried Transcendental Meditation for a while."

"Well, I don't generally recommend Transcendental Meditation, because they use a word, a mantra, that can sometimes work like an anesthetic. I think you need the kind of meditation that teaches you to sit with who you are, with whatever is there."

I felt comforted and intrigued. Even though it was certainly not well-articulated at the time, there was something in me that knew I was in deep spiritual trouble, that something was deeply wrong spiritually. At this point in my life I had no spiritual practice of any kind.

In the years since college, I had tried all sorts of things to fill my hungry soul. Political action, social service, individual psychotherapy, financial security, academic accomplishment, intellectual challenge, the companionship of lovers and friends—to say nothing of the grim and solitary consumption of enormous quantities of food—but none of these things, in themselves, seemed to be what I was ultimately looking for. I knew I was yearning for something deeper.

I had watched my mother struggle for religious meaning in her own life, and I was beginning to suspect that I needed to do the same thing. I began to wonder whether it was time to go back to church, time to find out for myself whether any of the glorious promises that I'd heard from the pulpit as a child were even remotely true, or just so much empty speculation and hot air. I wanted to know whether the Christian faith could be based on real-life experience—or whether it was nothing but a lovely fantasy, a finely spun structure of abstract doctrine capable of offering body and soul no more nourishment than a cloud of cotton candy, no more substance than pink chiffon.

So when McIntyre recognized that my dilemma was in part a spiritual one, I felt relieved.

"What kind of meditation do you suggest?" I asked him.

"The simple kind," he answered. "The kind of meditation that teaches you to watch the thoughts and feelings come and go. And that shows you that they do come and go. When feelings arise—and you and I both know that they do indeed arise—you learn to sit there and to tolerate them, to be with them. You begin to see that you won't die from them, that you don't have to run out of the room. You discover that they won't kill you and that you won't kill anyone else. With such a practice, you no longer run away. You learn to stay inside yourself and with yourself. You learn compassion for yourself, and you learn compassion for others."

"I could use some of that," I laughed wryly.

"Meditation doesn't fix anything, it doesn't solve anything, but it does cut through repression. Your anger, sorrow, longing—none of that has to be stuffed down your gullet with food. There's another way to live, another way to feel, another way to be with others and speak with others, another way to be with yourself."

By the time I hung up the phone, I was already beginning to sense within myself an almost imperceptible shift toward daring to face my life, a subtle but decisive tilt toward hope.

A few days later, Holy Week began. April 9, 1982, was Good Friday. On that momentous morning, I leaped out of bed in a rage. I put on loud music, Stravinsky's *Symphony of Psalms*.

Sometimes music can startle me awake. Sometimes when the boat is becalmed and the sails hang limp, music can blow wind into the sails. On this day, I found I had more resources than I knew. Although all things Russian had become intertwined and confused with my complicated relationship with my father and Harvard, still there was something in these Slavic sounds that buoyed me up and bore me forward.

I declared it. I sang it. I stood with my feet planted firmly on the ground and proclaimed one simple fact. I announced one basic truth: This is my life. My life belongs to me and to no one else. It is mine. I will face it, choose it, work with it. I will not live someone else's life; I will live my own.

The night before I'd had a terrible dream. I dreamed I was looking across a field. In the dream, I noticed that the sky was covered by a curtain. "Ah yes," I said vaguely to the friend standing beside me. "Doesn't it feel cozy, living this way, being safely closed in like this?"

I was propelled awake by an anger that burst through the curtain. I threw the curtain open. I tore it apart, as if all my aggression and my two bare hands had the power to throw off the blanket of melancholy and hopelessness that had been lying over me so heavily and for so long. I refused to be closed in any longer. I renounced the apparent safety of living inside a cocoon, behind a veil, out of touch with both pain and joy. I wanted reality, whatever that was, however painful it might prove to be. Anger spurred me on.

Resolute and raging, I dragged the quilt off my bed, tore back the blanket, and pulled off the sheets. I bundled the sheets into a ball and carried them off to the washing machine. While the machine was starting up, I put fresh sheets on the bed. I was brimming with anger.

I called a friend to announce the change. She laughed and said, "I'm glad to hear you're alive and kicking!"

"Definitely kicking," I replied. "I'm fed up with feelings! Feelings stink!"

But I knew that it was precisely my feelings that I had to face. And I was ready to do the work.

On that distant morning, I was already beginning to glimpse the intensity, the ferocity, of what I felt. The fact was, I was shocked, at times dismayed, at times terrified, by the torrent of feelings that was beginning to burst up in me, like a gas main that had suddenly ignited, like a forest fire raging all around me, like a flood from which there was no escape. I was beginning to see the force of what I'd been trying to hold down, and how impossible my life would be if I couldn't bring myself to face it.

I was beginning to see how much I had to confront. Near the top of the list were my long-ignored questions about the existence of God. Questions of faith, spiritual questions, were suddenly fiercely important to me, essential to explore. It was reality that I wanted, reality that I hungered for. What was real? What was *really* real? Was God real? I longed to know, to find this out for myself.

Looking back on that pivotal morning, I wonder whether the curtain that I ripped open as I woke from my dream was not merely the curtain between me and my feelings, between me and direct contact with the world. Perhaps it was also a curtain between heaven and earth, a curtain between me and God that was rent that Good Friday morning so long ago, as if a barrier between us had suddenly fallen away.

All I knew at the time was that I was suddenly passionate about looking for God, about looking for what was ultimately real. I wanted to make contact with the Holy, if holiness there was. I wanted to go back to the religion of my childhood and examine it closely, to find out if there was something true in it. I wanted—no, I *needed*—to know whether religious experience was ever authentic. Could my struggles with desire be connected to a hidden yearning for God? Was it God that I'd been searching for all along? Who was God, anyway? Could God have any interest in me, whose life was such a shambles? Was there a chance that God was actually with me, here in this craziness? How could I find out?

I was under no illusion that I was out of the woods. It would be months, years, before I could reclaim my own body, not to mention my own soul. Yet at the same time I knew that I'd made a decision to face what I had to face. At last.

On that Good Friday so many years ago, I realized that it was time to confront my life. It was time to learn who I was. Enormous anger flowed through me as I broke out of the depression, as if the anger were opening up, enlarging, and making firm some kind of inner structure within which it would be safe to grieve, to wonder, and to explore. For once, anger was not a stranger, not a thief stealing into my house. For once, the anger was *mine*: beside me, within me, recognizable, wearing my clothes, inhabiting my body, with my very own face. Here I was. This was me. I was angry. I saw myself. I recognized myself. I could live with this. For so long, I'd been trying to shut it out, and now here it was— in me, around me, defining the space that I lived in like a sturdy house built with my own two hands. This was me. I was home. I could live with this. I was mad as hell, but I was on my way.

I felt held by the recollection of McIntyre's voice on the phone earlier that week: it was so sad and lovely and clear. I felt held by the possibility of exploring Buddhist meditation and Christian prayer. I felt held by the prospect of joining the new therapy group at Mount Auburn Hospital for adult children of alcoholics. Later on, I would feel held by its leader, who insisted that, before the group got started, I begin attending meetings of Overeaters Anonymous.

A contemptuous voice within me laughed: "What a stew of self-help projects! What a lot of busy self-absorption! Why bother with that encyclopedia of self-improvement? None of it will work. You're only wasting your time." But I paid no attention to the voice of self-sabotage. I knew where I felt most clearly led. I no longer felt as if I were flailing around helplessly in space. I knew there were concrete, specific tasks that I must do if I wanted to live. I was willing, with every ounce of my being, to do the necessary inner work, however painful it might be. I had made my choice: I had chosen life.

That morning remains crystal-clear in my mind. It was as if I were breathing fresh, cool air into my lungs; as if I were drinking a tall glass of cool water; as if I were standing at a spring deep in the woods, knowing that I'd found the way out and that however costly it might be, however painful, however bumpy or brambly the road, the journey was worth taking. In the end, God willing, it might even guide me home.

I walked through the morning filled with clarity, focus, feeling, power. When the anger threatened to fritter away into mere annoyance and irritability, I centered myself again.

"Stay with the central rage," I told myself. "Let it build inside you. Let it create a safe space to hold your grief."

I promised myself one thing: "If I'm going to grieve, I'm going to do it with gusto. One hundred percent. I refuse to go back to that vague, half-hearted mood of melancholy, or the diffuse atmosphere of a binge."

In the language of the twelve-step program, I'd finally arrived at the point of being "sick and tired of being sick and tired." I was ready to face whatever I had to, ready to feel whatever I must, ready to do anything that was necessary, in order to let my unlivable life die and allow something new to be born.

. . .

That evening, for the first time, I visited the monastery of the Society of St. John the Evangelist, the oldest Anglican religious order for men. The monastery sits beside the Charles River, just beyond Harvard Square. I stood outside for a long while, contemplating the power of its architecture: bare walls, semicircular stairs, a door at the top. All the lines of the building point toward that door: it is the hub toward which everything converges.

I hesitated. Did I dare?

Timidly I ascended the stairs, pulled open the door, and stepped inside. The chapel space was strikingly austere, ascetic, stark, filled with patches of shadow and light. I suddenly found myself in another, highly focused world. The high granite walls seemed to hold all distractions at bay. No color caught my eye except for several stained-glass windows glowing far above.

The chapel was already crowded for the Good Friday liturgy. The only seats left were behind the metal enclosure that separated the back of the chapel from the nave. I looked nervously around. I didn't see anyone I knew. The altar was far off in the distance, behind the grille, and for a while I felt shut out. Did I belong here? Was I really welcome? The voice of self-doubt murmured within me: Was I good enough? Did I deserve to be here? I was briefly tempted to slip out, to mutter apologetically to the people around me as I tiptoed past, "Sorry, folks, I made a mistake, I shouldn't be here, I have to go."

But I held my ground. I stayed put. I wouldn't leave. I wasn't going anywhere. I was here to stay.

I reached down into my core, my angry, self-assertive center. In as powerful a declaration as I had ever made, I told myself this: "I want to exist. I want to live." I had found within myself a deep river of desire. I wanted to be a real person, connected to the real world.

Most of the liturgy escapes me now. I don't remember the words of the prayers, the text of the biblical readings, the lines in the hymns, or the message of the homily. It's not the words of the service that I recall, but what I did with my body, where I moved, how I knelt, how I stretched out my hands. It was as if my mind, my intellect, was able to grasp very little of what the service was all about. For the time being, my intellect needed to step aside and observe in silence, so that my body could lead the way. It was my body that was steering me, my body that would absorb whatever wisdom was to be found within this sacred place, my body that longed to relate to the body of Jesus in a kind of deep nonverbal communion.

As I knelt and stood, listened and prayed, everything in the liturgy seemed to urge me to face the pain that brings healing, to enter the darkness that births the light, to undergo the death from which new life can spring. I knew that there was plenty in me that needed to die, and I felt anxiety and dread at such a prospect as surely as I felt the hint of hope. What I desired, what it was I longed for so ardently, I didn't yet know how to express in words.

One day I'd come to understand that I was longing to encounter the One who had made that dreadful journey first. One day I'd understand that what I hungered for was to meet the One who promises to accompany and sustain us in our suffering and fear, in our dying, in our very death. One day I'd see that I was longing to believe that all my confusion, all my stubborn willfulness, all my anguish and distress, could be gathered up within the heart of God. That all my suffering could be taken up by the cross of Christ and there transformed, so that at last I'd be set free.

I didn't yet know how to articulate these longings in words

or thought, so for now my body "spoke" them for me. After the readings, the sermon, and the Solemn Collects, the congregants were invited to walk forward through the sanctuary, kneel three times, bend down at the wooden cross that lay against the steps before the altar, and kiss the feet of Jesus.

I was briefly alarmed. "Yikes," I said to myself. "This is too gruesome, too florid, too public, too embarrassing. I can't do that."

I heard someone behind me whisper to his neighbor, "This is where I leave," and I heard the rustle of clothing, felt the slight jostle and adjustment of position, as he surreptitiously made his way out.

I watched the worshipers in front of me take their place in line and quietly make their way, one by one, to the foot of the cross. I wondered what this moment meant to them, what this gesture signified, what they were feeling, what they hoped would happen. I felt myself holding back. "It would be hypocritical for me to kneel up there," I argued with myself. "My life is a mess. My faith is too weak. I'm not wholehearted enough to go public, to express a trust in Christ that is so complete."

And yet I wondered: Was it here, in this place, that I could admit my faults, admit the secrets and the shame? Was it here that I could express how far I'd gone astray, how lost I felt, how much I longed for healing and a way home? Was it here that my whole mixed-up self could be offered, gathered up, and blessed? Was it here that my confusion and pain might be met with love?

I didn't wait for the answers. Desire propelled me forward. The desire in me was stronger than my questions, more potent than my need to analyze or rationalize, more urgent than my wish to weigh the risks or know the outcome in advance. The longing in me was too great to allow me to wait on the sidelines until my mind had figured it all out.

I knelt three times, and I kissed Jesus' feet.

I hardly knew what my body's gesture meant, and I had no clue as to where it might lead, how it might affect my life. All I knew was that a hunger in my body, in my soul, was awakening and finding "speech" through the movements of a liturgy. A hunger too deep and too wide for words was opening within me, a hunger that—to my great surprise—actually filled me not with anguish but with joy.

When I stepped forward and stretched out my empty hands to receive Holy Communion, for the first time I noticed the sheer physicality of the sacramental bread and wine. You literally taste, you swallow, you take in God. I was amazed and moved to tears. It was as if Christ was willing to address me in the only language that I could presently understand, the language of food. Here was the bread that might give sustenance to the starving little horse trapped in the blizzard. Here was the bread that might lead me home.

Later that night, I wrote in my journal:

I want to get to the center of the universe. I want to get to the center of my body, to the center of my self. And I want to live there.

April 12, 1982, the day after Easter.

Leonard Bernstein is conducting Beethoven's *Missa Solemnis* on television, and the program is being simulcast on the radio. The music blasts through my dining room.

I set the table, set the stage, for an ambiguous liturgy. Its mood is hectic. The time has come to assemble and consume one final death-dealing dinner. The prisoner prepares her own last meal, as if tomorrow she will die.

I'm an addict. Nothing is simple. Confronted with the possibility of salvation, I sit down to my own last supper. "Hors d'oeuvres" come first: I eat one large Cadbury chocolate bar in the car driving back from the supermarket, and a second as I unpack the groceries. Next I prepare a "hot meal": a batch of pancakes with maple syrup. I feel the flushed, exalted mood of a binge, but there is an added edge of intensity: this one will be my last. A feast of fools—or in any case, a feast for *this* fool.

Is it the prisoner who will die tomorrow or the prison? I don't know. Don't care. Maybe it will be both.

Tomorrow night I'll attend my first OA meeting.

This is the bottom. I can't do this anymore.

CHAPTER 4

Putting Down the Duck

Many years after I stopped eating compulsively, long after I walked into my first meeting of Overeaters Anonymous, at once anxious and hopeful, wary and eager, with my eyes downcast, my heart pounding with anxiety, and my coat wrapped tightly around my bulging body (having gained twenty pounds in the past six weeks), I happened to see a clip from *Sesame Street* that made me burst out laughing. As I remember the sequence, Ernie is clutching his beloved rubber duckie when he comes upon a jazz band. Suddenly there's nothing that Ernie wants to do more than to play jazz too. He wants to join in, catch the rhythm and carry the beat, add his own distinctive voice to the cascading play of sound. He wants to pick up the saxophone and let his spirit soar. But there's just one little problem: His hands are already full. He can't play the saxophone if he's clinging to his duck. What should he do? Ernie is worried and confused, torn between conflicting desires.

At last, an unlikely assortment of advisers steps forward to release him from his dilemma. To the brisk and jazzy beat of the band, this improbable collection of newscasters, actors, musicians, and performers—including, among others, Harry Reasoner, Barbara Walters, Itzhak Perlman, Paul Simon, Ralph Nader, and some of the stars of *Taxi* and *Upstairs, Downstairs*—repeats one after the other the same, very simple advice: "Put down the duckie. Put down the duckie. You've got to put down the duckie if you want to play the saxophone." Their voices are sometimes chiding and sometimes kind, sometimes coaxing and sometimes stern, sometimes melodic and sometimes tuneless, but their message is always the same: If you want to make music, you have to let go of the duck.

Why did I laugh? Because it's so obvious: No one can play the saxophone and hold a rubber duck at the same time. Because I saw myself in Ernie: like him, I longed, when I came in to OA, to join with life, to let loose, to let my spirit fly free. And because, like him, I was afraid. I needed encouragement to do what was so obvious and yet so terrifyingly difficult, so simple and yet so terribly hard: to put down the food and live.

My early weeks and months in OA revolved around one simple message, one basic refrain that began to pulse through my mind with the regularity of a heartbeat: Don't eat, no matter what. No matter what, don't eat.

In the lexicon of OA, the verb "to eat," when it stands alone without a direct object, is shorthand for "compulsive overeating." To refuse "to eat" means to refuse the first compulsive bite, to refuse to binge. If I wanted to have a life, if I wanted to find out who I was and why I was here on this earth, if I wanted to learn how to love and how to let love in, if I wanted to be happy and at peace with myself, if I wanted my existence to have any sense of meaning or purpose, if I wanted nothing more noble or ambitious than simply to stop being so miserable and so filled with self-hatred—if I wanted *any* of these things, I'd have to stop eating compulsively. I'd have to put the food down. It was as stark, as simple, and as scary as that.

Addiction is now widely considered to be a threefold illness, at once physical, emotional, and spiritual. To some degree, our healing takes place on all three levels at once, but in the early stages of recovery, the addict must focus all her energy and attention on physical recovery. The enormous challenge in my first weeks of OA was unambiguous and unequivocal: not to overeat, no matter what. As far as physical recovery is concerned, it makes no difference what you're feeling. It doesn't matter if you're angry with your mother and don't know what to say. It doesn't matter if your boyfriend has left you, if your cat has died, or if you've just bounced your rent check. It doesn't matter if you think nobody loves you, if there's half an hour to kill before the plane takes off and you're worried about the flight, if you've blown or aced the exam, if your boss just chewed you out or handed you a bonus. It doesn't matter if you just found out you're pregnant, or if you just found out you're not. It doesn't matter if you're stressed out, bored, or lonely; if you're angry or ecstatic, sorrowful or joyful, excited or exhausted. In fact, it doesn't matter *what* you're feeling, or what's going on, or not going on, in your life. In any case, in every case, the same principle holds true: you don't eat, no matter what. No matter what, you don't eat.

Physical recovery isn't about nuances of feelings or insights into why you overeat. It's simply about behavior, about what a person does or doesn't do. Did the hand reach for the fork, the spoon, the extra food, or not? Was the lid screwed back on the jar of peanut butter, or not? Was the cereal box closed after one serving was taken, or not? Was the piece of cake refused, or not? For someone like me, long accustomed to handling every problem, challenge, and feeling by eating over it, this was a radical reorientation indeed. Day after day, the OA program asked me to accept the fact that although excessive food had once served me as lover and friend, companion and confidante, those days were over. For good. A line had been crossed. An activity that had once given me some measure of solace and satisfaction now brought nothing but misery. Food was no longer the answer. The answer was not in the food. Like every other addict, I had to put the rubber duckie down if I wanted to make any music with my life.

I needed to hear this message over and over again. In the

first months of recovery, I needed to hear it every day, and many times a day, because it so easily slipped out of awareness. Left to my own devices, I could easily fall back into the familiar cacophony of voices that always preceded a binge. What was one little bite after all? How bad could one little slip be? What was the big deal? Who would care, who would know, if I just helped myself to a few extra slices of bread, had just another spoonful or two of peanut butter? How bad could a few bites be? I could always go back to OA the next day and begin again—right?

I remember having lunch with an OA friend just one week after I'd come into OA, one week after I'd begun eating with moderation and care. I remember casually remarking that I was thinking about going on a binge that night. My friend lunged across the table, grabbed my elbows, and looked me squarely in the eye.

"Focus!" she cried. "Focus! You need to make two phone calls. You need to get to another meeting today." And then came the refrain that had slipped my mind, the refrain that cut through all the wheedling, seductive voices spinning webs of confusion within my head: "Just don't eat. Whatever else you do today, just don't eat. A good day is a day in which you don't eat compulsively. Even if you accomplish nothing else today—even if you don't do a stitch of work, even if you're a bitch all day, even if you lie around all day in your pajamas—if you don't eat, it's a good day. Just get through today without eating. That's all you have to do. Eat tomorrow, if you have to. But don't eat today."

My friend's fervor shocked me to my senses. I was startled that somebody cared so much about whether or not I self-destructed with food. Jarred awake by her clarity, I remembered who I was: a compulsive eater trying to recover, one day at a time. And I remembered, too, the insidious nature of an eating disorder: an extra bite here or there might not matter in itself, but before long an extra bite could swell into an extra serving, and then, like a sleepwalker wandering through her own private nightmare, within a few days I could be polishing off all the food in the house. In the wink of an eye I could find myself sliding back down into the chaos that so recently had been killing me.

So I did what she told me, what I now knew I *must* do if I wanted to save my life. I got myself to another meeting. I made two phone calls. I put together another day of abstinence.

It is friends like that, support like that, that empowers the powerless. It is friends like that, support like that, that carries each recovering person through another day of sobriety or another day of abstinence, until the days gradually become weeks, and the weeks, years. That incident over lunch was just one critical moment among many when my OA friends prodded me to pay attention and stay awake, giving me the strength to listen and stay faithful to my own deep desire for healing. On the days when I lost my desire to stay well, when I could find no motivation not to overeat and plenty of reasons why I should, my OA friends encouraged me to stay abstinent anyway, until I could again claim for myself the longing to be whole and to be set free. In the meantime, until that moment came, they would carry my heart's desire for me. Physical recovery came first, even if desire and insight lagged temporarily behind.

Just as my life had once revolved around food, so too did the early stages of recovery revolve around abstinence. Eating in moderation—what OA calls abstinence—had to become the central focus of each day, for it was the task that made any other task possible. Every morning I had to ask myself: What do I need to do today in order to maintain my abstinence? What must I do to keep food in its rightful place?

I remember being taken aback, in my early days in the program, by an insistent and solemn refrain that played through our meetings like a recurring motif: "Abstinence is the most important thing in my life without exception."

"Jeepers," I sputtered to myself. "What about your spouse, your family, your friends? What about world peace? Or social justice? What about God?"

Only after some experience with the program did I come to see that for a compulsive overeater, maintaining abstinence is like focusing a camera: If the image in the center is clear, the whole picture comes into focus. Only if my food is clear am I free to love self, family, and friends. Only if I'm abstinent am I free to give myself to larger goals, or to God.

In order to help keep that clarity at the center, the OA program offers a variety of tools. In order to maintain my abstinence, I learned I must use them all. For instance, I learned to go to meetings. In the first months of recovery, I went to at least one meeting a day. In church basements and hospital cafeterias, in classrooms and meeting rooms, in corridors and halls, I met with strangers from all walks of life who were somehow just like me in the ways that mattered—people whose struggles and conflicts, shames and fears, desires and hopes, I could recognize as variations of my own. Here was a resting place for me, a place to find welcome and acceptance, a place to tell the truth. Here was a place to gain inspiration and hope, a community in whose company I could begin the slow process of healing, even though in the early days I felt too shy to speak and could do nothing more than watch and listen.

In meetings I found a world quite distinct from the world of my family—a world in which I could take my first faltering steps toward telling the truth, making my pain explicit, taking responsibility for my choices, and slowly setting aside blame. I didn't know it then, but the more I saturated myself in twelve-step meetings, the more I was learning a whole new way of life, one that empowered me not only to stop eating compulsively, but also to find new ways of relating to myself and to my family. Twelve-step meetings can change you. When you reenter your family, step back into the fray, you're no longer the same person.

I learned to use another tool of the twelve-step program: I found a sponsor, a person who had more experience in recovery than I did and was willing to offer me personal guidance as I groped my way toward wholeness.

I learned to commit myself to a daily food plan. I learned to avoid binge foods and sugar. I learned to take time to plan and to fix in writing what I intended to eat each day.

I learned to "turn over" my food to my sponsor, to "give my food plan away." For all my embarrassment at sharing such an intimate part of my life with somebody else, I learned to call my sponsor every morning and tell her what I planned to eat.

I learned to make other phone calls too. Addiction is rightly considered a disease of isolation. When loneliness closed in, when I felt anxious or overwhelmed, agitated or upset, I learned to pick up the phone instead of diving into the food. I learned to ask for help. I learned to carry a little notebook with me, which I slowly filled with OA members' phone numbers and first names. I learned, despite my shame and anxiety, that it was in fact possible to call someone I barely knew, possible to ask for a few minutes of someone's time, possible to talk about what was "eating" me until the urge to eat had passed.

I learned that it was possible to be abstinent if I took each day one by one; if I chose to live, as the program puts it, "one day at a time." The thought of giving up sugar forever was intolerable. The thought of a lifetime without Halloween candy, Thanksgiving pie, Christmas cookies, Valentine's Day chocolate, or cake and ice cream on my birthday, was more than I could bear. Just thinking about this loss was enough to evoke such anxiety and self-pity that I was tempted to plunge headlong into a binge. So I learned not to dwell on words like "never," "always," and "forever." Maybe one day I would eat sugar again, I told myself, but just for today I needed to protect my abstinence. I learned to focus on what I must do to stay abstinent just for now, just for today. If a twenty-four-hour stretch of abstinence seemed too long to endure, I focused on what I must do to stay abstinent for the next hour, or the next five minutes.

At various points during my recovery, I brought my own food with me to wedding receptions and on airplane flights. I weighed and measured my food, both alone at home and with others in restaurants. Sometimes I ate with chopsticks. Their awkwardness made me eat more slowly, tasting every bite. In the intense first weeks of the program, when my body was enduring some analogue of a drunk's going through detox, my mind topsy-turvy with the stress of withdrawal, I needed to simplify my life—to cancel unnecessary appointments, refuse dinner engagements, turn down projects—so that I could focus all my energy on the challenge before me: to eat with aware-ness, to eat with care.

For a long time, "working the program" meant being will-ing to look weird. I remember a friend of mine watching with bemusement as we prepared lunch one day at my house shortly after I joined OA. She wasn't one of my handful of "eating friends." She was one of the friends who thought I was fairly normal around food, someone who hardly gave my eating habits a second thought. In her presence, I'd always eaten sen-sibly, waiting until I was alone before pulling out all the stops and gorging on whatever I could find. I'd already planned what I would say if she or anyone else ever commented about my having gained some weight. I'd shrug and look perplexed, as if she had presented me with a mystery that I myself didn't understand, as if I had no idea how it could have happened, it must have been something in the air I breathed.

Now that I was abstinent, I handled food in public the same way that I handled it in private. A day at a time, the ancient deadly split between my secret self and the self I showed the world was being mended. I was done with lying about food. So in front of my astonished friend I did exactly what I did when I prepared an abstinent meal alone. I pulled out a measuring cup. I stuffed as much cooked broccoli into the cup as it could hold. I pressed the broccoli down. I mashed it into a shapeless pulp. I squeezed in every bit of green bud and fiber, until the measuring cup was packed to the brim. Then I took a knife and slid it carefully across the top.

My friend raised her eyebrows quizzically. "Is this what recovery is all about?" she asked.

How fussy this was, she seemed to imply, how patently greedy. Of course she was right. And I was stricken with shame. (Now she knows how greedy I really am! How strange I am around food!) Yet even in those early weeks in OA, I knew that I had been given the tools—the map, the compass—that could lead me out of the woods. But only if I was willing to use them and put up with looking like a fool. Only if I could face my shame and not let it stop me.

I explained my new routine to my friend. I'm sure I was defensive. I couldn't help but be embarrassed, but there it was; this was what I needed to do, if I was going to save my life. I'd "committed" my food for the day, I told her. I'd promised my sponsor I'd eat a cup of broccoli as part of my lunch, and so one cup I'd have, no more and no less. I was entitled to a full cup of broccoli, and I didn't want to feel deprived. When it came to food, I told my friend, I needed total clarity. For now, at least, I couldn't trust my eyes to tell me what "one serving" of broccoli might be. For me, eating "one serving" of anything meant eating the whole thing, entire, all at once. Something external and objective—a measuring cup, a teaspoon, a portable scale—could let me know where the limits lay. Then I'd be free to taste and to enjoy my food. I'd know that it was safe, that it wasn't more than my body needed, that it wouldn't lead me to binge.

Was all of this rigid? Without a doubt. Was it obsessive? Certainly. Was it necessary? I'm convinced of it. Like a house whose foundation has eroded and whose walls are toppling, I needed to be braced by an external scaffolding that could hold and contain me while the basic repairs were being made. All the insights and good intentions in the world weren't enough to stop my addictive behavior. Food had a way of slipping into my mouth even before I'd made any sort of conscious choice. Somehow the spoon was licked clean, the extra helpings were grabbed, the hand was already in motion toward the mouth, before I knew it or clearly intended it. I needed a structure outside me to help me stop—guidelines to follow, a path to walk, a net to catch me when I slipped.

More than fifteen years have passed since I came into OA, and how I work the program has changed radically. I no longer need a scaffolding to surround me so closely. There's room now for some flexibility and spontaneity when it comes to food, although I still never touch sugar. I figure it's best to let sleeping dogs lie. No more battles with Cerberus at the gates of hell. I never want to tackle that beast again.

I no longer go to many meetings, no longer follow the guidance of a sponsor or turn over a daily food plan. I no longer weigh and measure food before it goes into my mouth or travel with a measuring cup and scale. And no, I don't mash my broccoli into a pulp anymore. I eat three moderate meals a day and keep second helpings and snacks to a minimum.

Do I have to stay alert with food? Absolutely. Am I still a compulsive overeater? Yes, although a day at a time I live in balance, in grateful recovery. Am I anxious about food, worried about my weight, absorbed in the struggle to make peace with what I do or do not eat? No. The tools of OA have done their good work. The house is standing. Its windows are open wide to the world. Its doors are able to open and close. The walls of the self are durable again: there are clearer boundaries to me now, an outside and an inside, the capacity to say yes and the capacity to say no. I can eat with pleasure when I'm hungry and stop eating when I'm full.

And yet, although I don't use the OA tools as I once did, I still know they're nearby whenever I need them. If the roof springs a leak or a wall begins to sag, if food begins to call me again with its siren song, to lure me with its phony promises and deceptive deals, I know what to do and where to go. I pick up the tools at once. I get on the phone and talk with an OA friend. Recommit myself to abstinence. Pray. Write. Ask for help. If need be, I go to a meeting.

But the first step in the long process of recovery, and the foundation of a food addict's subsequent well-being, is putting down the fork, putting down the food, one day at a time. No insight into self, however subtle; no analysis of the dynamics of addiction, however accurate; no understanding of the nature of desire, however sophisticated or enlightening—none of these fine things can substitute for action. The healing of addiction depends, first and foremost, not on what we know, nor on what we feel, but on what we do—a fact that remains as stubbornly true for "old-timers" as it does for newcomers.

After spending a certain amount of time in twelve-step meetings, almost anyone can master the language. We may learn to speak eloquently about the value of "surrender to a Higher Power." We may be able to rattle off glibly the tools of the program and explain their use. We may grasp the fine points of the Big Book of Alcoholics Anonymous, the basic text of all twelve-step programs. And yet if we take no action, if we don't use the tools about which we speak, if we don't put into practice the principles that we espouse, full recovery will remain elusive.

When it comes to addiction, it's easy to kid ourselves and to settle for talk. That's why I learned in OA to mistrust so-called fat serenity, the pipe dream of being spiritually healthy and at peace, even though we continue to overeat as compulsively and chaotically as ever. OA taught me that physical recovery must come first. Action gives birth to insight. It's only when we put the food down that a deeper level of healing can arise; only when we stop our restless, random, greedy munching that we can begin to listen to the desire of our heart and to learn anything about what serenity might really be.

As the months in OA went by, the extra pounds dropped away. My body gradually returned to its natural size, and stayed there. I was used to my weight going up and down by fifteen, twenty, thirty pounds, while I alternated periods of bingeing with dieting and fasts, exercising ferociously all the while. I suppose in my lifetime I've put on and taken off many hundreds of pounds. And weighed every single ounce of flesh as it came and went.

But once in OA, I did what my sponsor requested: I began weighing myself only monthly. Gone were the days of making charts, the days of daily, twice-daily, thrice-daily weigh-ins. Gone were the days of removing clothes, glasses, earrings, and wristwatch before I stepped nervously onto the scales. Gone were the days of clinging to the towel rack and lowering myself gently down, one ounce at a time, as if a slow descent might magically lead to a lighter landing. Gone were the days of standing on the scales and leaning ever so slightly to the right, so that the remorseless arrow whose verdict I dreaded would swing just a tad further to the left. Gone were the days of weighing myself only after I had moved my bowels, emptied my bladder, blown my nose, exhaled every trace of air from my lungs. It was my food that was weighed and measured now, not my body.

OA takes physical recovery seriously, but it also recognizes that an obsession with weight is a distraction from the inner work of healing. Long before coming to OA, most overeaters have learned to dread the scale, handing over to its unforgiving eye the power to measure our worth, to weigh our failings, to proclaim us worthy or unworthy as human beings. Many of us have hooked our self-esteem to an arbitrary number on an external scale of measurement: Weigh less than a particular number, and we're "good." Weigh more, and we're "bad."

Of course, people come to OA with a range of eating disorders—from the systematic binges of compulsive overeating, to the binge-and-purge of bulimia, to the self-starvation of anorexia. For some members, it's a struggle not to get too thin, and they need the help of the program to maintain sufficient body weight. As one anorexic young woman wryly observed, "Before I came into the program, I was proud that I could get down from a size 7 to a size 5, and then a size 3, and then a size 1. And then one day I woke up and said to myself: What's next? To get down to a size zero? And I began to ask: What's so great about trying to make myself disappear?"

Whether we hope to gain, to lose, or to maintain our present weight, many of us discover that it helps us to stay sane if we weigh ourselves only occasionally, and always within the context of a loving relationship. I learned to call my sponsor right after my monthly weigh-in. Whether the news from the scale made me feel crazy and threw me back into self-hatred and self-doubt (because I thought I was fat) or left me giddy with anxious exhilaration and pride (because I thought I was thin), she listened to my feelings and offered me reassurance and a larger perspective.

Even more important, the twelve-step program helped me to jettison the notion that my value as a person was inextricably tied to how much I weighed. Never mind what society had to say to me and to other women. Measuring my body was no way to assess whether I "measured up" as a person. In fact, OA called into question the whole concept of "measuring up." It challenged me to let go of my perpetual frantic efforts to size up my value as a human being; my struggle to prove, once and for all, that I deserved to be loved. OA, like all twelve-step programs, seeks to help its members realize that we're *already* loved unconditionally, that we don't have to do something special to deserve to be loved, that we can fall down and make mistakes, that we can confess that we've blown it and receive forgiveness, that we can begin again.

The love that can be found in twelve-step meetings is astounding. I remember one woman telling me how grateful she was for her sponsor.

"The thing I can't stress enough," she said, "is how much her kindness means. The other day I ate an extra handful of soybeans, and she didn't come down hard on me. She helped me let it go and begin again without hating myself. I have enough whips and chains of my own. I don't need anyone else's."

OA members try to love one another. God knows, we don't always do it well, don't always get it right. But most of us find more love extended to us in an OA meeting than we're able, at first, to extend to ourselves. And the power of that love helps to wean us from depending on external things—a high grade point average or a large paycheck, an impressive résumé or a low number on a bathroom scale—in order to know that we have "weight" in the world, that we have value and significance as human beings.

Certainly many people come to OA because they want to step on a scale and see the number go down. If they're overweight and work the program, certainly they'll lose what they need to. But the focus of OA isn't on losing weight. It's on learning to live. In the words of one OA member, "OA doesn't want you to be obsessed with being thin. If you're going to be obsessed about anything, be obsessed with growing up."

With the program's help, I learned to stop incessantly weighing my body, to let it rest, to let it be, even to accept it at its current size and shape without bitter self-recrimination. Ever so slowly I learned that if I was kind to my body, if I treated it with gentleness and respect, if I refused to judge it harshly or measure it against some external ideal of perfection, I could begin to live more peacefully inside my skin. I could begin to discover that my body was my home, begin to listen to what my body had to tell me.

And there was plenty that my body wanted to express. For months, for years, my intense craving for food had blotted out every other desire; obscured, even obliterated, my awareness of other feelings. The moment I stopped eating compulsively, the moment I stopped silencing myself with food, I discovered that the rest of me had plenty to say. Feelings bubbled up in me, all sorts of feelings, large and small. I couldn't make sense of most of them. I had no clue what they were about or why they were so intense. But with the support of OA and the guidance of my therapist, I did what I could to notice them, feel them, name them, let them in, while at the same time holding fast to my commitment not to overeat, no matter what. Like blood flowing into an arm that had gone numb, like color flooding the sky at dawn, feelings began to stream through me.

The longer I didn't overeat, the more spacious I grew inside. It was as if, every time I was able to stop and turn my attention to the feelings moving within me, my inner house could grow a little larger, another inner door could be pushed open, another room could slowly be filled with light. The more I held fast to the resolve to eat no more than my body needed, the greater grew my capacity to let feelings arise and pass through me without trying to fix them, change them, or drive them away.

Needless to say, this wasn't easy. It's no more comfortable to tolerate the twinges of sensation that precede full emotional release than it is to endure "pins and needles" when blood flows back into a leg that has fallen asleep. For example, let's say I feel a pressing urge to eat. Thoughts of food fill my mind. I know it's nowhere near mealtime and that my body isn't really hungry. I'm clear about my commitment to being abstinent today. I can't eat right now. But what's going on inside? Am I willing to find out? Am I willing to feel it? Uncertain, uneasy, I have to stop what I'm doing and begin to listen inwardly. Almost always, the first thing that pops into my mind is, "I hate this!"

The decision not to eat but instead to face your feelings, however unpleasant they may be, is a decision not to bolt, not to run or dodge or flee. It's a decision to stay put. You must be willing to resist all the urgent inner voices that exhort you to hustle. "Keep moving!" they implore. "Keep running. Keep busy. Whatever you do, don't stop! What's coming is too awful! You couldn't bear it! Don't look around! Don't feel it! Don't feel anything!"

To resist the internal pressure of anxiety, you must be fierce. Like a warrior on the battlefield, you must stand fast. You must refuse to run. You must instead turn and face your "enemy," the part of yourself that longs to have its say, longs to be heard, longs to be made welcome. If addiction cuts us off from our feelings, recovery demands the costly work of letting them back in.

And so, even if every particle of my being is clamoring to run, to eat, I've learned that I must stop and find out what's going on. OK, I ask myself, if I wasn't obsessed with food just now, what might I be feeling? Can I stay for a while with this itchy sense of restlessness? Can I breathe into this vague state of tension, letting it be just what it is, until a clearer feeling emerges? Can I feel my way into the possibilities? For instance, am I sleepy? Lonely? Angry? Sad? Where's the feeling being held in my body? Is it a constriction in the chest, a wrench in the guts, a tightness in the throat? Can I let that feeling speak to me? Can I give it a little airtime? Am I willing to discover what I'm really hungering for?

Sometimes I discover I'm sad and need to cry. Sometimes I discover I'm sleepy and need to go to bed. Sometimes I discover I'm angry and need to fume, pound a pillow, talk it out with someone, find a way to address the situation. If I can't eat over the feeling, if I can't stuff it down with food, I'll have to find some other way to work with it. Fortunately, just as there are an infinite number of ways to blot out feelings—by eating, smoking, shopping, watching television, working, having sex, taking a drink, what have you—so are there any number of ways to express and accompany ourselves in times of strong emotion. We can do something receptive—dig in the garden or go for a walk, take a bath or listen to music, dance or draw, gaze at a tree, weep with a friend. All these activities can help us listen to our feelings, face them, bear them, learn from them, without having to run away.

In order to stay open to my inner experience, I sometimes find it best to do nothing at all, to just sit and breathe, to give the feeling space, to explore its contours, to give it my full attention with none of the distractions of my usual busyness. I may need to listen to the feeling, however painful or disjointed, with the same attentiveness that I'd bring to a Brahms symphony.

All this was new to me when I began in OA. One fumbling step at a time, I learned the art of listening to myself. And before long, I began to see how miserly and pinching I was with myself, as if I doled out pleasure by the teaspoon. For heaven's sake, when was the last time I'd gone out for a walk or taken a leisurely bath? Before OA, I'm sure I would have objected, Who has time for such things? Who has room in their lives for such self-indulgence? But as I clung to abstinence, I began to see that if I didn't want to act out with food, I'd have to find other ways of feeding myself, other ways of offering myself nourishment and care. I needed to be generous to myself, to make room in my life for such "treats," if I didn't want to resort again to the edible "treats" that had made my life a living hell.

I also began to realize that for years I'd misinterpreted every bodily sensation, every twinge of emotion, as a signal of hunger. Was I bored? Sad? Frustrated? Lonely? The one-size-fits-all interpretation was always the same: You're hungry! Go eat! But now I learned that I must question that automatic interpretation and reexamine my bodily experience. I had to explore whether what I'd read as physical hunger was in fact the glimmer of a feeling, a hint that something needed my attention. On rare occasions the urge to eat was indeed a sign that I was hungry, but more frequently it signaled a feeling just below the surface, only beginning to take shape.

There were a lot of them, especially in the beginning. I have yet to meet an addict whose recovery didn't begin in emotional turmoil. What didn't I feel, in my first weeks in OA? Like every newcomer, I felt it all. I was afraid I'd never get well. Afraid the program wouldn't work. Afraid I'd fail. Afraid I'd feel deprived. Embarrassed about weighing and measuring my food in front of other people. Sad that I couldn't handle food the way that normal people can. Angry that it took enormous effort to do what normal people seem to take for granted—to eat moderately, to have an uncomplicated relationship with food. Frustrated that my normal friends didn't understand my terror and greed around food. Ashamed when I tried to explain it to them.

Feelings of all sorts began to erupt in me, and OA gave me a place to admit them, encouragement to express them, a context within which to sort them out. Here I could talk about my fear of exposing my "angry bones" and count on several heads nodding yes. Here I could speak about the anguished split between my overly intellectual, perfect, false self, and my humiliated, out-of-control, secret self. Here all of us could tell our stories in a place where the fear and loneliness, anger and sorrow, could be named, expressed, and released at last. Physical recovery was important in OA; we didn't have to settle for fat serenity. But we needed emotional recovery too. As people in OA put it, we didn't want to end up being "thin and sick"— that is, physically slim but emotionally sick. There was inner work to be done, and we did it.

How? We talked. Shared feelings. Confessed secrets. Ventured hopes. We listened, wept, laughed. We held hands at the end of the meeting, recited aloud the Lord's Prayer or the Serenity Prayer, repeated the familiar chant, "Keep coming back. Give a lot of love. It works." We offered one another as much love as we could, doing our best to create a safe space for healing, for truth-telling, for supporting one another in the labor of learning to live without food as our primary consolation and support.

Stories spilled out of us. One woman spoke about a hot, muggy summer day when the thermometer had hit 96 degrees, but she'd nonetheless bundled up in layers of heavy clothing to hide how much weight she'd gained. Someone else told us about the time she got into a car accident: she was unable to get both hands on the steering wheel in time because she didn't want to drop her ice cream cone. A newly slim woman came close to tears as she talked about her anxiety. That morning she'd tried on her pants seven different times, with and without pantyhose, with and without underpants, with both pantyhose and underpants, over and over, every which way. She was never satisfied with what she saw.

"Finally," she confessed, "I just took everything off. I comforted myself by wrapping up in a heavy wool coat. Now that I've lost weight, I don't know if I'm skinny or huge. I feel so exposed."

We listened, we nodded, we understood.

A man who was just coming back to OA talked about his futile attempts to handle food on his own, his failed resolutions not to overeat, his desperate effort to save himself through brute willpower. At last, baffled and despondent, he telephoned his former sponsor, who simply asked him, "What's your food plan for today?" And he gave it away, he turned it over, he discovered again that he didn't have to struggle alone.

"This isn't about weight," he concluded. "This is about sanity."

The people who came to meetings were in every stage of recovery. Some of them had long-term abstinence. Others were new to the program, or newly abstinent, or struggling to recover from a relapse. Some were filled with joy because they'd begun to taste the fruits of serenity, the peace that comes from refusing to eat more (or less) than your body really needs, the simple pleasure of inhabiting a body no longer wracked by the restless urge to eat. Their witness offered courage, strength, and hope to members who were still wrestling with the feverish lust for food. For many people, maintaining abstinence feels like recovering from a chronic low-grade fever: Suddenly you notice that your body feels peaceful. A constant, fidgety preoccupation has quietly dropped away.

Some of those who came to meetings were filled with pain. They talked about the anguish of losses, past and present; about the fears and sorrows, resentments and setbacks, that are part of daily life.

"My life is painful right now," one woman observed, "but you know, at least now I *have* a life. I'm not eating over my problems. I'm facing what's here and feeling it, and I know that this pain will pass."

Were OA meetings perfect? Did they work beautifully every time? Was every member of OA a paragon of insight, a model of maturity and healing? Did every sponsor say the right thing, offer the surest guidance? Of course not. Some meetings were stronger than others, more focused or more inspiring. And that turned out to be all right. None of us was perfect, none of us was whole, but together we could help each other to stay on track. Together we could remind each other that recovery was possible, recovery was real, and the tools to claim it for ourselves were in our hands.

OA gave me an experience of community, a network of relationships that penetrated the hard shell of my isolation. Gradually I learned how to listen to what other people said at meetings, even the ones I didn't like very much. I learned to listen for the wisdom hidden in each story, the hope hidden behind the pain. I learned to listen for whatever each individual could show me about the process of becoming more real, more human, more fully alive. I learned to identify with some part of every person's story. I learned that if I felt shocked or troubled by something someone said, I was probably coming face to face with a part of myself that I hadn't yet met.

Emotional recovery takes place within community, because part of it is discovering just how inextricably linked we are to each other; how much we influence each other; how much our own willingness to tell the truth, to feel the pain, to express the joy, helps free other people to do the same. In OA I discovered the healing power of participating in a community that is mutual rather than authoritarian, reciprocal rather than hierarchical; a community in which we are all equals, all suffering from a similar pain, all fired by a similar longing, all sharing a core desire to get well. By myself, I couldn't stop from compulsively overeating. In fact, when it came to staying abstinent, I could do nothing on my own. But in OA I discovered that I could help someone else, and that someone else could help me.

Through the power of our relationships with one another, healing could happen and new energy could be released.

One afternoon, several months into recovery, I found myself veering toward self-destruction. I'd done no productive work on my dissertation that day; in fact, I had done nothing that made the day at all worthwhile. I was lapsing into isolation, self-hate, and depression, and I was starting to obsess about food.

"Well, I might as well make it a perfectly bad day and start eating tonight," I muttered angrily to myself. I decided not to say anything about this to my sponsor when I called her for my daily check-in late that afternoon. I was vague with her, evasive. I committed my food for the following day, but I said nothing about what I was feeling or the binge that I'd secretly planned.

To my surprise, my sponsor listened to me quietly and then began to speak about her own loneliness and sorrow. Lured into honesty, I said a few words about the pain that I was carrying in my own heart. The truth set me free. A few moments of listening to her truth and of telling my own, a few moments of offering each other a handful of words that expressed what was really going on, released in me, in both of us, the willingness to say yes to life. I accepted her invitation to meet that night at an OA meeting.

When we spotted each other in the group, both of us smiled. Through the power of relationship, we'd helped each other to stay alive: abstinent, open to the moment, engaged with life.

"Not such a worthless day after all," I said to myself as I drove home that night.

Through regular attendance at OA meetings, through daily contacts with my sponsor, through frequent OA phone calls, I slowly took in the presence and companionship of these new friends. I began to experience myself not as an autonomous individual who lives over and against everybody else, not as an isolated monad, not as a self-sufficient individual who goes out into society but then withdraws into the "real" world in which she is fundamentally alone, but rather as a person whose basic identity is relational. I discovered that I was most truly myself when I was open to relationships with others, when I knew that I belonged to a community. I was most truly *me* when I felt my participation in a web of relationships that extended far beyond my own little life, my one little self.

The only way to know this on a visceral level was not to overeat. When I ate compulsively, the world around me instantly shrank: there was no one here but me and nothing but the desperate, urgent need to fill myself with food. When I refused to eat compulsively, when I refused to consume more than my body really needed, I could perceive a community of others who were willing at a moment's notice to offer me their love and support. I could see I wasn't alone. A circle of healing could begin its gentle work. The more I opened myself to others and tried to be of service, the less I felt the urge to stuff myself with unnecessary food. The less I stuffed myself, the more fully I could take in the companionship of other people and in turn offer them my friendship as well.

When I was alone in my house and just beginning to feel a restless urge to browse through the refrigerator, or beginning to entertain the idle thought that I might just wander over to the pantry to see what goodies were stashed on its shelves, I learned to bring to mind all my friends in OA, all my fellow seekers who were trying, like me, to stay abstinent one day at a time. Their invisible but almost palpable presence gave me support. And if this awareness was not powerful enough to bring me back to my senses, I could activate my community by picking up the phone.

Conversely, when the phone rang in my quiet house, when someone in OA gave *me* a call and was obviously looking for connection, daring to hope that I might be willing to listen and share in the person's joy or pain, what fierce and quiet happiness I felt in being able to offer help. The phone call confirmed my leap of faith. Even though I was alone, I was part of a community; even though no one else was in the room or even in the house with me, I belonged to something larger than myself.

This may not be news to those who aren't addicts, but to those who are, it's the stuff of revelation. Abstinence is all about relationship, because it begins with a willingness to ask for help. Abstinence springs out of community and is sustained by community. And abstinence, in turn, tends to form and enlarge community. Ask anyone in a twelve-step program, and they'll surely tell you the same story: Because one person was abstinent (or "clean," or sober), he or she could help someone else. And because that person was set free, he or she could then help someone else. And so the stream of light passes from one person to another, one person's life touching and illumining another's, until our web of interconnection is complete. Thus we are healed and made whole.

It seems to me that abstinence is a profoundly transgressive act, an act of resistance, a direct and daily challenge to the status quo. Refusing to take in extra food is a step in saying no to all the inner and outer voices that urge us to fill ourselves not by making contact with each other, but by consuming more than we really need. These voices urge us to shop, take, grab, amass, acquire, because otherwise we're empty, otherwise we're nobody, otherwise we're alone. Refusing extra food is a way of saying no to the lie that we're cut off from each other, that we're fundamentally isolated and can give each other no real nourishment.

When I stand my ground and refuse to overeat, I'm saying yes to a life that is lived in relationship. I will listen to my body, and I will listen to its needs. I will live in connection with others, without closing up, shutting down, or hiding out. I will face the truth of my experience. I will face what I feel. I will face what is here, trusting that I'm not alone, trusting that a community of love supports me and surrounds me, even though at the moment I may not be able to see it with my eyes or touch it with my hands.

Which brings me, of course, to the question of faith. Coming into OA, I wondered who this God was whom I could neither see nor touch but whom I yearned to know. This God that members of the twelve-step program referred to—vaguely, it seemed to me—as a Higher Power. In what sort of deity was I supposed to believe? In what sort of deity would I want or be able to believe?

These were hardly frivolous questions. There's an old joke that makes the rounds in twelve-step groups, a saying about the difference between religion and spirituality: "Religion is for people who are afraid of going to hell. Spirituality is for people who've been there." I was definitely in the latter camp. The externals of religion—adherence to custom, tradition, rituals, and laws—could have little meaning for me unless they sprang from a deep seriousness of purpose, unless they were connected to an awareness that the captive who needed to be set free, the patient who needed healing, the sinner who needed saving, was not someplace else or someone else. She was here and she was me. I'd been to hell already, I was trapped in hell right now, and I wanted out. I wanted help. I wanted God.

The twelve-step program is all about spirituality. I don't think anyone enters a twelve-step program without being desperate. For most of us, it's the method of last resort, the place we turn to only after we've tried and failed at every other conceivable way of changing our lives. The spirituality of the twelve-step program is a spirituality for people who've known anguish, for people who've daily confronted the choice between life and death and discovered, time and again, how mortally difficult it is to make the choice for life. It begins with the shattering admission that our lives are out of control. We've tasted hell, and left to our own devices, we are more than likely to stay there.

By the time I limped into OA, I was ready to admit defeat. In the language of the twelve-step program, I'd "hit bottom." I was ready to admit that I was in serious trouble, that I was powerless over food, and that I badly needed help. I was ready to explore what it means to put one's trust in a Higher Power and to depend on that Power for insight and strength.

To my relief, I discovered that the program didn't require me to accept any particular religious doctrine or worldview. It simply asked me to keep coming to meetings and to keep an open mind. I was surprised to see the variety of ways that OA members spoke of the divine. For some people, "H.P." was some version of the God represented in mainstream Judeo-Christian religions. For others, it was a goddess figure, or the energy of compassion, or simply the power of the group itself. As we mused one day about Step Three, the step in which we "made a decision to turn our will and our lives over to the care of God *as we understood Him*," one woman offered a disarming description of her Higher Power.

"People generally think of God as some kind of enormous, impersonal force," she observed. "You know, the omnipotent God out there in the cosmos who makes the planets turn. I can't relate to a God like that. So I made up one of my own. Her name is Donna. She's divorced. She's got two kids. She's very down home. When I go shopping for groceries, it's Donna that I talk to as I walk down the aisles. And let me tell you, it's Donna who's keeping me abstinent."

It was possible, I could see, to imagine God in more intimate, even playful ways than I'd ever dared. For those of us who found the word "God" an empty symbol devoid of meaning—or what's worse, a symbol filled with negative or punitive connotations—it was liberating to pose new questions about our faith. We could ask ourselves: Who do I wish God were? What do I wish God were like? Who is the God that I'm longing for? Who is the God that I don't want, the God in whom I no longer believe? How does the God I seek relate to the God of my own faith tradition? Slowly, tentatively, we began to listen to the longings of our souls. Sometimes we inspired each other, goading each other to dream bigger dreams.

"The reason I want you to sponsor me," one OA member confessed to another, "is because I like your Higher Power."

Some of us stayed with our inherited images of the sacred. Others gave themselves permission to imagine the deity in new ways. But always the twelve-step program gave one simple, potent message: however we imagined the holy, however we conceived of the sacred, God wanted to help us stop our compulsive eating. In God we had an ally, a Power that could save us. Whether we met our Creator on a pew or a prayer bench, on a zafu or a prayer rug, in a church, temple, zendo, or synagogue, in nature, in twelve-step meetings, or anywhere else, the Power that was higher than we were—greater, deeper, larger than ourselves—offered us the strength to stop eating compulsively. OA challenged us to begin to put our trust in that Power; to depend on that Power's capacity to care for us, to protect us, and to set us free in all the daily choices of our lives, but especially when we were beset by the deadly urge to overeat.

I began to practice a very simple, frequent, and honest form of prayer, no doubt a form of prayer that has been uttered by human beings since the dawn of time: Help me! I learned the power of turning, both in words and in silent inner gesture, toward the One who alone could get me through the next five minutes without my diving into the cookie jar or the bread basket. If I needed to pull my car over to the side of the road, if I needed to step out of a conference, if I needed to lock myself in a stall in the ladies' room in order to collect myself for that simple, secret, urgent prayer, then that is what I'd do.

Addiction to food is different from other substance addictions. For starters, unlike heroin or cocaine, food is legal and readily available almost anywhere that people gather to work, play, shop, and live—from the rows of candy at the gas station to the beer and bags of peanuts at the baseball stadium, from the gum machine at the Laundromat to the bowl of peppermints on the receptionist's desk. In the prosperous United States, food is everywhere, which means that in the course of a single day a recovering food addict must confront her drug over and over again. But not only that. Unlike substances such as tobacco or alcohol, which are also readily available, food is necessary for survival. A recovering food addict can't simply swear off food. She must learn to interact with it: to handle it, prepare it, and eat it in a way that keeps her sane, in a way that keeps her alive, both when she's with others and when she's alone.

The only way for me to do this is to pray. Prayer slowly became the undercurrent of my life, sometimes serving as its quiet backdrop, sometimes leaping into clear relief in the foreground, as I went through each day and asked for help not to overeat. I remember one OA member explaining that her kitchen counter had become her altar. There, as she sorted and sliced, seeing and smelling the food that had once flowed murderously straight into her mouth, she found that she must surrender utterly to God. Only with the help of God, only in the presence of God, could she handle food with care and self-restraint. Illuminated by her desire for God, this woman's kitchen became a space as sacred as a sanctuary.

Just as I learned that the urge to eat was usually the signal of a feeling that needed to be explored, I also learned that the urge to eat was a signal to pray. Since the urges to eat were frequent, so too were the reminders that I must turn to God. From moment to moment, day in and day out, I had to return again and again to my desire for God, my dependence on God's help, my need for a saving relationship with the Source of life. There's nothing like addiction to teach us that we can do nothing by ourselves.

And yet I also learned that just because I was powerless over food, I need not—no, I *must* not—be passive. Passivity implies a shrug of resignation, a disingenuous "Oh well, what can you do?" It invites the almost devil-may-care attitude of "Let's just wait and see what happens, shall we?" Passivity wears a mask of resigned acceptance, the compliant, docile face of the victim who refuses to take any responsibility for the cravings that beset her. It is a setup for eating compulsively: since I'm helpless over my bingeing, I might as well go out and do it again.

"Powerless," on the other hand, suggests profound defeat, an admission of utter failure that goes deeper than the sense of being passive and helpless. When I confess that I'm powerless, I recognize that I've come to the limits of what I know how to do. I face the fact that my autonomous willpower is unable by itself to stop me from overeating. Out of the depths of this powerlessness bursts a cry for help, a willingness to reach out for a relationship with some trustworthy Other that has the power to save me. I may not know exactly who that Other is; I may not know how or when that saving power will come. But I do know that I can't save myself, that I must throw myself upon the mercy of the Power who can. And there is plenty that I can do to align myself with that Power: I can drop the fantasy of handling my addiction alone. I can ask for help. I can use the tools of the program. I can practice each of the twelve steps to the best of my ability. Above all, I can pray.

After coming to OA, I struggled day after day to surrender to God. I struggled to trust that even when I was alone, I was still intimately connected with a Someone who loved me, a mysterious Someone who was longing to enter into a relationship with me, if only I were willing to ask and to consent.

One night, four weeks into the program, four weeks into abstinence, I sat down for supper alone. I looked down at the plate of food that I'd committed to my sponsor. The meal looked so small. There were two poached eggs, a cup of turnip cooked with a tablespoon of butter, and two cups of salad with a tablespoon of low-fat dressing. That was it. No rolls, no rice, no potato, no crackers, no wine, no second helpings, no sweets— and nothing else to eat until breakfast the next morning.

I was tired and hungry, and I wanted to binge. There was no way that this pathetic little meal could fill me. But then I remembered to say grace. I took a breath, turned to God, and offered what paltry, halfhearted thanks I could. And suddenly love flowed into me. Suddenly I felt immensely cared for. In my mind's eye I saw the face of my sponsor and the faces of all my friends in OA. I looked down again at my plate, and now this moderate meal with its clear limits was a sign to me that someone outside me was helping me. Someone was letting me know just how much food I needed to nourish myself. This meal was not a deprivation; it was a gift, a sign of love. I sat down to a feast.

Gratefulness welled up in me for all the support that I was receiving and for the fact that, mystery of mysteries, I was finally allowing myself to receive the help I needed. Tears came to my eyes. I ate the meal attentively and slowly. I ate it in the company of God and with the invisible companionship of my friends. I found the food delicious. I was filled. I was satisfied. I'd been given just as much as I needed.

"So this is what it means to have enough," I said to myself. "This is what 'enough' feels like."

Spiritual recovery in OA is characterized by humble stories like this one: stories that aren't glamorous, spectacular, or heroic; stories that would never make the evening news or the local newspaper. Spiritual recovery is often not dramatic. It's made up of little moments like this one, moments when we open ourselves to relationship rather than turning away, moments when we dare to perceive and to trust the love that's within us and around us.

Twelve-step spirituality is grounded in our caring for these little moments. In the past, I would have overlooked them as unworthy of my attention, too insignificant to notice. Who cared what happened while I ate a moderately sized meal? And what was the value of moderation anyway? I was used to—and in some ways I preferred—the drama of extremes: a wild binge or a lengthy fast, the lurid excess of a no-holds-barred, blow-out feast or the transparent purity of near-starvation. Why? Because, when it came right down to it, I had no awareness at my core that anyone really cared about me. I didn't believe that I was really seen and known and loved. Most of the time I wasn't sure what I really wanted or really felt. Perhaps at some level I even wondered whether I myself was real.

Both bingeing and fasting erupted out of a great inner emptiness. Maybe, through one extreme or the other, I could make something happen. Maybe I could prove to myself that I was alive. Maybe I could make God show up. Maybe I could make God real. Maybe I could play the central role in a drama in which I was either the wanton sinner or the glorious saint, either eternally damned or surpassingly holy. Maybe, through the practice of excess, I could capture God's attention, I could be someone in the eyes of God. Maybe I could find a place in the drama of salvation.

OA challenged me to drop the dramatics. My self-created drama wasn't necessary. Like everyone else, I did indeed have a part to play in the drama of salvation, but I would never discover what it was if I kept on hurting myself with food. OA could help me to make healthy choices, so that I ate what I needed. I had to learn to connect with God, with the living Source of my life, not through a violent reveling in extremes but through the practice of moderation. I had to learn to stay patiently with my inner emptiness. I had to enter it, taste it, pray from within it, cry out for a God who could meet me in my loneliness, a God who could accompany me in the ordinary, quiet, undramatic moments of day-to-day life.

Maybe then I could begin to thread my way through the thickets of my family relationships, begin to find the words and cultivate the silence that would help me to create a self that was my own.

CHAPTER 5

Clearing a Space

One morning in early May shortly after beginning OA, I received a phone call from my mother.

"I haven't seen you for a while," she said with affection. "How about coming over for lunch today? Maybe around 12:30?"

"Sure," I replied. "That sounds fine."

After we said good-bye, I telephoned my OA sponsor: I needed to change the food that I'd just committed for the day.

"It turns out that I'm eating lunch with my mother," I explained. "So here's what I'll commit to you now: I'll eat a moderate portion of whatever she serves."

"No way," my sponsor replied. "You've already committed your food for the day. You can't change it now."

"What?" I sputtered. "But that's crazy. I'm not talking about a binge. I'm talking about having a regular lunch with my mother. I'll eat a moderate amount of healthy food, OK?"

"No." She was adamant. "That's not the way to work your food plan. You've already committed your food for the day. You can only make changes if your committed food has run out or if it's spoiled. Other than that, if you change your food, you are taking back your will."

By now I'd learned some of the vernacular of the twelve-step program. I knew that "taking back one's will" was a no-no, the prelude to a binge. One might as well lean over into the driver's seat, grab the steering wheel, and send the car careening off the road and over the edge. My own experience of such willfulness was all too recent. I knew the taste of defiance and its dreadful cost. Still, I chafed at my sponsor's decree. In proposing to change my food, was I in fact taking back my will? Or was I listening to my own inner wisdom? If I did as my sponsor told me, would I be abandoning my own common sense and granting her too much power?

Years later, with more experience in OA under my belt, I'd know that a different OA sponsor might have responded to this situation in another way, offering a more collaborative conversation as we worked out together the best way to handle the change in food. Another sponsor might have agreed easily to the change. But the sponsor I had then was quite strict. At the time, I was annoyed with her inflexibility and found her rules rigid. In hindsight, though, I'm grateful for this interchange. It showed me something that otherwise might have taken me a long time to see.

As I stood in silence with the phone in my hand, stopped dead in my tracks by my exacting sponsor, irritated by her petty rules, an image of my mother swam into awareness and floated before my eyes as smoothly and quietly as a fish. For an instant, I shivered with anxiety. I suddenly saw what was at stake. The issue was not my sponsor; the issue was my mother. I didn't want to make waves with her. I didn't want to cause trouble. I didn't want to disturb the placid surface of our relationship. It seemed rude, a hard-hearted refusal of hospitality, to call my mother back and say that she needn't cook anything for me, that I was bringing my own lunch. But even worse than that (and here a cold ripple of fear wound up my back), bringing my own meal seemed to announce with unbearable clarity that something had gone wrong between us in our transactions around food and that I now needed to do things differently. I knew that my mother must have noticed over the years that my weight tended to go up and down like a yo-yo, but I'd never talked with her about my compulsion to overeat. I'd never mentioned to her the desperate appetite that awoke in her presence, the longing to receive something more, the frustration when it never came. Such things had never been speakable between us. How could I begin to speak them now?

For as long as I could remember, my mother and I had been like two fish swimming side by side in the same vague sea. If she dipped to the right, I dipped that way too. If she glided to the left, I followed with a smile. We moved as one. Like a fish whose blood temperature varies with the surrounding water, I took my cues from my mother's moods. If she was relaxed and happy, I could be happy too. If she was tense or withdrawn, I was on edge too. Since I never knew for sure what she was feeling or what was going on within her, I learned to tune my awareness to every hint, every gesture, every signal, and to adjust my behavior accordingly.

Only I knew the cost. When I sat down to eat with her, I couldn't taste my food. Tasting only takes place inside the body. Salty or sweet, sour or bitter, crunchy or smooth—all such distinctions of taste and texture can be registered only if one has some degree of interior awareness. But when I ate with my mother, my awareness was focused outward: Why was she grimacing? Why did she put her fork down so abruptly? What was the meaning of her enigmatic smile? What was really on her mind? What was she feeling? Was she angry? Was she sad? What was going on inside her? What did she see when she looked at me? Horror of horrors, was she watching me eat?

Most of the time I'd leave the table exhausted and unsatisfied—no matter how many helpings of food I'd absentmindedly consumed—and go home and choke off the surges of panic and anger in a binge.

And of course I said nothing of all this to my mother.

I hated my sponsor for her stupid rules. The OA program was disrupting everything, unsettling the waters, spooking the fish. Bring my own food to my mother's house? Impossible. Can't be done. That's not how we do things in our family. I felt the tug to repeat a familiar pattern, a pattern as old as any in my life, one that I'd learned in infancy perhaps, that now, years later, seemed as irresistible as the moon's pull on the tides: the pattern of a child hovering anxiously near her mother, longing for authentic connection with her, endlessly hungering for the nourishment of spontaneous intimate contact.

Years later, my brother and I laughingly branded this family pattern the Unconscious Hypnotic Flu, or UHF.

"Be the first on your block to get it!" I once wrote him in a letter.

Watch these thrilling scenes play themselves out! It's easy! It's fun! It's inevitable!

One smiles . . . they ALL smile.

One is nice . . . they're ALL nice.

One is earnest . . . they're ALL earnest.

How much would YOU pay to get UHF? But wait! Don't answer yet! You also get this game, too:

Who is the wisest of all?

Who feels the least?

Whose face will freeze first into a permanent (and yet thoughtful) grin?

Like a school of fish, our family members swerved and swooped as one. If intimacy among us wasn't possible, then we would settle for fusion. I would imitate my mother in every way I could. I would be like her. I would please her. I would be close to her in the only way I knew how: I would swim in my mother's sea.

But the decision brought me no rest, no peace. Beneath the frozen grin, I was uncomfortable, restless, full of fear. I dimly sensed that I was trapped, I was stuck. I was fighting for my life, and I could see no way out. If I separated from my mother and went my own way without the resources of her presence and emotional support, I felt as if I'd die. I'd starve. But if I continued to merge with my mother, I might as well be dead already. I would never have a life of my own. I would never make my own footsteps, never be my own self. Some deep part of me would pass away, because it had never been fully born.

The dilemma held me fast. Death was all around me. Whichever path I chose, something in me was going to have to die.

My sponsor interrupted my reverie. "Well?" she said. "So what's it going to be?"

I took a breath. Threading a path through the intricacies of human relationships—especially one as intense as the mother-daughter bond—is no easy task. In a skein of knots, OA can work like patient fingers that gently separate the tangled threads. In the dance of sick human relationships, when we are trapped in the same old moves, waltzing around wearily with the same old partner in the same old ways, OA can invent a new melody and show us the steps for a whole new dance. When a family is suffering from an extended case of Unconscious Hypnotic Flu, OA can provide the medicine that breaks the fever, so that family members can begin to see each other as distinct and separate beings, as persons with their own individual personality, their own particular destiny.

I heard my sponsor's challenge, and I felt the lure of life. The longing to come out, to step forward, to brave an entry into the world as my own separate self was too strong to deny. Maybe I'd die if I did it, but it was a risk that I'd have to take. It was time to separate from my mother. My sponsor's request probably *was* absurd. Probably I *was* letting her dictate a decision that should really be my own. One day I'd have to re-negotiate our relationship, or go out and find a new sponsor. But OA could wait. I'd deal with those issues later. Right now

I needed to lend my sponsor enough power to provide the wedge between me and my mother that I so badly needed. My sponsor's refusal to budge helped me make my first, small effort to disentangle from my mother. Could I find the muscle to stay true to my own separate experience? Could I find the courage to follow the movements of my own separate mind and heart?

I didn't know, but I would try. At 12:15 I packed up my OA food and drove over to my mother's house. She greeted me as kindly as ever, offering me a plate as I unpacked the food from its plastic containers. I murmured something about OA, and to my relief she seemed willing to leave it at that. I was glad she didn't ask me anything more. Enacting or dramatizing my need to separate from her by bringing my own food to her house was at this point about all that I could handle. I had no words yet, no apologies, no explanations. Like so many of our significant transactions, this one was accomplished by gestures rather than speech. We simply sat across from each other at the kitchen table. She ate her food and I ate mine. We talked about other things.

But for me this meal was unusual. It was unlike any other that I'd ever experienced. I wasn't depending on my mother as the source of my food. I had brought what I needed with me. I was thirty-one years old, I'd lived independently for years, I'd done all my own cooking in my own apartment ever since my junior year in college, but somehow this was new. I was in my mother's house, and I was eating my own food. I was eating a different meal from hers, eating something in her presence that I myself had chosen and prepared. I didn't need to worry whether I'd get enough to eat. I'd brought my own meal, my own sustenance. I'd discovered that I could nourish myself.

I don't remember a word of our conversation that day, but I do remember the taste of the food, the crunch of the celery, the sweetness of the butternut squash. I had some room now to taste my own meal, a little bit of freedom to let go of my perpetual anxious inquiry into what my mother was up to and to begin to attend to my own inner experience. I had never before noticed how separate two plates lying on a single table can be. Here I was on this side of the table, and there she was on that side. With the relief of knowing that my food was taken care of, I found that I could be more steadily aware of my own separate body, more conscious of the boundary of my own skin. I could begin to take air into my own separate lungs.

After all those years of merging and flowing, of darting to and fro in my mother's wake, I was uncertain how to be a separate person. What would happen if my mother made a move to the left and I didn't follow? What if I just waited in one place, or headed off in another direction entirely? What would happen if I changed the subject, objected, or contradicted her? If I didn't keep the conversation harmonious, flowing, and smooth? If I didn't smile when she did? What if I didn't put on the sweetly sympathetic face that I usually wore when she spoke of someone's troubles? What if I scowled instead, or looked unmoved? Or what if I was so deeply moved that I alarmed her by bursting noisily into tears? What if I refused to read her glimpses and hints and asked her to be more explicit? What if I told her how anxious I sometimes felt with her, how constrained; how eager I was to please and be polite, because I was so afraid that she'd disapprove of me or find me wanting—or simply bolt, like a deer into the forest or a fish into its watery hole? What if I spoke and gestured and expressed emotion not according to how my words and silence might affect my mother—or anyone else, for that matter—but according to their congruence with the desires and feelings of my own authentic, separate self?

I wish I could say that I tried some of these experiments

during that lunch at my mother's house. But I did not. Simply to be in her presence while I ate my own food and breathed my own air was all that I could manage in one day.

OA didn't resolve the dilemmas in our relationship, but it did give me a space within which to see them more clearly. My work in OA gave me a new vantage point, a fresh perspective on some lifelong predicaments. Abstinence empowered me to begin the work of differentiation: to begin to discover who I might be as a separate self, to search for what was mine. Bolstered, sustained, even in some sense emboldened by my abstinence, I began the hard work of taking back the parts of myself that I had disowned and rejected, and of relinquishing what did not belong to me.

Like a toddler who delights in taking her first steps away from Mother, I found myself drawn in those years to stories and pictures of the separations that set us free. On the bulletin board in my study I tacked a picture of a bird walking away from its cage. On the living room mantelpiece I put a white ceramic egg standing proudly erect on two tiny, pale-yellow legs: the chick was about to be hatched. Again and again I burst out laughing over an absurd cartoon of a carrot rising from the ground, sprouting arms and legs, and striding purposefully away from the garden. Did I dare to trust my own longing to sprout legs and walk away from the family patterns in which I found myself planted—however unnatural my family might think me, however disloyal? Could I learn to listen to my own inner voice, to pay attention to my own desires, to move into life in my own way and under my own power? Was I willing to walk, to run, perhaps even one day to soar?

I didn't have the answers yet, and I wasn't always sure that I wanted to find them. There were days when I wished that consciousness had a reverse gear, days when I wanted only to revert to the familiar, blurry patterns of hiding out, going along, getting by. But day after day I attended my OA meetings, and in the space created among this new community of friends for speaking with honesty and listening with care, I began to hear the sound of my own voice. As I continued to eat with moderation and the wild craving for excess food gradually weakened and grew dim, I began to hear an insistent inner urge to get on with it: to follow the grain of my own particular life, to grow into the unique person that I was intended to be.

What this meant for me, most immediately and concretely, was that one way or another I had to finish up at Harvard. Legends abounded on campus of hapless graduate students who had attended Harvard for ten, eleven, even twelve or more years, never quite getting around to finishing their doctoral dissertation and yet never quite deciding to leave, either. Sometimes one of these poor souls would be spotted in the library stacks, poring over yet another dusty volume of poetry or literary criticism. Or one would be sighted in the graduate school cafeteria, musing abstractedly over a cup of coffee. But mostly we hardly ever saw these folks, as if (or so we imagined) they were too ashamed to be seen on campus. We imagined that their most vivid existence was on paper, on the list of enrolled students that was published every fall. Beside their names, the digit indicating the number of years of graduate study would painfully, inexorably increase: G9, G10, G11 . . .

Secretly I promised myself that it would never happen to me. Imagine my shock when I realized that what I most feared had already taken place: I'd become one of Them. By the time I reached OA I was already a G7. The rigors of course work and the terrors of general examinations were thankfully behind me, but as for coming up with a subject for my dissertation, I didn't have a clue. I couldn't seem to find a topic. I couldn't think of anything about Russian or comparative literature that I really wanted to study or to say. Like a recalcitrant horse that refuses to jump the hurdles, I found myself balking, my feet planted firmly in place.

Oh sure, I knew the routine. After all those years in school, I knew perfectly well how to be obedient. I knew what I was supposed to do. I could prance and strut with the best of them: write a coherent essay, construct an argument, compare and contrast one idea with another. But I felt like Melville's odd character, Bartleby the Scrivener: something deep inside me kept quietly and firmly insisting, "I would prefer not to."

Many of the motives that had pushed me toward Harvard in the first place—the desire to prove myself in my father's world, to please him, to impress him, to gain his love and respect, to find out once and for all whether I could measure up, whether I could win—had gradually begun to lose their power. They no longer energized me. The thrill was gone. Once in a while I still got hooked by the lure of trying to win his love at last, but—especially since the intervention into his drinking and the beginning of my own recovery in OA—the pursuit of my father's approval was beginning to look more and more like another endless, addictive quest that led only to heartbreak and ruin. My own.

In the meantime I no longer knew whether I wanted to finish my doctorate or whether I wanted to become a professor after all. I was no longer sure I wanted to live my life in the academic world. Mired in a stew of ambivalence, I couldn't make up my mind whether to stay or go. I hadn't lost my love of literature. I hadn't lost my love of writing, research, or thinking, or the pleasure that I felt in teaching and making contact with my students. But what I *had* lost somewhere along the way was the willingness to use my time, talents, and energy to please other people. I was beginning to see how little I knew about doing work that was mine, work that was done to please myself first and others only later, work that was more than a performance for the benefit of onlookers, but that emerged instead from the depths of my own passions, commitments, and concerns. Work that was my own. Work that mattered to me. Like a show horse that has trotted obediently, on command, countless times around its little ring, I began to look longingly toward the fields beyond. What would it be like to go where I pleased, to run where I cared to; to let my nose and my intuition lead me wherever I, rather than my master, wanted to go? What would it be like to be my own master?

I had no idea. Even the gifts that seemed most truly my own—my love of words, for instance—were alienated from me. The language in which I'd been so thoroughly trained was in some ways not my native tongue. Like every other dutiful college and graduate student, I'd learned that the best writing and thinking were essentially combative. We were taught to thrust and parry, to master a subject, defend an argument, make a point so elegantly that it effectively crushed the opposition. We learned to avoid the first-person pronoun at all costs, to write from above and afar as if we were disembodied intellects floating at a serene distance from any direct personal involvement with the subject at hand.

I remember studying Dostoevsky as an undergraduate at Stanford. In one work after another, we read haunting, disturbing stories about spiritual desolation and longing; stories that evoked the despair of a person drifting to the edge of suicide. From the comments of the teaching assistant and the class culture itself, I quickly figured out that the students who were considered intellectually serious were the ones who analyzed the story as if it were pure text, the ones who examined Dostoevsky's creation as if it bore no discernible or potentially interesting relation to themselves or the actual world of flesh-and-blood people who perhaps had their own experiences of anguish and despair, their own episodes of battling the impulse to slip over the edge of a high-rise balcony or slam the car into a tree. If suicide happened to be a topic of genuine personal concern, it was not supposed to leak out into classroom discussion, not if you wanted to be taken seriously as a budding scholar.

By the time I reached Harvard, I'd pretty well mastered the dominant discourse of academics. I knew how to replace "I feel" with "one feels" or, better, "one suspects." I knew how to disappear myself behind a screen of words, so that nothing showed but my capacity for rational analysis, poised like a Stealth bomber to attack whatever subject might be set before me. Analytic, systematic prose was what was wanted, prose that was masterful and vigorous, prose that was—how shall I put it?—*masculine*.

After my father read one of my graduate school papers, he nodded with satisfaction.

"You write like a man," he told me, smiling warmly.

I relished this rare compliment from my father, but I also felt confused, as if his praise concealed a putdown, as if I'd bitten into a piece of cake and a hidden shard of glass had cut my tongue. I "wrote like a man." What did that mean? Did it mean that I should thank my lucky stars that I'd successfully erased any sign that I was female? That I should be grateful because I'd learned not to spoil my writing by sounding too much like the person I was—a woman? That I should be thankful for being welcomed into the ranks of academic writing and scholarship, never mind the cost of leaving some huge part of my identity behind? Had I so absorbed the language of the master that I'd forgotten—or perhaps not yet even begun to learn—my own native speech?

What was it that I wanted to say? Was there something that I secretly longed to but had never dared express? Were there words that I needed to speak, words that were shamelessly subjective, personal, emotional? What words might I speak if I began to speak as a woman and as someone who was genuinely, visibly, and wholeheartedly engaged in what she was saying? I had to ask myself: Were there words that were *mine*?

Memory swings me back to a family meeting at Mount Auburn Hospital several months before the intervention. Alcoholism counselor Jeffrey McIntyre is there, along with my father, my stepmother, and her adolescent son. And I am there too. It is one of several meetings that will precede the intervention, each one charged with its own atmosphere of urgency and desperation. We are talking about my father's drinking. Sometimes he is willing to tell the truth: He describes how, on Thursday mornings when he was Master of Quincy House, he'd finish his last class of the week and walk with some faculty friends to Chez Dreyfus, the restaurant that sold the largest martinis in Harvard Square. Then he'd get very drunk, go back to his office in Widener Library, and fall asleep.

He describes the morning of his last day as Master of Quincy House, when he got up at 7:00 a.m. to sign the diplomas of his graduating students: he was exhausted and hungover, and he couldn't keep his hands from shaking. Even when he pressed down hard, he couldn't sign his name. The nub of the quill pen broke and ink went flying across the paper, blotching the signatures of the president and secretary of the Harvard Corporation.

But mostly he denies everything. No, he doesn't remember any blackouts. No, he doesn't remember the morning after his sixtieth birthday when, flushed and silent, he skipped breakfast and almost lost his balance as he got into the car to drive his son to school, clinging to the car door until his dizziness had passed. No, he doesn't remember the time he forgot to pick up his son at a friend's house. No, he doesn't believe that he has any difficulty controlling his drinking. In fact, he's experimenting with consuming no alcohol after dinner. The only problem is that now he can't sleep.

"No beer, no sleep," he complains, shaking his head. He does confess to a tiny bit of worry: he's not under any particular stress right now, because the semester hasn't begun yet, but how will he get by on three hours of sleep when the time comes, as he puts it, to "attack" Harvard? (We don't ask him what this means to him; why he, a senior professor and former master of a Harvard house, has to "attack" his work, his place of employment, his colleagues, as if he fears he won't survive unless both guns are blazing.) No, he declares, he doesn't believe that his insomnia has anything to do with his withdrawal from alcohol, or anything to do with being in the middle stages of alcoholism.

I've been silent for a long time, but now McIntyre shifts his focus. He wants a word from me.

"Could you describe exactly what it is about your father's drinking that bothers you?" he asks. "How is he different when he drinks? Can you help him see what changes in him when he's drinking?"

I hesitate for a few moments. I search for words, grope for speech, glance at my father.

My father's eyes are twinkling with irony. He flashes me a knowing smile, egging me on, daring me to open my mouth.

"If you're going to be a writer," he grins at me, "you're going to have to know how to describe these things."

I feel speechless, confused. I don't know what to say.

"Go ahead and speak," he seems to be saying to me. "Go ahead. I dare you."

He crosses his arms and gazes at me, sizing me up. His smile is cool. His eyes are defiant. I know that the gauntlet is down. The challenge now is twenty paces, turn around, and shoot. He is aiming at me and I am aiming at him. He is saying, "Go ahead, draw." To save his life, I'll have to shoot.

How has it come to this? What has brought us to this deadly duel? I want only to save his life and not to lose my own, but I feel paralyzed. Fear grips my throat. I love this man. I've loved him all my life, and I want him to love me. I can see that he's angry, and I feel the sting of his taunt. What will happen to us, what will happen to *me*, if I tell the truth? Yet I can guess what lies behind his anger. Behind his bluster and bravado, he too is probably afraid. He's watching me search for the words that he's afraid I will find.

A duel is a life-and-death encounter. So is an intervention and all the meetings that lead up to it. To save his life, my father would have to lose the one he had. And I would have to pull the trigger.

I wish I could tell you that what I said to him was so eloquent, so persuasive, so undeniably skillful that my father took one long look at me, broke down in tears, and confessed the truth of who he was: a man who desperately needed help. But I can't remember what I said, and whatever it was, I'm sure he didn't cry. I don't believe he showed any sign at that meeting of agreeing that his life needed to change. All I know is that I spoke the truth as best I could and that when we all gathered after Christmas for the final, formal intervention, our collective words did have the power to inspire a reluctant, if temporary, change of course: he entered a thirty-day treatment program and for the next twelve months managed to maintain a white-knuckled sobriety.

But he never admitted that he was dependent on booze. He never acknowledged that he was powerless to control his drinking, or that drinking had damaged the important relationships in his life. When my father returned from the treatment center, his anger was boundless. He seethed. He was *not* an alcoholic, he said. He had loved me well. He had struggled with his life. Yes, he'd made some mistakes. Yes, he'd admit to some flaws of character. But we had betrayed him; *I* had betrayed him. Like piteous, patient old King Lear, he was a man "more sinn'd against than sinning." And I? I was the ungrateful daughter who had broken his heart. I was Goneril, Regan, and Cordelia rolled up into one. The women in his life—and me especially—had done him a grave injustice.

"Unnatural hags," he said to me, a Shakespearean spit in the face.

The memory of this moment sends me back to my worn paperback copy of *King Lear*, its margins full of the penciled comments of a young high-school girl. Back at boarding school, I hadn't underlined that phrase from the second act. I could not have known then that one day Lear's words would be addressed to me; that one day my own father would stand before me "as full of grief as age," his voice trembling, his tone shifting like Lear's between sorrow, love, and rage, as when the old king cries,

> *I will not trouble thee, my child. Farewell.*
> *We'll no more meet, no more see one another;*
> *But yet thou art my flesh, my blood, my daughter,—*
> *Or rather a disease that's in my flesh,*
> *Which I must needs call mine.*

The fact that I had spoken, as he saw it, "against" him, meant that I had betrayed him. To find my voice meant to betray my father. If I spoke what I felt, if I spoke what I saw, if I spoke what I needed and longed for, if I tried to save my own life and his life as well, then I was a faithless, treacherous daughter. I had double-crossed and deserted him. I was a stool pigeon, a renegade, a tattletale, a harpie. What's more, I had broken his heart.

What he perceived as my betrayal of him only got worse. When he came back from the treatment program, he was sober but unrepentant. He would experiment, he said, with not drinking, at least for a while. He might follow up with the aftercare program, he said, and go to a few AA meetings. But he adamantly refused to admit that he had a problem with alcohol.

Not long thereafter, his second marriage, which had for years, it seemed to me, been held together by only the most tenuous of threads, finally fell apart. My stepmother told him to leave the house. But where was he to go? He came to me. He asked me to take him in for a time while he looked for a more permanent situation.

I have no memory of how he asked me, where he asked me, or exactly what I said in reply. I have rummaged around in my mind, I have poked through old files, but I've come up with nothing, not a clue. Did he ask me over the telephone, or were we having lunch together in Harvard Square? Did I answer right away, or did I beg for time to think about his request? Did I turn him down outright, or only after some days of painful thought? My journal, like my mind, is a blank. Some memories are just too difficult to bear. They disappear from consciousness, they never make it to the page. All I remember is that I said no. I turned him away. And I remember his bitter words as we said good-bye.

I'm sure that what I was wrestling with was survival. My own. Hindsight tells me that I was locked in a battle with my father, who was drowning. By then I'd tried everything I could think of to save him. In every way I knew how, I tried to speak the words and take the actions that could save his life. But he only shrugged or laughed at me in reply, as if he thought I had it wrong, he was not drowning at all, he was just fine, thank you, flailing alone out at sea. Or as if the decision to drown was his and his alone—and die he would, if he so chose.

And in the end he was right. What he did with his life was his own business after all. I might wish with all my heart that he would choose not to drown, that he would come to his senses, that he would fight against the waves, cry out for help, take hold of an outstretched hand, board a life raft, and come at last to a safe shore. I might do everything in my power to persuade him to do these things. But eventually the time would come when I had done all I could, and there was nothing more that I could do; the rest was up to him. And now, it seemed to me, that moment had come at last. That time was here.

As I look back on that pivotal decision, I can't help asking myself if I betrayed him by not letting him live with me. Did I leave him out in the cold? And the answer that comes to me is: Yes, probably. Definitely. Did I think that if I didn't take him in, he might well die? Yes, I did. Did I have the power to throw my arms around him and drag him forcibly to shore? Could I swim the whole distance, cross-chest carry him all the way to land? If I tried, if I kept on trying, if I persisted in trying until he finally succeeded in pushing my head under the water for the last time, I suppose that some might have called me a hero for the attempt. But I discovered that I wasn't willing after all to drown with him. I did not want to die. I could not save his life, but at least I could try to save my own.

For me the intervention was a crossroad from which there was no turning back. It announced the death of the old, unconscious patterns of relationship, the death of secrecy and silence, the death of hiding out and getting by. It announced the possibility of something new. I loved my father as ardently as ever, but I knew that I must protect myself. I needed distance from him, I needed boundaries and borders, I needed a place that was clearly mine. I had to find out who this new self was who dared to speak her truth. Only then could I begin to discover who my father and I might be for each other, which parts of our relationship might be salvaged or reworked and which had died for good. I had no idea what *was* now possible between my father and me, what degree of communication, what level of understanding. But one thing at least was clear: I could not save his life.

Perhaps I could save my own.

I don't think my father ever forgave me.

I remember his parting shot, after I told him that he couldn't live with me: "My hands were shaking, that Commencement Day at Quincy House," he told me coldly, "not because I had had too much to drink and was hungover, but because I was saying good-bye to the woman I'd been having an affair with for years."

I drew back as if I'd been slapped. If his intention was to shock me, I suppose he was satisfied. Until that moment I'd never known about his extramarital affairs. I was stunned. And furious. How could he have deceived my mother like that? What a betrayal. What an insult. And what an insult to me, to throw this news so brazenly in my face.

I recalled a long-ago evening back at Quincy House when I saw my father reach out drunkenly to my mother. I remembered seeing her flinch and turn away. She murmured an excuse as she slid deftly out of his arms.

The image spoke to me both of his loneliness and of hers. It brought back to me all the unspoken loneliness that pervaded our home as I was growing up. I realized all at once that I had no memories of my parents embracing, no memories of them touching or kissing or greeting one another with open-hearted joy. And so, beneath the anger at my father's infidelities, I began to feel the edges of a great sorrow, as if I'd suddenly come upon a vast inner lake, long hidden not only from the world but from me.

It was a relief to know that my house was mine and to know that my father would find somewhere else to live—as, in fact, he did. For now, at least, I needed space from him, a safe space where I could listen to my own needs and longings without fear of ridicule or rebuke. A space within which to discover and to sort out my feelings, so that my own authentic self might arise at last and find a language in which to speak.

By then I'd begun to read the work of the psychoanalyst Alice Miller. I knew that I couldn't expect my "true self," as she called it, suddenly to emerge in me full-blown, to pop out all at once like a jack-in-the-box. Miller showed me that the true self is a potentiality within each child that only comes into existence as the child is noticed, understood, and taken seriously by its parents. Within an atmosphere of respect and care, children grow up feeling a whole range of spontaneous emotions. They feel vital and alive; they are authentically themselves. The true self is revealed. But without that atmosphere—and here I would lean forward, poring over every sentence, absorbing every page—without that atmosphere, children lose touch with their inner vitality. If, for instance, a child feels that she must earn her parents' love by behaving a certain way or by expressing only certain needs and feelings—if, in short, she must construct a "false self" in order to be accepted and to survive—then, however successful and accomplished she may grow up to appear, inwardly she will be fragile, anxious, depressed.

Reading Miller's work was like finding a long-sought-for road map in a strange land, or a landmark in the wilderness. Suddenly the snarl and muddle and muck of my life began to make sense. When her *Prisoners of Childhood* appeared in 1981, I read it with such amazement and gratefulness that even before I finished it, I could see that it would be one of a handful of books that would change my life. I'd never read a book that took so seriously the suffering of children. No book had ever given me such an understanding of my despair. Suddenly I understood that my own loneliness, which had always seemed vast and incomprehensible, was somehow being taken in hand by this exquisite observer of children and given genuine respect and attention.

Miller writes with a clarity that is almost fierce. In the light of her burning words I saw the path that lay ahead: the only way to come to wholeness was to mourn what I hadn't received as a child; to face and grieve the inalterable fact that, like all such children, I had not been loved just as I was. Her account of childhood illuminated my own. When I found myself in the pages of that book, I wept with the relief of recognizing myself at last, as if Miller had held up a mirror to my face and I could finally see myself with all the grief and heartache that I'd never been able to accept and understand.

And that night, when I cried, I knew that some part of my life was over. There had been a huge death, one that would take me years to understand. But I also knew that it was a new day.

I remember working in my garden one summer afternoon after reading one of Alice Miller's books. My hands were busy pruning and weeding while my mind roamed quietly here and there, now attentive to the task at hand, to the feel of the soil and the warmth of the sun; now wondering about my tangled relationship with my parents; now musing on Miller's account of how we lose and find our true selves. In the space that only receptive tasks such as gardening can give, I was listening for myself, quietly waiting for clues, ready to keep myself company. With a garden fork I dug weeds out of the path. I tore open a bag of fresh gravel, poured it out, and raked the pebbles into place. Gingerly I began picking Japanese beetles out of the roses, two by two, and, with a rush of anger, I plunged them into a jar of kerosene. I watched the insects move until they died.

Gardening, like living, like sorting out our important relationships, can be a lethal enterprise. Not everything in this garden was going to survive. Sometimes it's only the killer instinct that saves our lives. Sometimes we're locked in combat, fighting for our lives, and can only survive if we let our opponent die.

As my hands worked and my imagination played, the gardening became a kind of liturgy.

"I am setting limits," I declared firmly to myself as I trimmed back the ivy that was hell-bent on invading the lawn.

"I am saying: This is who I am," I whispered as I propped up a fallen tomato plant with a stick.

"I will not pretend anymore. I will not be false," I promised myself as I pulled out weeds.

When we see someone gardening alone, we do not know what private rituals she may be performing. Who knows, in the humble gestures of weeding and planting, pruning and raking, what vows are being made or what insights disclosed? Who knows what transforming power is perhaps being called forth in the gardener as she connects with the earth and with the longings of her heart?

I took my shears and began trimming the tendrils of ivy that were crawling up the side of the house. It was a small house, just a cottage really, that had been built more than a hundred years before as an art studio for the wife of a prominent Boston architect. I loved this little house for its quirky, fairy-tale charm: its mullioned windows peeking out toward the street; its walls made of stone, with a slate roof perched on top like a hat; its tiny dilapidated greenhouse; its handful of little rooms, no two on the same level, that meandered here and there with nary a bow to architectural convention or common sense. I loved the garden spaces that still survived: the grape arbors, the roses, the small stretch of lawn, the ancient green hedge that enclosed it all. I enjoyed thinking about the woman for whom this place had been created. For all I knew, she had come here every day to paint, to gaze, to muse, to find the lines and colors that expressed the vision of her inward eye.

As I roamed around the perimeter of the house, pruning back the overgrown ivy with my clippers, I suddenly caught my breath with surprise. Nestled against the southern side of the house was a little semicircle of cement. I'd never noticed it before. Someone years before must have planted a small garden plot here. Someone had taken the time to set up this small enclosure. Someone had come here to prepare a space that would nourish life, a space for growing lovely living things.

I was filled with delight. I had found a secret garden. I tugged away the overhanging ivy and pulled out thick clumps of rotting leaves. I knew at once what I wanted to plant in this sunny corner: red tulips, something festive and bright. With mounting excitement, I pushed the debris out of the way, and after I'd finished clearing the space, I leaned back on my heels to gaze at the open patch of earth.

Suddenly I was overcome by both thankfulness and sorrow. Tears sprang to my eyes. I felt as if someone from long ago were greeting me, as if someone were showing me something special that I'd possessed all along but that had long been hidden, something beautiful that I welcomed with joy but that I also grieved for as well: how long I have waited for you, how long I have ached for your coming.

Whenever we first come upon the traces of our own true self, I imagine that it is something like this. What delight there is in knowing that its neglected soil will one day bear fruit and bring forth blooming flowers, but oh, what sadness we have to feel first, what grief we have to endure before that land can become truly our own.

CHAPTER 6

What Comes Up

W hen I'm waiting for something new, full of expectation, an African song I used to sing as a child sometimes pops into my head: "We've been invited to
Henrietta's wedding, tho' she can't tell us when it will be."

In the second verse, the mystery deepens: "Tho' we're
invited to Henrietta's wedding, no one knows who the bridegroom will be."

I can picture the wedding guests milling about, eagerly trying to guess the identity of Henrietta's beloved. "Who will it
be?" they ask each other. "Who will it be?"

By the end of the song, we still know nothing about the
mysterious bridegroom. We don't know—will the wedding
take place? Oddly enough, Henrietta herself seems to know as
little about it as the rest of us. Only one thing is clear: we're on
our way to a celebration, and we're looking for someone. An
important someone.

In those years of searching for a self and a life that were
mine, I too felt as if I'd received a mysterious invitation. An
invitation to look within. Could I finally let go the effort to
please my parents, earn their affection, be the person they
wanted me to be? Could I seek, and find, what was real in me,
what was truly my own?

For many years, I thought that only a splendid marriage
could make me happy. But now I realized that before taking
anyone else into this madhouse, I needed to go inward. I needed

to find the other half of myself—the better half, I think. I yearned to meet this long-lost self, to fall in love, to marry, and to live more happily ever after than I presently was doing.

If I could have walked into a church and seen my own self waiting for me at the altar—radiant, alive, in love—I would have asked the organist to play, and, believe me, I would have marched down the aisle. I was on the lookout, searching for clues, waiting for some glimpse of this "me" who was fully alive. Who was this stranger whose coming into being aroused in me this deep longing, this fierce ache? Would I recognize her? What would she be like? I didn't know, but I awaited her coming with the eager anticipation of Henrietta and her guests.

Pay attention! I told myself. For starters, notice what's going into your mouth. There's no way in hell you'll find out who you are, what you're doing, if you're eating compulsively. Every escape into food is a delay, a retreat, a decision to close down. So get with it. Work your program or die. Stay awake. Open your eyes, not your mouth.

I began to notice how itchy and irritable I felt whenever I simply mouthed my lines. I began to ask: Who's writing this drama anyway? Is it me? My parents? My family? Am I caught up in some time-worn tale that has been repeating itself for years on end, passed down from hand to hand through the long line of ancestors that preceded me? Does this interminable story stretch all the way back to the *Mayflower* and into the invisible past? Did someone divvy up the parts and slip the script into my pocket when I wasn't looking? What the hell am I up to here? I don't know. But I'd better find out. This story has been killing me. I've been eating off this story addictively my whole life. I've been stuffing this story into my face and down my gullet. I've had my fill of it.

I'm desperate for a new story, a new role. I crave them. I want new words to speak, a plot that holds a surprise or two.

I'm tired of knowing exactly what will happen next, since it has already happened so many weary, predictable times before. I'm ready for a new family scrapbook with pictures of entirely new characters. Or maybe a fresh, blank book with no faces in it, no captions under the photographs, no story that isn't written in my own hand. This is it. I'm not going to leaf through this old album one more time and smile at these pictures. It's time to pull the mask off my face and step off the family stage. I'm going to look for some other stories to give my life meaning and purpose. And not only that. I'm not going to try to fix this family anymore. I'm resigning. I quit.

One month after starting in OA, I wrote my younger sister: "I want to walk out onto a bigger stage, directed by a creative genius who sees more of me than I do. I want to play every role I can think of—shrew, vengeful killer, sexy bombshell, brilliant intellectual, meddling boss. I want to make room for them all."

I signed up for a six-week acting course with fifteen other people. Every week we tried on new faces, new voices, new identities. One day the instructor asked us to roam the room in silence and greet the others without saying a word. We were nervous. We laughed. None of us had ever done this sort of thing before.

The drama coach, a small man with keen eyes, silently wandered around the room with the rest of us. When he got to me, I saw him give me a quick, penetrating look, and then I saw his face change: his chin tilted slightly down, his eyebrows lifted, his eyes widened, his mouth turned up in a half-smile. Written all over his face was an expression of shy eagerness. Even his body changed: he shifted his weight a bit from side to side, hunching his shoulders, swinging his arms. Suddenly I saw that his body was a mirror image of mine. I saw my face in his face, the movements of my body echoed in his. With a shock of recognition, I burst out laughing. How astonishing to see myself standing before me in a separate person.

The instructor mirrored me for another moment or two before dropping back into his own skin, slipping out of the role, flashing me a warm smile, and melting back into the group.

I puzzled over this odd encounter for days. What was he showing me? What hadn't I seen before? What did I need to see? What was I expressing that I couldn't see? Did I really have a particular way of walking, a way of moving my hands and turning my head that was uniquely me?

I could barely admit it, but this encounter left me feeling almost friendly toward myself. Not too much, but a little. Was I confused? Yes. Ignorant and out of touch? Absolutely. But I was starting to emerge as me, some particular self, and that is what he was showing me, gently and without a word, in a way that was both friendly and revealing, full of acceptance. Maybe I wasn't fully myself just yet. Maybe I still had a long way to go. But this was who I was, at least for now. Maybe I wasn't so bad after all. Maybe I could even feel a bit of affection for myself. Sure, the drama coach was a man I barely knew. I felt unexpectedly exposed, embarrassed that he had seen me so clearly. And yet his friendliness, the way he'd seen me, the way he'd handed me back to myself, delighted me. Even thrilled me. Bit by bit, this unknown shadow in the mirror was beginning to come clear. I was beginning to see my own face.

One day, the instructor asked us to take turns sitting onstage in front of the class. I don't remember what roles we were supposed to play. All I remember is suddenly being overcome with acute self-consciousness. My attention was riveted to the faces of my classmates looking at me. My cheeks burned. I forgot my lines. I was dumbstruck, at a loss for words.

The instructor took all of this very matter-of-factly.

"Step away from the stage," he told me. "Take a few moments to go inward. Connect with a feeling, any feeling at all."

Chagrined, I crept away from the group's curious eyes.

"Well, right now I am anxious and embarrassed!" I blurted out.

"No, go deeper than that. Find a feeling that lies below self-consciousness."

I could hear that he was coaxing me now, pulling it out of me. I closed my eyes and sat in silence for a few moments. Gradually I made out the faintest outline of a feeling. Yes, here it was, now I could sense it: a bit of sadness was moving through me. No, let me see: really it was quite a little river of sadness, a slow blue stream of sorrow winding its way right through the center.

"Have you found a feeling?" the instructor asked.

"Yes," I said quietly.

"All right. Now stay in touch with that feeling and come back to the stage. Let's try the exercise again."

I stepped back up to the stage and played the assigned part without difficulty. Acting, I began to see, was like living. There is no faking it.

On a cool fall day six months after starting in OA, I go out for a run. I love running around Fresh Pond. When I'm running, I feel five years old again, or maybe nine. I'm a horse cantering across a field, her flanks gleaming, her muscles taut, the wind blowing in her mane. I stamp my feet against the pavement. I draw deep breaths. When I run downhill, I stretch out my arms. I could be an eagle, gliding through space, diving, plunging, rising again, soaring above the earth on outstretched wings.

I run all the way home. When I reach the front yard, I slow to a walk, catch my breath, start to cool down. I slap my legs with satisfaction. My legs. They can run. I press my thumbs into the muscles of my thighs. Like a child discovering her body, eager to know the shape and feel of her own flesh, I lean over and rub my hands over my kneecaps. My thumb touches the small scar on my knee.

I was eight years old that spring. My younger sister was on her red tricycle, pedaling hard, and I was the tricycle's outboard motor, one foot pressing the bike's back step, the other pumping the ground. We were laughing. What a team we made! How fast we could go! A moment later the bike lurched forward and I fell down hard, my right knee landing on a piece of gravel. Blood flowed at once, then tears, but I still smile to remember the moment just before I slipped: the sound of my sister's laughter and that exhilarating ride.

My hands slide down my legs. To shave or not to shave? A marble-skinned Venus or an Amazon athlete with hairy legs, take it or leave it? What a lot of time I've spent since puberty debating whether to take a razor to these legs. At the moment, they're rough with stubble. Maybe I'll shave them tomorrow. I grasp a calf with both hands. It feels too big. I want slender calves, sexy ones, and perfect feet clicking around in three-inch stiletto heels, dancing the night away. I used to hate the way kneesocks slid down my fat little calves, bunching over my brown penny loafers as I stood at the corner waiting for the light to change on my way to school. But I can live with these calves. This is not a bad deal. They look a bit like my father's—a man with good legs, as a matter of fact. He looks handsome in the photograph my grandmother gave me. The picture's getting faded now, but I can still make out a sturdy young man in a bathing suit striding the length of a dock. He is smiling. A towel is draped around his neck. His calves are shapely and strong.

Here are my ankles. My poor ankles! I remember the day I binged all morning and then went out for a ten-kilometer road race. I tried not to notice how swollen they were. I started out with the pack, but after only a few blocks they began to ache so badly I had to sit down. From the curb, I watched all the other runners' legs go by—their feet, their shoes, the dust they kicked up. I kept my head down, I was so ashamed. After everyone had passed, I clambered to my feet and limped slowly back to the parking lot.

And here are my feet. I think of all the miles I've put in. All the running shoes, all the flip-flops that made me trip in the deep sand of the beach until I flung them away and walked with bare feet, all the shiny black patent-leather shoes. All the dancing lessons in junior high school, all the soles I wore smooth and flat by sliding across the linoleum floor—not that I would have dared to do that in front of the boys. And the dark blue flats I wore for my Christmas piano recital. Like all the other children, I was dressed to the nines. When it was my turn to play, I climbed up on the piano bench, checked to see if my slip was showing, listened to the rustles in the audience, and, feeling the blood pounding in my ears, lifted my hands to the keyboard, my foot to the pedal. Out of the hush burst the first chords of Schumann.

I go inside the house. Leaning against the bathroom sink, I stare into the mirror. My cheeks are still flushed. Who is this person who looks back at me? For a few moments I simply gaze at myself, wondering, Who's there? Who's behind these eyes? Feeling what? Seeing what? What do these eyes express? I play with the possibilities. Just look at yourself! I open my eyes wide. What am I seeing? Who am I looking at? Do I see panic, wonder, absorbed attention? I lower my eyelids and look into the mirror. Now I see a sultry gaze, a suspicious look, a tired face. These lips. These teeth. I try puckering for a kiss. I touch my lips to the mirror. I give myself a little come-on. I bare my teeth and take a little nipping snarl at the woman in the mirror. Then I take a bite. I feel like an animal ready to pounce. I try one face after another. How many faces there are that are not sweet and smiling and oh-so-tidily polite!

I peel off my sweaty running clothes, step out of my underpants, unfasten my bra. I cup a hand around each breast, letting my thumbs graze the nipples. I let the soft weight of flesh rest for a moment in my hands. I slide my fingers down my belly, along my hips. Bare flesh. My own. I like this. I want this. But no sooner do I reach out to touch myself than I hear a little voice that says: "Don't do it. Don't touch yourself there." I recognize that voice. And today I don't listen. Today I want myself. I slide my hands down my thighs, let my fingers press against the mound of hair, let them slip between my legs. I feel the warmth in my body. Deliciously feminine. Me. Mine. I squeeze my thighs, feeling them press against my hand as the fingers stroke. I linger for a moment. This pleasure is mine and I give it to myself. I know how to do it.

I step into the shower stall. Water sprays over my upturned face, washing away the sweat, the tang of salt on my lips. Opening my mouth, I drink gulps of water. Water rains down over my breasts, belly, back, buttocks. I am drenched from head to foot. I lay my hands flat against the tiled wall and look at the freckles, the knuckles, the hint of bluish veins. I never noticed before that my palms are square.

Today my hands are full of energy. I play the piano, I garden. I can turn a doorknob, hold a pen. I like my strong hands and nimble fingers. I like what my hands can do. Someday I want them to hold on to someone I love, but first I need to love myself. If I don't like myself, I'm not going to like anybody else. And if someone likes me, I won't really believe it. I'll just be going through the motions of love, faking it all the way. And wondering why I always feel so lonely.

I squeeze my hands shut, making fists. Hands flat against the wall, I push against it, hard. I want to be as solid as this wall. I want to be in touch, just like this, with everything. I don't know whether I've ever put my hand to my own life, touched it, taken hold of it, felt I had a grip on it. Most of the time I feel my hand sliding down the wall, losing my grip on life. But I'm done with that. I want a grip. I've got to get a grip. I want contact. Like this. Direct. Clear. Really there.

What I remember most about that day in the shower is pounding against the walls, just pounding, feeling the exultation of breaking out of the box I found myself in. Suddenly I knew I could beat down any barrier I'd set up. I could break through, break out of any trap, any expectation, any role. That I'd done it to myself, I'd let people shut me up, I'd let people wall me in. Only I can break it down. And so I will. I will!

I pound on the walls and I laugh to hear the sound. This is no quiet escape. And I don't want it to be. Give me some tympani. Give me a horn. I want noise, and I'm making it.

I could have been a one-woman band in that shower stall, and anyone who had been walking by that day would have wondered what the racket was. That cacophonous noise? That beating on the wall? It was me, breaking free.

I kept showing up at OA. I kept going to the weekly group for adult children of alcoholics. I brought to the work of therapy a focus and intensity that was impossible during my bouts of binge eating. I began a class in Buddhist meditation, learning to pay close attention to each breath, each moment. Could I begin to notice what was here, what was present for me, without instantly judging it, or grabbing for it, or pushing it away? Could I learn to become more sensitive to the actual texture of experience?

I was a woman with a mission. I'd been in espionage all my life, living in the midst of strangers, caught in some kind of bad cloak-and-dagger novel. Now I was in reconnaissance—an adventurer, an explorer, both looking for myself and studying the terrain. What did I have under my belt? I had a body under my belt. And not a bad one at that. It had come awake. And I had a handful of instructions, a program to stick to, some buddies to keep me company, and a map—my own map—that I was beginning to put a few lines on, one that I hoped to God would take me home, wherever that was. As I looked over the terrain of my life, I had a better sense of where it began. I could mark an X to show where I started from and draw a line to here. And I could begin to ask myself: What do I want to do with this life? Who do I want to be?

It was spring. Ice was thawing, and so was I. Crocuses were beginning to bloom, and so was I. Rivers were running full, and so was I. Sometimes anger welled up in me, sometimes passion, sometimes sorrow. Sometimes I didn't know what it was. But I kept on going. And I kept my eyes open. I was looking for meaning, for connections, for what was true. I was looking for *me*.

How was I going to discover myself? By paying attention? By studying every move of my body and what I was feeling? That wasn't always easy to do. I'd become expert at stuffing a feeling between two slices of bread. I knew how to sit in front of the television as if it were the only company I'd ever find, listening to the drone of the voices, the canned laughter, the high-volume ads. I didn't know much, but I knew I wanted to quit doing that.

I remember watching TV late one night, lonely and restless in my quiet little house, staring dully at the images that flickered only inches from my face, waiting for them to fill me magically and give me comfort. I wasn't eating anything, I was abstinent, but I really didn't want to know what my body was trying to tell me.

At last, near midnight, I had to face facts. I had to put my cheek down on the kitchen counter and admit, I wish someone would put me to bed.

At times like that I felt palpably the small child that I was no longer, didn't want to be, could no longer be. I realized again what an effort it takes me sometimes to shake loose just a little bit of inner truth. But I was learning to look at those feelings; to feel them, face them, let them wash through me. I didn't have to eat over them. I had choices. Why? Because I had somebody to discuss them with. Myself.

The next morning it is raining. I get up early. I want to pull up the onion grass beside the fence. I don't know the real name of this weed, but its tiny bulb is as smooth and sleek as a scallion. You can't get it out unless you are patient. It takes real skill. Pull too hard, and the long, oily stems break off in your fingers. I have to dig down below them with the three-pronged garden fork—not the kind that holds a piece of pie. Then I shake the plants gently from side to side. If I'm lucky, I can get out a whole clump intact in my hand. I sit on the wet grass and work at it patiently. The rain tapers off. The sun is rising. I can hear the birds begin to sing. I am happy. I am honestly happy.

After a couple of hours, I stand up and go inside. I wash my hands. The soap is slippery, and I watch with pleasure as the suds grow fat in my hands. Water splashes over my hands and into the sink. When the water runs clean, I tighten the faucet and dry my hands on a towel. Time to put on fresh clothes. The cotton blouse feels cool as I slip it over my shoulders. I close the buttons, tuck the blouse into my skirt, thread the belt through the fabric loops at my waist, and fasten the buckle. What a simple pleasure it is to have the same shape every day, to use the same hole in my belt buckle week after week. I comb my hair. The comb gets stuck for a moment, tugging at a knot. I don't mind.

Since I stopped overeating, I've been taking unexpected delight in being able to touch and taste, to smell and see and hear. It's as if all those years of overeating had cut me off from direct contact with the world. Now everything is sensuous again. Physical, bodily life, once attenuated and faint, is slowly being restored. Every sensation seems interesting and fresh. I feel as if I've never lived so thoroughly in my body before. It's all a wonder to me.

When I'm finished with my hair, I go in search of shoes. I've decided to go to church. Not so long ago, I would have been surprised if such a desire had crossed my mind. For years I thought of church as pretty dull: nicely dressed people, stiff as boards, listening to mind-numbing moralisms and pious clichés. Church? I gave it up after high school. But since joining OA, I've actually found myself wanting to go to church. On one or two Sundays, I've actually sat in the pew and enjoyed the hymns, a certain lyricism in the words of Scripture, a certain tenderness in the prayers, and the eagerness, or hopefulness, that people seem to have as they go up to the altar rail, open their hands, and receive Communion. There have been times when I thought I could, just possibly, take this to heart. Maybe there was something here I needed. Maybe there was something here beyond myself. Maybe.

At church, I listened to a lot of stories from the Bible. I wasn't sure how those stories spoke to my life, to the stories of the others I listened to in OA, the stories of people trying to save their lives. I knew about *those* stories: stories of temptation and ruin, hope and disaster. I'd known quite a few people who had lived, died, and been buried alive, and as far as I could tell, they hadn't come back to life—not yet, anyway. But they wanted to. And so did I. I was one of them. I was trying to save my own life. Was there a story here, in this place, that I needed to hear, that could make a difference? A story that I could be a part of? A story that could somehow gather up all the little bits and pieces of my own fractured life and give it back to me whole?

I never know what will happen in church. Some days, nothing. On other days, something—upheavals, a burst of clarity perhaps—and I grasp a new way of seeing things, or fill with a gratefulness that spills over into tears. It's as if worshiping opens me sometimes to something larger than the self I know every day, something deeper than my reasonable, rational, conscious mind. In church I sometimes hear from parts of myself that I've never heard from before. Sometimes I even sense the presence of a mystery that maybe—just maybe—is more than my own imagining. I feel a responsive love spring up in me, a longing to give thanks.

This Sunday I savor the air in my throat as we stand to sing the opening hymn. It feels good to stand up, the weight of my body balanced on my own two feet. The blue hymnal is a comfortable weight in my hands. I like the sound of my own voice singing. I like hearing myself in this company, among these other voices, feeling the presence of other worshipers beside me, all of us looking together for God. When I sit down to listen to the readings and settle in to hear the sermon, I lean back against the pew. I glance around briefly, scanning the attentive faces. I fan myself with the service leaflet. It's warm in here. The ceiling fans never seem to work very well. When it's time to pray, I kneel down, my knees pressing into the bench's worn red-velvet cushion. I wonder if anyone else finds this position as uncomfortable as I do. I lean forward awkwardly and rest my forehead on the pew in front of me.

I'm trying to pay attention to the service, but my efforts are flagging. I don't feel particularly joyful singing the hymns. I don't feel especially penitent saying the confession, or even particularly interested in the absolution that follows. I can't seem to keep track of the sermon, and however often I haul it back, my mind keeps wandering off into a miscellany of random thoughts.

Kneeling in the pew, I notice that I feel uneasy inside. Something is yanking up a memory, a bitter memory, pulling it insistently to the surface, like hands that pull up reluctant onion grass.

"It must be something I ate," I think to myself, "something I swallowed."

I can't keep it down. I feel it surging in my gut, up through my chest and into my throat, piling up in my mouth. I want to throw up. In a flash, it all comes back. My body, twelve years old. My parents, leaving me alone, dropping me off in boarding school in a foreign country. Watching them go. Vomiting. Being told to clean up the mess myself.

Here in the church pew, I think I'm going to throw up. I feel streaming through my body the feelings from that distant night in boarding school, already twenty years past: my suitcases in a pile beside my bed, my new roommates looking me over, my parents leaving me.

As I kissed them good-bye, I didn't say to them, "Don't go. Don't leave me here. I feel sick without you." I didn't object. I didn't cry. The only clue I had to my distress was the cheese that came up later. I was sick to my stomach after my parents left me, my body rebelling against the strange and sticky fondue that I'd eaten with them just an hour before. It was an involuntary wrenching, my gut's mute protest: How can you leave me? Where am I? What is this place? And in case I wondered whether I was really lost, really left alone to fend for myself, the stranger who now had charge of me briskly told me to wipe up the floor myself. How did I feel just then? Lonely, anxious, ashamed?

I now saw that all of this had been buried somewhere in my body's memory and was capable of surging back into awareness decades later at the most unexpected moment.

· · ·

When it comes to stories about church, I usually expect to hear something noble and uplifting, not a story about someone sitting in the pew, recalling an old memory and wanting to vomit. But the confusion and sheer messiness of that moment speaks to me now about the spirituality I was just then beginning to apprehend—a spirituality that does not take leave of the body, does not transcend it or annul it, but instead includes and welcomes it, finding in the body itself a deep connection to the divine.

I was just beginning to learn to listen to my body and my inner life, to welcome into awareness the whole range of felt experience. I was just beginning to trust that here, in my body, were the truths I needed to know. Right here, in the closed-off rooms of memory, in the anxieties and hurts locked up in the attic or buried in the basement, I might find not only my own long-lost self, but the One who inspired my search for self in the first place, the One who longed to embrace everything in me, to bless and heal it all, and to lead me out into a new life and a new way of being.

I wasn't sure yet of any of this, but after almost vomiting in church that day, I at least knew that there was a trail that winds its way through the body, back into the past. There are stories, images, events, housed in everyone's body: things come up when you least expect them to. I began to suspect that if I followed the trail carefully, if I looked here and there, if I felt my way along and didn't get lost, I'd find the place where I needed to go.

How often I'd seen a faraway hill and wondered how to reach it, only to discover that it was in fact very close, vividly, physically at hand, if I could just pay attention to it, face it, feel it. If the trail led me to a cliff, maybe with groping hands I could find a tunnel, maybe I could find a way around. I'd been taught as a scholar to start at the top, to reason my way down a hill and around a crevasse, to find a logical way to get from fact to fact. But this hand that pulled the onion grass knew better. I knew where the truth lay. On the ground. In these feet that stamped. In these hands that reached. There are truths that come only from below, as we learn to trust the body, as we learn to listen to the language of image, intuition, sensation, feeling. I needed to learn that lesson now, before my days were up and every logical thing had turned to dust, gone back to the worm.

I realized at last that I'd never "figure out" the story that was mine. I had to let it speak to me on its own terms, in its own time. My job was to make it welcome and to give it room. What was the story my body was trying to tell? Did it have a plot? What plot? Like the stones that are calved and dug up every spring in New England fields, like the tubers that are harvested every fall, my memories and feelings rose insistently to the surface. I searched them for clues, examined them for patterns of significance. Day by day I told myself that if I didn't eat compulsively, if I stayed connected to my feelings, my life's story might eventually come clear, and a new chapter, a new path, would open up before me at last.

CHAPTER 7

Telling Stories

Slowly but surely I got down to my dissertation, hunting through stories that might help me understand how other people put their lives together. Mostly I liked stories of defiance and dissent, stories of people who'd found the courage to say no in order to say yes to a more authentic life.

I remember a story my mother told me about the writer Archibald MacLeish, who was a family friend. His picture hung in the family portrait gallery. It showed a man my grandfather's age who still cut a dashing figure in his Bermuda shorts and straw hat. He was ruddy, vigorous, and smiling—a man at the peak of his powers.

As my mother tells it, when MacLeish was in his twenties, he made an appointment with the head of the prestigious law firm where he worked, in order to tender his resignation. Stepping into the boss's office, he was startled to find everyone assembled—all the partners, all the bigwigs. They'd gathered to announce his promotion to full partnership in the firm and to offer a toast.

"But I've come to say that I'm resigning," MacLeish explained.

He walked all the way home that day, from Boston back to Cambridge. I wonder what went through his mind, whether he was elated or dumbfounded by the decision he'd made, eager or anxious about the unknown future that lay ahead. This much was clear: He didn't want to be a partner. He didn't even want to practice law. He wanted to be a poet. "The heart's necessity compels me," he wrote years later. "Man I am: poet must be." He was off to Paris. He was going to write.

Here was a story I could feed on: a story of someone who dared to walk in his own footsteps, to follow his own inner light.

I was lucky when someone suggested that I write a dissertation about the memoirs of Alexander Herzen. Herzen, I dimly remembered, was one of the great Russian revolutionary democrats. He was an essayist, a literary critic, and a newspaper publisher, an ardent champion of the serfs who'd worked for their emancipation in 1861. Deep in the stacks of Widener Library, I found the book I was looking for: Herzen's autobiographical masterpiece, *My Past and Thoughts*. I pored over its pages. What was Herzen saying about his childhood, about himself? How did he make sense of his life? What stories could I dig up here?

At the beginning of the book, Herzen warns that its meaning is hidden in its pages, that only he knows the secret code; only he can unlock the message within the hieroglyphs of his text.

What were these hieroglyphs? Could I find them? Make sense of them? Could *I* find the key? Was there a story here that I could find, that I could tell? I even wondered if the story might make sense not only of Herzen's life but of my own.

I began to read about Herzen's life. How, as a small child, he begged his nurse to tell the story of Napoleon's 1812 invasion of Moscow, not long after his birth. I read about Herzen's early years among the wealthy aristocrats of Moscow. How he overheard someone saying that he was illegitimate and therefore had no right to his father's name and power. How he decided that the circumstances of his birth were irrelevant and refused to relegate himself to the shameful position of not belonging. All this at an early age, when he was only ten years old.

It made me think about being ten, how *I* was at ten. How I had never quite felt I belonged to the formal world of Quincy House. How I too had tried to dispel the sense of not being quite good enough. Though I could tie my shame to no clear facts, overheard or otherwise, it had eaten away at me nevertheless.

I loved reading about Herzen's liveliness, how he refused to let his spirit be crushed despite being repeatedly humiliated and mocked by his father. I knew something about growing up with a father like that. I savored Herzen's rollicking tales of visiting the servants' quarters, of shouting and playing pranks, of finding people who treated him with affection and respect. They reminded me of the people and places from my own childhood who'd kept me company and kept my spirit alive.

What amazed me more than anything else was that Herzen presented the terms of a conflict I knew only too well for myself. A battle was going on inside his family, inside his soul— a hidden battle without cavalry or gunfire, without swords, boots, or epaulettes, but a battle nonetheless; a real battle that could produce real casualties, a battle of psychic life and death. He was fighting for his life. Fighting to stay connected with his feelings and inner truth in a culture and family that shut children down.

Herzen's memoir showed me what was at stake, what can happen if children lose this war, if their vitality is throttled, if they're robbed not only of their joy but of their anger and their grief. What happens if children are forbidden to protest or mourn. Such children are likely to fall ill or silent. When they grow up, they breed their discontent, unwittingly inflicting on their offspring the pain that they've endured.

I read Herzen. Reread Herzen. Puzzled over the text with

keen interest. What did this story mean to its author? What did it mean to me? And what about those hieroglyphs? What did it mean to read the story of someone else's life and to find the secret of my own life unlocked, given back to me? For all our differences of age and gender, of temperament, nationality, and culture, it wasn't only Herzen that I met in this memoir. It was myself. I started to see myself in his text, to find my own life revealed in a way I hadn't thought possible, to find in Herzen's words a treasure trove of resources for my own remaking of myself.

I thought about my own childhood. I thought about my mother's childhood too. Had her childhood been anything like Herzen's? Our lives, in their generational unfolding, I now saw through Herzen's life, through the power of his words on the page, his willingness to speak the truth.

What fascinated me about Herzen's telling of his life was the way he gestured and hinted, the way he cryptically embedded the truth like little treasures stuck in the knotholes of a tree, leaving the reader to search for them.

Maybe there was a clue here about my mother. She too would only hint. When it came right down to it, I knew very little about my mother's early life; she spoke of it elliptically, letting fall a memory here and there, letting us glimpse only the barest trace of feeling.

I remember when I told my mother about vomiting after I arrived at my Swiss boarding school and being forced to clean up the mess myself. In protest I said to her, "Imagine! There I was, a sick child, having to clean up after myself!"

I remember how my mother smiled, looking off into the distance. Was she remembering a similar story? Often I wondered what was being called up in her when I spoke of my own life. Was she thinking about her life in relation to mine? Was she reminiscing about her motherhood, or about her childhood? Was she looking for fragments of her own life?

On this occasion, my mother let me see her train of thought. She turned back to me and commented, "Maybe it was part of the culture. I remember Mamselle making me do the same when I was little and didn't make it to the toilet."

I knew a thing or two about Mamselle. She was the starched and proper French governess who came to live with my mother's family when my mother was six or seven years old. She took the place of Fraulein, the nurse who had cared for my mother when she was very small. The new governess was nothing like Fraulein. Fraulein had a sweet face and a simple, loving disposition. Fraulein enjoyed caring for little children, and to this day my mother remembers her fondly. But in time Fraulein was sent away. Older children needed a proper education: to acquire manners, to learn French, to master the ways of the adult world.

Mamselle was just the person for the job. A small, slim woman who wore her gray hair tightly gathered in a bun at the back of her head, Mamselle brooked no nonsense. Mamselle required order of her young charges: order, obedience, propriety, and decorum.

One evening when my mother was still very young, a sudden stomachache sent her hurrying on bare feet to the toilet. Up came her dinner, splashing all over the bathroom floor. Mamselle took one look.

"Wipe it up," she commanded.

As my mother tells the story, she bent down, dizzy and sick, to clean the floor. I've often wondered: Did it make her angry? Did she think Mamselle cruel? Did it make her sad? Or was she full of apologies, sorry for having made such a mess, for being such a nuisance? Did she vow to do better next time? Had she learned that neatness was essential to being a member of this family? The more I puzzled over my mother's life, the more I wondered what she felt as a child.

I've often wondered what my mother thought about childhood in general. Having given birth to four children whom she raised in difficult circumstances, what image did she have of her own childhood, and of ours? What image do any of us have of ourselves as children? In what ways does it change? Did my mother look back on her younger self with friendly eyes, or with impatience, indifference, even shame? Did she harbor an unspoken complaint against the gods of her childhood, those well-meaning but ill-advised caretakers who "brooked no nonsense," who would tolerate not even a small child's unkempt feelings?

I wonder sometimes if it's in the genes. I've often asked myself if they're in our "wiring," these family patterns. Who says that wiring isn't social? I wonder if the way my mother was brought up was as durable and fixed as a sort of genetic plate that was stamped on each generation of offspring. More than once I've wondered: What if I could see it and crack that genetic code in my own family, in my own life? Could I, can I, can anyone, crack the code in his or her own family?

I know I'm not the first daughter—nor, I suspect, am I likely to be the last—who needed to find her mother, her mother's story, in order to find herself. It wasn't so much my father's early life that I needed to know right now; it was my mother's. If only I could see clearly what had happened to her, what choices she'd made, what battles she'd fought. Maybe then I could begin to see her as separate from me, as a woman with her own story—a story that was distinct from mine, clearly not my story, yet one that surely would illumine my own.

If I could decipher what really happened back there, would that give me a way of reading my own childhood as well as hers? If I could crack the genetic code that shaped us both, mother and daughter, would I be set free? Could I crack it for myself, even if I couldn't crack it for anyone else?

What needed cracking as much as anything else, I suspect, was my own self-righteousness. I needed to find my mother's story not only so that I could see her as separate from me, but also so that I could learn some compassion. So I could quit harping on the ways I felt she'd let me down, quit laying the blame for my troubles at my mother's feet. Perhaps there were mistakes she'd made that I'd made too. Perhaps there were hurts she'd suffered, victories she'd won, that I knew nothing about; and not because she meant to withhold anything, but because she valued tact and self-restraint. Perhaps there were decisions she'd made that I could begin to imagine from another point of view. Hers.

Perhaps if I could see my mother's separate life with clarity, I could find a new way to connect with her. Could learn a little something about love.

It is Mamselle's voice that echoes in my ears as I listen to my mother tell the story of her life.

"Les coudes!" Mamselle would announce sharply whenever the elbow of a small child crept up onto the dining table. Swiftly the offending elbow would be withdrawn, the head bowed, the eyes cast down. Be as inconspicuous as possible, eat neatly and quietly, don't draw attention to yourself. Compliance, tidiness, self-restraint—these were the values that children must learn.

Along with the cook, the upstairs maid, and the butler, Mamselle took up residence on the mansion's third floor. She immediately became a hovering presence in my mother's young life. Sometimes at breakfast the children would be joined by my grandmother, or even my grandfather, who ate his toast silently as he studied the newspaper propped before him in a silver holder; but generally Mamselle presided over the children's meals, which were served in the breakfast room adjoining the main dining room. It was Mamselle who saw to it that the children were properly fed, dressed, and sent off to school. It was she who made sure that homework was completed, hands washed, teeth brushed. Every evening Mamselle brought the children downstairs to the library to bid their parents good night. This was one of the few times my mother could count on actually seeing her parents. Otherwise they were absorbed in their own affairs, in the respective challenges of running a newspaper business and overseeing a household.

I imagine my grandmother standing up with a smile to greet her children, the gleam of her emeralds, the smell on her breath of cigarettes and Scotch. My grandfather looks up from his armchair, a plume of cigarette smoke encircling his head, one hand clasping a drink, interrupted in midsentence from a conversation about race relations, the Senate elections, the balance of trade. Here are their children: prompt, neat, obedient. Good children. Give each one a kiss. Offer a reprimand, a reminder. Send them off to bed.

Mamselle seems to have done a good job in seeing that the children's manners and behavior passed muster. Still, I have no idea how much Mamselle knew or cared about the inner life of the children in her charge. Feelings, like the contents of their stomachs, were to be kept to themselves and only secretly discharged.

My mother tells me that after the kidnapping of the Lindbergh baby in 1932, her mother and father, like other wealthy parents around the country, worried about their children's safety. Mamselle was instructed to accompany my mother to school. Every day they walked together to the local public school. Every day my mother was late.

I can only wonder just what it was that detained Mamselle in her duties. Was she enjoying this bright little child on the way to school? Was there some small pleasure that distracted Mamselle from her duties? How did my mother make sense of this ironic little mistake of Mamselle's?

"Mamselle didn't know how awful it was to be late," my mother explains.

"Didn't you tell her?" I ask.

My mother grimaces. "I may have suggested it to her, but she didn't seem to hear. I wanted to skip ahead, I wanted to run to get there, but Mamselle would not be hurried."

My mother falls silent, and it seems to me that for one brief moment her eyes grow sad. She looks at me, and then she says in a quiet voice, "I died a thousand deaths."

The bout of scarlet fever that my mother suffered when she was three years old coincided with what turned out to be the first of many trips that took her parents away from home and the children. Her father worked long hours, often twelve hours a day, and there was concern that the stress of running the newspaper was taking too great a physical and emotional toll. The doctor prescribed rest: annual six-week vacations alone with his wife, both summer and winter.

My mother already saw her parents only at the margins of the day, in a brief morning visit at breakfast and in the evening when the children were presented for their goodnight kiss. Now twice a year she would go for weeks at a time without seeing her parents at all.

Under the strict guidance of Mamselle, my mother learned what she could and could not reveal to her parents in their absence. Letters could be written—they were in fact required—but they should be cheerful letters. No child should complain or tell a "bad" little story. A child's letters to her parents should be cheerful, upbeat, even uplifting. A child should put her best foot forward. She should not distress her parents while they were on holiday.

And so my mother would bend to the page, the neat round letters slowly uncurling from her pencil, as she told her parents cheerful stories, showing them her nicest self, her most pleasant feelings.

Did she believe the stories she wrote, their lighthearted tone, the sunny anecdotes? Did these stories satisfy her parents and comfort her? Did she assume they were the only stories worth knowing or telling, since they were apparently the only ones her parents wanted to hear? Did she forget, or never quite let into awareness, the other ways she might have told the story of her days?

I know I certainly did. I remember all the stories I used to tell myself when I was little, particularly the story about having a happy childhood, being part of a happy family. This story served me well for a while, giving me strength to get through each day and connecting me to the people I loved most. After all, this wasn't only my own private story; it was the family's story, the story that held us together. At some point, though, these happy stories lost their power to persuade. They began to seem only fanciful to me, far-fetched. Too much of the truth—the painful truth—had been left out for me to believe them any longer.

Even before children learn to write, they learn what truths are acceptable to express. From the very beginning, my mother had to learn to quiet herself. She remembers having a temper tantrum once. I don't know what touched off her fury, but she ended up crying in her bedroom. She remembers someone standing outside her door and observing in a detached tone of voice, "My goodness, doesn't she have healthy lungs."

The little girl was surprised by the comment and startled into silence. Suddenly it all seemed clear. Being noisy, expressing passionate feelings with gusto and conviction, would never work in this family. The important people were not likely to take her feelings seriously or give them much attention. She would have to find another way to navigate through life, another strategy that was more effective. She wouldn't be noisy anymore. She'd be quiet instead. She'd be nice.

Whatever anger might be seething within her, whatever sorrow or outrage she might be feeling, my mother remained calm and self-contained as she grew up. When I was a child, I learned to guess my mother's moods in the flickers and hints in her face, but I never saw her lose her temper. I never saw her cry, I never saw her lose control. It was an alarming day indeed if we heard her raise her voice: if that little bit of anger had managed to slip out, how much more might be hidden away?

Of all my mother's childhood toys, there was one that she loved best: a china doll with golden hair. It looked like a real baby, my mother tells me, with a long lacy outfit like a christening gown. It was my mother's special possession, the treasure of all her toys.

One fateful day, Admiral Kitt and his family came to visit. The admiral, who was an old friend of my grandmother's, was dressed impressively in his military uniform. Granny was delighted to see her friend again, and Grandfather was eager for news about the navy.

The visit went splendidly until late in the afternoon, when everyone was standing outside in the garden as the admiral and his family prepared to leave. My mother made the mistake of carrying her doll with her as she stepped outside to say good-bye. The admiral's daughter took one look at it, and instantly she wanted to touch it and stroke its golden hair. She wanted to hold it. And then, to my mother's consternation, the little girl burst into tears. She wanted the doll. She wanted to keep it. She wanted to take it home with her. The girl's parents tried to distract her, but it was no use. The girl would not stop sobbing. She had to have the doll.

As my mother remembers it, her father looked at her mother and then her mother looked at her. Who actually spoke the words she can't recall, but finally one of her parents said it: she should give her doll to the other girl.

I don't know if Mother objected, if she blanched, or if she wept, either then or later. I wonder if she ever dared to love a doll again. I wonder if she considered it risky to form another such attachment, to feel again that degree of passion for a doll. My mother says she did accept the doll that was given to her as a replacement sometime later. She did play with it, did like it well enough. But still, she says, when her parents made her give up the thing she loved most, something in her broke.

Over the years, my mother occasionally told us anecdotes about her early life. Bit by bit, we children pieced together what we heard. My mother offered these morsels calmly, almost casually, as if they had no emotional charge. She seemed genuinely bewildered when her stories brought tears to her children's eyes. She was taken aback, I think, to see that these events of her early life, to her so familiar, so completely normal and ordinary—indeed so trivial as to be almost unworthy of note—could stir up in her children such tenderness, such sadness, such fierce anger on her behalf.

It was as if we were hearing in these stories some terrible, poignant melody that my mother did not hear; as if these stories packed a punch that my mother didn't notice, didn't even feel. It was as if my mother had invited us to wade into the coldest lake we'd ever known, into water so cold it made your skin turn blue, your ankles ache, your teeth chatter, your bones throb from the sheer chill of it. It was as if my mother were standing waist-deep in these chilly waters, quietly poised there, and saying to us, "This is simply how life is, there's no need to say anything, no need to react." The thing to do was to stand as still as you could, as still as a statue, until you went numb.

Sometimes my mother's stories about her childhood startled me not because of what she told me, but because of all she *didn't* say, her need to remove herself from the text. It was a need that anyone might feel, growing up in a house where the whole world came to the doorstep—particularly such an illustrious world, a world of presidents and governors, journalists, publishers, politicians, and business leaders all eager to seek counsel, to gain the confidence of a man of influence and privilege. My grandfather was a man of many words, many talents, many opinions; a generous man too, a man who cared about justice and was deeply committed to bettering the community; a man whose wife had a flair for hospitality, the skills to regulate her husband's life, and the capacity to know what was wanted and needed even before he spoke. My grandmother was a leader, even a pioneer, in a wealth of civic causes, from family planning to racial justice and human rights.

What gravity should we give to a child's yearnings, even the small unspoken ones, that amount to nothing more than an elbow misplaced on a table or a sharp word from a governess, even if it seems to her that the whole world is collapsing? Do these things matter? Set against the larger drama of her parents' busy, demanding lives, what weight should be given to the needs of one small child?

. . .

It was always a major event when my mother took us to the house where her family had lived since she was twelve. It's an amazing moment in a child's life to visit the house where her mother grew up; to sit on the same chair where Mommy sat as a young girl; to eat at the same table; to look at the same objects that surrounded her years ago; to imagine her young life, so near at hand, feeling that at any moment that child might reappear in these rooms where she once lived. There is a moment of fascination, of seeing, that comes over a small child when a historical perspective takes root in her mind and sensibilities; when for the first time she realizes that her grandparents are also the parents of her mother, and that she herself is just one small part of a family that stretches back into the past and, through her, into the generations ahead.

I remember wandering, no longer a child, not yet a woman, from room to room in the mansion in Minneapolis where my mother was once a young girl. Paintings by Picasso hung on the walls, along with others by Klee, Matisse, Gauguin, O'Keeffe—more artists than I could possibly name. Each painting had been chosen with exquisite taste. There was a plum-colored carpet running up the front stairs. Pale curtains drawn across the windows, muffling any sounds from the street, softening the light. The sheen of antiques—rosewood, mahogany, teak. The luster of silver. The soft, plump curves of upholstered chairs. The glint of gilded mirrors taller than a child, reflecting back the subdued glow of delicate porcelain bowls, cut-glass candelabra, needlepoint cushions, yellow mums in a vase.

I run my hand along the velvet slope of a sofa, peer into the family photographs in silver frames: a bride all in white, two children looking through a telescope, Eisenhower grinning as he holds up the small-mouthed bass he caught at Grandfather's lakeside retreat. I inspect the shelves of books—fiction, political commentary, the volumes of an encyclopedia lined up like soldiers. I look over the inlaid table; the secretary desk with its display of knicknacks brought back from trips abroad; the sculpture by Modigliani of an impassive woman with an impossibly long nose; the Henry Moore statue of a warrior after battle, holding up a shield with the one arm left to him. Wherever I look there is comfort, order, and wealth. All these artifacts, as gorgeous as any you might find in a museum. Everything is perfect. Every surface is immaculate. I know better than to touch anything on these tables. I know not to leave a fingerprint.

Everywhere there is abundance in this house. And nothing to feed on. At least not for me. Everywhere there is more than any one family could possibly need, and yet there's famine in this house. Perhaps no one in this family would agree, but I say there's hunger here. I feel hungry in this house.

In the dining room hangs a portrait of my grandparents painted by Oskar Kokoschka, the figures—all jaggedy lines— full of startling oranges and greens. Grandfather is leaning back somberly with one hand resting on the sofa, the other hand in his lap; Granny is sitting erect and animated, her arm outstretched to gesture toward him. The two of them are larger than life, an imposing couple in a young girl's eyes.

We sit below this portrait at the dining table, a chandelier glowing over our heads, silver and linen spread out before us. My grandfather presides at one end of the table and my grand-mother at the other, ready to press the buzzer with her foot and signal the maid to begin serving dinner. I sit at the table as correctly as possible, back straight, hands in my lap, careful not to touch my fork until my grandmother has picked up hers, careful not to upset the water glass or let my knife scrape against my plate.

My mother has trained us well how to eat politely with our grandparents. We know the story of the hapless guest who ate his entire artichoke, prickles and all, because he'd never seen one before and didn't know the right way to eat it; the story of the guest who raised the finger bowl to his lips and drank it down, thinking it was some kind of clear soup. We laughed when we heard these stories, partly because our own grip on propriety was so precarious. What did we know about manners? We ate with our eyes on the grown-ups, watching to see what they did next.

The best of times was when the adults were content to talk among themselves. But whenever my grandfather announced the beginning of General Conversation, a hush would fall over the table. Smiling benignly at the assembled throng of family and guests, Grandfather would declare that the time had come for us to take turns naming something, perhaps the justices of the Supreme Court or the capitals of each state. For him this was no doubt a pleasant diversion, his way of making everyone at the table feel included. But my grandfather's announcement instantly emptied my mind of any particle of knowledge it might once have contained. A clean sweep. Nothing in me but bare floors, vacant walls.

One of my aunts still laughs when she tells the story of her first dinner with my grandfather. She was being courted at the time by his eldest son, so she was seated in the place of honor at my grandfather's right hand. When the time came for General Conversation, Grandfather announced that everyone around the table would take turns naming the members of the cabinet. Graciously he turned to my aunt-to-be and informed her that she could go first.

"A cabinet? What does he mean by 'cabinet'?" my aunt remembers thinking anxiously to herself. "A chest of drawers? A bureau? A highboy? Lowboy? *What?*"

To her credit, my aunt responded brilliantly. "I tell you what," she said to my grandfather, leaning forward to lay a gentle hand on his sleeve. "Let's begin by asking one of the younger relatives, shall we?"

It was a quick-witted move. I suppose it wasn't only the children who were anxious at that table, struggling in one way or another to look good, make a favorable impression, and at least appear to be poised, witty, attractive, intelligent. We knew this game, and we knew its stakes. To earn whatever share of love might deservedly be your own, you felt you had to pass a series of tests, prove your prowess, establish your worth, and succeed.

Randolph, the African-American chauffeur, was always the first to greet us when we came to visit my mother's parents. He would meet us at the airport, collect us and our luggage, and guide us to a sleek black limousine with tinted windows. We children would tumble into the car, scrambling for the pop-up jump seat or settling back into the plush cushions. Randolph would be quick to see that everyone found a place, that everyone was happy, and then he would sweep us away, the Cadillac pulling soundlessly from the curb and gliding out onto the highway. As we watched the world whiz silently by, we would laugh with pleasure at Randolph's jokes. Sometimes being with Randolph was the warmest, most enjoyable part of our visits—these moments of sitting with him and swapping tales, sharing the news, as the cornfields flew by.

Randolph was probably the most affectionate person in my mother's childhood world. He was head of the household staff, expert at everything he did. He kept harmony among the staff, he insisted that they maintain the high standards expected of them, and he anticipated his employers' every request. To my grandparents, Randolph offered respect and attentive care. To my mother and her siblings, he offered enormous kindness.

Randolph *liked* children. When the family gathered every summer at the lakeside retreat in northern Minnesota, Randolph gladly accepted the company of any small child who wanted to join him in fishing for sunfish off the dock.

After my grandmother died, my increasingly frail grandfather lived "alone" in the big house, surrounded by a small band of paid and staff. When Grandfather passed away, my mother flew out to help settle his affairs. The work of the staff was obviously over. They could now retire comfortably on their pensions from the family. By this time, Randolph was more than seventy years old. He had worked for the family for forty-five years. He had seen several generations pass through this house, and for decades he had offered his warmth and quiet steadiness to anyone in need. He had seen an entire family through a lifetime.

Who knows what Randolph thought about this family? In another time and another place, perhaps thirty years later, Randolph might have been an executive in charge of a large organization, or a psychiatrist whose skill and insight led his clients to a deeper understanding of their lives. Now that his working life was over, Randolph was saying good-bye to the family to whom he had devoted so much of his time, so much of his care. He handed his house key to my mother. He was going home. Randolph had his own house to go home to.

When the door closed behind him, my mother found herself alone in the house for the first time in her life. Her parents had always seen to it that no family member was ever alone in the house without a servant present to open the front door or answer the telephone. Now, as she crossed the front hall, my mother's footsteps echoed loudly on the marble tiles. When she stood still, the empty rooms were hushed. I wonder if the loneliness of that moment was different from the loneliness she had often known in that house, even when it was bustling with people. I've often wondered, did she feel "at home"?

My mother told me a story once that has stayed with me. Many years ago, on a Friday afternoon, Randolph was preparing to go home. The children stood by listening as he gave a last word of instruction to the cook. Then he put on his coat and started for the door. My mother's younger brother watched him go with the saddest little look on his face.

"I wish I were in your family," he said to Randolph wistfully.

Randolph stopped and turned around, his face open and curious. He took off his cap. A tall, lanky man, he had to bend down, as he customarily did when speaking to children, stooping way down until his eyes looked straight into the young boy's face.

"And why is that?" he asked the child. "Tell me why that is."

"Well," said the boy, "because if you were my father, I'd get to be with you. I'd get to see you. We could do things together."

"I see," said Randolph. "Yes, that's exactly what we would do."

It's a sad and poignant business, this hunger to belong. Not easy. It's never been easy.

When I sat down to write my thesis, I realized that I had found what I was looking for. I had found the code to decipher the hieroglyphs not only of Herzen's life but of my own as well. Reading Herzen enabled me to read my own life and to feel it, to feel the grief and the anger that welled up as I began to see who I was in the midst of my family. It was my grief and anger that had cracked the code.

Sometimes we have no access to our feelings, we can't get hold of our lives; we can only find ourselves as we read our way through the stories of another writer, another teller of a family tale. Maybe it was the distance—Herzen being a man removed from me by a century, whose mother tongue was not my own—that helped me see my own life so sharply.

As I read Herzen's account of himself, following along in the story of my own life, I saw suddenly, clearly, the loneliness and emotional deprivation that had been concealed, hidden within a life of privilege. As I listened to this man tell his story, I listened in a new way to my mother telling hers, the way she told the truth of her childhood, the way I reflected now on my own.

I realized that I had not been able to separate my mother's childhood from my own or her childhood loneliness from mine. I can't say exactly how I finally came to see that my mother had indeed survived her own childhood, but I saw clearly that I needed to survive my own. Always when I'd looked into my mother's face, my mother's eyes, I'd seen the face of the little child she was along with my own, the two superimposed, the two intermingled and blurred. Now we could stand side by side: mother and daughter.

As grief poured through me, and a longing to express it, I now had my own place to stand. Like my mother, I too had been shocked into silence. Like so many others around the world whose voices are ignored or rendered mute, I too had inherited the silent tradition, the legacy of saying nothing and feeling less. But I was done with it now. I would write my way out. I was hungry for meaning, hungry for words. For once, I would pick up my pen, not my fork. I needed to write my heart out.

It took me decades before I found my mother, even as I stood right there beside her in her own company; decades before I read my mother in the text of her own words. It took me the better part of a lifetime to read the secret, unuttered text, the story of my mother's life that I could only conjure, only infer.

There were times when I used to wonder whether my mother would disappear completely, becoming so faint that at last she'd vanish soundlessly into thin air. I wrote a story once about a woman who became translucent, transparent, her flesh and bone immaterial, until finally nothing at all was left, only a trail of vapor. It was a story that made me wince with horror.

What happens when people treat us as faintly unreal, not quite there? What happens when someone repeatedly looks in our direction but doesn't quite see us? What happens in the exchange of gazes that causes us to lose our image of ourselves? What happens to us? Where do we go? Do we somehow cease to be?

Had my mother's parents never quite seen my mother? Had her parents' distracted gaze never made her feel quite real? Or was it perhaps my father's gaze, sometimes intrusive, often drunk, that led my mother to take inward flight when I was young? It was years before I learned what it had been like for her to live, day after day, from her marriage on her twenty-second birthday through young adulthood and into early middle age, with a man increasingly muddled by booze. It was years before I learned how close my mother came to losing her life.

One day my younger sister, my brother, and I, all of us now grown, sat down with our mother to talk about the worst of it—our years together as a young family, what she'd been through, what it had been like for her. That day she told us how, in the most awful of times, she had planned to take her life on May 1, 1966.

It was our last year at Quincy House. Gulp by gulp, my father was drinking up a storm. The rest of us were wrapped in silent misery, trying to duck his unpredictable moods, his startling swings, with drink in hand, from high-flung elation to melancholy and despair. We steered away from his bitter laughter and explosive anger, his leering jokes and vacant stares. Sometimes I was infuriated, sometimes full of pity, sometimes just plain scared.

I'd never dared to ask my mother what she'd endured in those years, caught up in the complexities of a life of privilege and possibility that had brought her to a living hell; raising four children, married to a man of enormous talent and energy. Both of them were trapped: my father, gripped by an addiction that had no mercy; my mother, faithful, long-suffering, desperate for a solution, dying for some way to change all this, to stop all this, wanting so badly to wake up from this nightmare, but with no way to walk out of her life and no one to turn to for help.

I listened with amazement to the story of how my mother made it through the days, how she moved from meal to meal, morning to night, sunrise to sunset, each move carefully planned, the date of her death circled on her calendar, her only reprieve from an unlivable life. Each day was another day crossed out in the calendar, one day closer to the end.

When the day arrived, she decided not to kill herself. No, she would not put an end to her life. But she would put an end to her life with my father. In a moment of pristine clarity, she decided to walk out of their unlivable life so that she herself could live. Whatever self she did have would survive, but only apart from their life together. Rather than kill the body, my mother laid aside her unlivable life.

It's a heroic act to have the wherewithal, the courage, to leave a deadly marriage. My mother refused to crash with everyone on board. If he was going to go down, kamikaze-style, she could not go with him. This trip was over; this story, finished. My mother would begin again, start over. She turned the page.

By autumn my mother had left my father. She had taken her life into her own hands and decided to live it. She had become a survivor.

. . .

I am grateful to my mother for what she told me that day. For me it was a coming-of-age story, the day my mother took me into her confidence as a daughter and as another woman, both of us thoroughly grown up. I think of it as the day my mother told me the real facts of life.

The greatest gift my mother gave me that day was self-disclosure. It was a moment of revelation. My mother had been willing to tell me her suffering. She became human to me, with real blood coursing through her veins, just like mine. Real sorrow had broken her heart. Mine too.

Today, more than thirty years after the date of what could have been her suicide, my mother is vibrantly alive. She is a woman who has seen a lot, someone who can sit in a room with real suffering, a woman who offers wisdom, solace, instruction, and conversation to young and old alike, to people from all walks of life, to those who are confused, seeking, or on the brink of death, to a steady stream of people who make their way to her door. I see my mother offer her many gifts—a helping hand, a wise word, a sense of life. I see her deep in conversation, attentive and alive; I see her throw back her head and fill the room with her laughter; I see her, at the age of seventy, take a slugger's swing at a baseball. And I give thanks for whatever stayed her hand, for her courage in finally walking away from a marriage that was killing her.

She made it. She survived. And so did I. I give thanks for her life. And for mine.

CHAPTER 8

At Sea

Would that my father had been able to save his life. Even before he was diagnosed with cancer, my father was in a tailspin, and he knew it. His first marriage had failed, and his second one too. His children were wary and estranged. His scholarly work had never taken off as he'd hoped. And drink was slowly but surely getting the better of him, taking the best of him. You could see it in the lines of his weathered face. His ruddy cheeks, burned by years in the sun, were now often flushed with alcohol. His red beard and hair were turning gray from age and stress, and sometimes he couldn't stop the shaking in his hands. I could see a look of lostness flashing across his face. Behind the bluster, behind the articulate web of words, behind the fierce blue eyes, I sometimes glimpsed the face of a frightened man, directionless, drifting out to sea.

My father will always be linked in my mind with the sea. He was more at home deep-sea diving than he ever was in a classroom, more at peace in a sailboat than at a podium or behind a desk. I remember the awe I felt as a little girl that I should have a father who was so at home in the sea. Marveling, I would inspect the treasures that he'd collected and laid out on a table in the front hallway at Quincy House: sprays of coral fans from the Caribbean; heavy pink conch shells with fat, bulbous lips; broken pottery from the Sea of Galilee; spikes made by Paul Revere and salvaged from an old sailing ship that went down in the Atlantic years ago.

From one of his diving expeditions in Greece, my father brought back a large clay amphora. It stood on the porch of our summer house on a cliff overlooking the waves of the Atlantic. I liked its curves. I wondered what stories it might tell if it could speak. Was it very old? Was it valuable? Whose hands had touched it? What had it once held? My father treated the amphora in the same offhand manner that a naval officer might treat the spoils of war: he used it as an ashtray. Even so, cigarette butts managed to land all over the lawn. Before hosting a party, my father would pay us a penny for every ten butts we retrieved. We'd collect them in brown paper bags, our own tiny treasures, and spread them out for the count, trading them in for our father's coins.

When my father grew older, he gave up scuba diving. He never said so, but it occurs to me that even then, perhaps, his lungs were beginning to fail. He taught himself to sail. He took courses with the Coast Guard and learned how to navigate. He learned to read nautical maps and to predict the pull of tides, the depth of channels. He learned to decipher radio signals and to understand the language of foghorns and buoys. He read the patterns of the stars. He learned to tie knots, to hoist sail, to pull up anchor on a beautiful morning and sail away to destinations unknown.

My father loved to tell the joke about a yacht speeding out of the harbor and overtaking a sailboat. The yachtsman leans over the side to yell triumphantly, "I'm going to get there in one hour, and it's going to take you ten!" The sailor looks up calmly and smiles, "Ah, but you don't understand. I'm already there."

I know my father found more peace in the rise and fall of a boat on the waves, on the endless expanse of blue sea, than he did anywhere else on earth. But even now, looking back at him, I can see there was something about the way my father was rigged: no boat could hold him, no sail could contain his restlessness. There were always high seas and storms in my father that he just couldn't ride out. It wouldn't be long, once we were under way, before critical or contemptuous words were flying from his mouth, beer cans popping, while he fiddled with the radio, dialing for foul weather, so that he could head the boat straight into it to test himself against its winds.

Even on a calm day, my father could find trouble. Even if he wasn't looking for it, it would find him. There were accidents, in fact disasters. One of them occurred on a trip toward the Isles of Shoals. My father was taking my brother and younger sister out sailing on a day trip. A storm was coming in. Just as they left the mooring in the harbor, intending to set sail, the boat's propeller got caught in the rope of a lobster trap. In a moment, the boat was hopelessly snagged. Rising winds grabbed hold of it and turned it around, slamming it against a reef of rocks in the middle of the harbor. With every wave, the boat crashed broadside against the boulders.

My father, brother, and sister clambered off the boat and onto the rocks. They were stranded out there, marooned in the middle of the waves, until the harbormaster rescued them, ferrying them to shore. But the boat was left behind. Battered by the sea, it eventually broke into bits and sank.

I have a photograph of my father standing helplessly on the shore, watching his beloved boat get smashed to smithereens. A journalist from a local newspaper took a close-up of my father in his rain slicker, a safety harness still buckled across his chest. He is standing there staring with open mouth, a man with a grim, tormented face.

Sometimes I saw my father as a character straight out of Hemingway: brave, indefatigable, impatient with self-pity and complaints, as heroic even in defeat as the protagonist of *The Old Man and the Sea*. Other times I tended to write my father into Melville—more like Ahab, the crazy sea captain whose single-minded quest for an elusive prey eventually destroyed not only himself but the ship and almost everyone on board. I often thought it wouldn't be long before my father took our whole family down with him. On days when I had more sympathy for my father, I figured him as the Ancient Mariner, compelled to repeat the same life-in-death story over and over again.

When my father woke up one morning in 1984 and discovered he could no longer speak, I suspected that a page had turned and he was stepping into the last chapter of his life, that the end was in sight.

Only months before, I had finally finished my Ph.D. at Harvard and said good-bye to my father's world. It had been an exultant farewell. Now I saw that I must prepare for a larger parting, face the fact that the time would soon come when I had to say good-bye to my father.

"It seems I have a bit of a problem," he whispered to me over the phone, his once-resonant voice now husky and faint. No, he was not in any pain. But my stepmother told me that when she asked him if he was scared, he croaked out one word: "Very."

Before all the biopsies, the CAT scan, and the bone scan, before the diagnosis of a fast-moving, lethal form of lung cancer, my father gathered us four children at his house in Marblehead, just a block or two from the beach.

I remember thinking to myself: This is not real. None of this is real.

We ate a picnic on the rocks. My father spoke about fighting the cancer and about facing up to the fact that he might soon die. He asked us which of his possessions had special meaning for us. He wanted to know which ones to pass on to us after his death. Did we want the portrait of his mother as a young woman? Would we like the wooden statue he'd brought back from Korea at the end of the war? What about the diving watch he'd worn on so many trips into the sea? Would we want these things?

I remember staring at the objects he'd assembled in words before us and feeling sadness descend on me, on the four of us, his grown children sitting beside him helplessly, our eyes downcast. Our father, listening to our silence, sensing our grief, admonished us immediately not to grieve until he had gone. His grip on himself, on us, was tight, but even so, one of my sisters began to weep. The rest of us fumbled for words to cover it over, wanting to control ourselves, to choke back the tears, to speak only lightly, ever so lightly, smiling all the way; wanting not to upset him, not to cry; wanting not to anger him by making our sadness too plain.

Me? I couldn't contain myself another minute. I yanked off my sneakers, tore off the clothes over my bathing suit, and ran, ran as fast as my legs would carry me, ran over the rocks, across the beach, and dove into the sea.

As I hit the water I was a woman in her mid-thirties, grief-stricken that her father, standing on the shore, was dying; but in the same moment I was ten, thirteen, the young girl who used to run down the beach, flinging herself into the water. I'd done it a thousand times before: my father on the rocky shore behind me watching; me swimming as fast as I could, making my stroke as long as I could, kicking my legs as hard as my muscles would allow, being as brave as he was, silently calling out, "Daddy! Look at me!"; wanting to show off for him and be claimed by him, and knowing, as death loomed now before my frightened eyes, that I loved my father fiercely, that as long as life was in me, I was the daughter of this man.

I remember coming home late one afternoon after a long day of sailing with my father. I jumped out of the boat and swam the last fifty feet to the beach. I wanted to get away from him fast. I was sick of the smell of beer, sick of being trapped with him in such a small space. I wanted desperately to get away at once, to leave him behind. But also, if the whole truth be told, I wanted him to watch me from the boat, to see me as I moved through the waves, to recognize what was in me—the life he'd passed on, an unsinkable exuberance.

And now I was swimming for all I was worth, trying to swim out beyond this disaster that was going to claim his life and, in some way, mine. I honestly couldn't imagine my father going under without taking all of us with him. I wanted to swim away from the vision of my father helplessly marooned on some other shore where I couldn't speak to him, couldn't hear his voice. At the same time, I knew I had to swim against the current, every current of despair that threatened to swamp me, sink me, send me to the bottom, diving headlong into food or some other addiction with its false promises of safety and escape.

I wanted the water to wash away everything, all the grief, all the despair. Could this water bathe away my fear, my sorrow? Could it soak out my pain? Could this sea, this life-giving sea, rising and falling with every tide, pulsing in and out like our breath, could it wash away everything that was past, wipe out all the words spoken in anger and contempt—my father's words, the words meant to kill—as if they'd been written in sand that would be swept clean by the incoming tide? Could this seawater wash away all the hurt?

It was words that linked my father and me, just as it was words that drove us apart. We were alike in loving words, the play of meanings, ideas, and sound. Only last Christmas he'd given me a dictionary with an inscription inked in his own bold hand: "To a fellow scribbler." Could I reach into the depths and find words to speak, words as polished and particular as stones, as fluted as the shells that waves gather up from below and spread out along a beach? I would dip into the dictionary that my father gave me. I knew all the words were there, all the words I longed for—words to bring new life, not death; words to heal memory, salve wounds, redeem the time. I would seek those words. I would find them, if I could. I would let them find me. I longed for my voice to join the voice of the waves, the life-giving energy of the sea.

As I swam, I could feel the cold sting of salt water spraying against my cheeks, into my eyes, my lips, my teeth. I was out over my head, and I knew I must take care. I could not go out too far and hope to come back alive.

Maybe, I thought with a shiver of fear, maybe the sea was a harbinger of death, not life, with its chilly waters, its unexpected eddies and swells, its riptides, rogue waves, and breakers, its hidden shoals and freakish storms ready in a million ways to kill anyone venturing too near for too long, ready to pull us down, swallow us up.

Suddenly I was angry, angry at death as I kicked against the waves, raging at suffering, my hands pushing against the sea, pushing it away from me, shouting down everything that cramps and limits and holds us back. No. I did not want my father to die. He must not die. I would never accept it, never agree to it, never give my consent to his death. I would find words for this too—the protest of every creature against all that hurts and wounds and terrifies, all that cuts life short—leaving behind, when I was done, the last words uttered, the last lines put to the page, a silence filled with love. Yes, there were many times that I'd hated my father, feared him, felt sorry for him, avoided him, been wounded by him. But I loved him still, I loved him deeply. I did not want my father to die.

Like a depth charge exploding in the center of the sea, the

anger in me turned to love, love for this impossible man, my father; and not only for him but for me, for all of us, for all creatures who have to die. A love passed through me that seemed meant for my father, yes, but not only for him, not for him alone.

When I stood for the first time at my father's hospital bed, I didn't know what to do with myself. For years it had seemed safer to love my father from a distance, safer than being up close, face to face. When I was actually with him, I felt constrained, circumspect. We had between us a long history of hurt, so I was careful in his presence, fearful that the tiny flickering dagger of his contempt might at any moment sink deep between my ribs and find its way again to my heart. He could be a killer, my father.

I kissed his cheek. I showed him the begonia that I'd bought for him and put it on the windowsill. Then I timidly handed him a card. The day before, I'd spent ages in the drugstore riffling through the racks of cards, looking for a good one, a perfect one, a card with just the right blend of sympathy and humor, just the right tone—affectionate but not cloying or overbearing, not too casual but not too intense either. What a weight of communication this card would have to bear. My father could be so quick with sarcasm, so dismissive of emotion. How could I express my love but do it lightly? What words would he let in? How much love could I share before he pushed me away?

I found a card that passed the test, at least as far as I could tell, and I wrote a few words inside, wishing my father well. To my horror, after he opened the envelope and read the card, he silently, carefully tore the card in two, right down the fold in the middle.

Oh no, I gasped, he hates it. What have I done? He's angry at me for something, I've annoyed him somehow, I've said too much, said it wrong.

But no. My father gestured silently: Would I get some thumbtacks and tack the front page of the card to the empty bulletin board at the end of his bed? And tack up the inside page too, which had my message on it? And then tack up the envelope as well?

He took a look at the result and smiled with satisfaction. "Good," he whispered. "Now there are *three* things up there."

I was taken aback. What did this gesture mean? It was what a young child would do—or a battered man, now reaping what he'd sown. Perhaps he was wondering if any of his other grown children would bring anything, or even come to the hospital to pay him a visit. Perhaps he was making as much as he could of this moment of love.

I found myself grinning with relief, like a kid who has just been forgiven, like a child who flinches from a man's raised fist and then realizes she won't be struck after all. What seems most poignant to me, every time I remember that scene in the hospital room, is that there was no way for me to stand in my father's presence as a woman, a grown daughter struggling to come to terms with his dying and the life he'd lived with us. It was not only my love that I dared not experience or express fully in his presence, it was my power, my adulthood, my authority as a woman. Even in my mid-thirties, well on my way to middle age, I still flinched in his presence, cowered, in fact, as if I were a placating child, eager to soothe, to please, still fearful of his biting eyes, his annihilating words.

What had my father and I come to, that our love for each other was expressed so strangely, so obliquely—in a gesture as violent and bizarre as ripping a card in two, in the grin of a grown woman who discounts her power and is suddenly ten years old again? How complicated our transactions seemed, as if we were tiptoeing a wary zigzag down a road salted with land mines, or peering at each other from behind fortress battlements, ready to let our arrows fly.

Standing at the end of my father's bed, I could see his suffering, his anxious eyes. How close was he to death? When would it come and how? What words could connect us? What words could convey our love?

In our family, we usually express affection by saying vaguely, "Much love." It's friendly enough. It's safe. It's indirect. It looks good, as neat and tidy as the closing salutation on a letter. The phrase hovers in space for a moment, as if uttered by no one in particular, addressed to no one specific, a detached, floating phrase as light as a beachball, affecting no one, changing nothing. Sometimes we add a cheery wave, a hearty laugh, and then, with a sigh of relief, we beat a hasty retreat.

In an unguarded moment, one of us might venture to say "I love you," adding a subject and object to this desperately vulnerable verb. When the words slip out, the trick is to say them very fast, squeezing them into the middle of another sentence, so that you hardly hear what was just said, as in "It's been good talking to you *Iloveyou* good luck on that project," the speaker sliding the phrase into a flow of words as if he or she were slipping into your bland bowl of oatmeal a raisin that goes down so fast you hardly realize the raisin was there, and even if you did notice it in your mouth, it's too late, you've swallowed it, it's gone, you didn't have a chance to taste it, and it would be rude to draw attention to the raisin and brazen to ask for another one, you greedy girl, so the thing to do is to hand back a similar bowl of oatmeal with its own buried raisin. That's a fair exchange; you're not stingy ("Thanks for calling *Iloveyoutoo* let's talk again sometime").

The basic family instructions: If you have something important to say, make it quick. Don't let anything more than the tip of your tongue touch the words. Don't get inside them. Toss off the words or squeeze them in, but never mean them fully as you speak, because then you are unutterably vulnerable. Precarious. Exposed.

And so now that I was overcome with love for my father, I was speechless. I had no words that would say a thing, not as a throwaway line anyway. I didn't know what to say, what to do. I stood at the foot of his bed like a supplicant, like a small child, feeling stupid and small, hemmed in, forbidden to express what was in my bursting heart.

I reached out my hand and touched the blanket that covered my father's foot. I didn't dare hold his hand, didn't dare stroke his face, didn't dare look him in the eye and tell him how much I loved him. What was I afraid of? That I would start to cry. That he would draw back in alarm, gently or roughly push me away, tell me to go cry in the bathroom if I had to.

So I stood by the bed feeling my silent, helpless love for my father—a love that stubbornly refused to go away—not knowing what to do except snap at the tired doctor who seemed distracted, almost too casual as he talked things over with my father.

"You're talking to a *person*," I angrily informed the physician. "In case you haven't noticed."

I wanted to be a real person with my father. I wanted him to be a real person with me before he died. I wanted to tell him the truth of what I felt. I would have liked to take as long a time as I needed to say, "Daddy, I love you. Do you know that? Do you know that I've always loved you?" And sit there and feel my words come out, one at a time, knowing that he was listening carefully, taking in each one.

Isn't it amazing that grief is universal and yet at the same time so particular? No two people do it the same way, and the members of my family were no exception. We each had our own way of facing the panic and anger, the grief and love, which were so tied up together, so intertwined.

I remember going out to a movie with my sisters after my father got sick. Each of them bought a large tub of popcorn and gobbled the kernels down fast.

"I think I'm eating to escape," one of my sisters said.

I nodded. I knew all about that. I'd done that too. I couldn't afford to do it anymore. Sometimes I wished I could. Just then, for instance, right there in the darkened movie theater, with my father's death waiting for us outside the door. Couldn't I ignore it for a while? Tune out? Run away? Escape?

No. I couldn't. I wouldn't. I knew I'd have to bear this moment, this movie, this darkness, this fearful future already knocking at the door of my consciousness, demanding to be let in. I wanted to feel my way through the truth of what was here without stuffing down my feelings, swallowing them whole along with the food.

My mother seemed floored that my father was so sick. How many years had it been since she left him, ending their marriage? Was it eighteen, nineteen, twenty years ago? And yet, she told me, she was startled to find that she loved him still. She didn't regret the decision to leave him, but at the same time she was amazed to realize that she loved him all these long years later, unconditionally, without reserve.

The first weekend after my father became ill, my mother was flat on her back with a sudden high fever.

As for me, I suddenly came down with laryngitis. My throat was sore. I could hardly speak. Hearing the strain in my father's voice, I tightened my own throat.

My father's deep voice once filled the largest lecture hall

at Harvard without a microphone. Now he couldn't utter a word.

"I hate this," he whispered. "What's happening to me? I would rather be blind than mute."

Perhaps my father had discovered that he didn't know who he was except as he spoke himself into being every day. Speech had been his weapon—a hand grenade to toss, a shield for self-defense. Spoken words had also been his way of caressing, spinning stories, cracking jokes, drawing his spellbound listeners into a charmed circle in which he was always the center. Now he had to negotiate the clumsy new language of gestures, grunts, whispers, and silence. I saw fear in his eyes, and anger, grief, loss, though neither of us spoke a word about it. Nor did I tell him what I was feeling. It all seemed too much, too fast, too soon.

Instead, my body spoke for me. My father's throat was tight, and as if echoing his silent cry, my throat responded by tightening up too.

One morning I felt a sudden cramp in my right foot. Just a moment before, I'd remembered my father's telling the doctor that he was having trouble with his circulation, that his right hand and foot often seized up in cramps.

I so badly wanted to be close to my father, it was as if I were turning into him. I wasn't surprised. I'd had years of training in losing myself. I'd been expert in making my life track the ups and downs of my father's life, in tuning myself to his mercurial moods while trying to figure out how much liquor was in him. Now that he was actually dying, not just slowly killing himself with drink, it was tempting to give myself away again, to focus everything on him. So I worked even harder to stay separate, to keep inside my own separate life. I repeated a litany to myself: "My lungs are clear. My throat is fine. My father has cancer. I do not."

I reminded myself that my path was not his path. For one

thing, I'd chosen to seek help for my addiction. My father had gone down a different road.

I got ready to go down the road without him.

It's a still, cool Labor Day, shaded with sadness and love. There is bread rising in the oven, draped with a wet cloth, its round little body lifting quietly in the dark. For the last six weeks, ever since my father's diagnosis, I've had an urge to bake bread. Here come another pair of loaves. I can think of nothing better to do right now than to quietly bake bread, slice it up, and give it away. Bread rises. But fathers don't. Not from their deathbeds anyway.

My father's not a man who would ever go to church for comfort. He certainly would not go up the aisle to receive Communion. But he loves the bread I bake for him. And for me it's consecrated, a love offering to my family. Last week I wrapped up a fresh piece of bread and offered it to him. He smiled with surprise and affection. Shyly—or so it seemed to me—he took the bread, pulled up a chair, and sat down to eat.

Yesterday I went sailing with my father and my new friend, Robert Jonas. Jonas, as I call him, is sturdy like my father, a natural athlete too, I think, with eyes as blue as my father's but without their sting. Jonas has a warm laugh, a gentle face. He makes me laugh. He makes me think. And he is not afraid of emotion.

Jonas can spot the hidden anger that sometimes lurks behind my smile, and playfully he teases it out of me, inviting me to let it show.

Not long after we first met, he saw me quietly seething over something, noticed my valiant but futile effort to grin my way through.

"I can see you're good and angry," he observed.

I stared at him.

"*Good and angry?*" I asked, startled. "I thought that was a contradiction in terms."

Feelings did not seem to faze this man. On our first date, Jonas came over for supper, and we talked about what was going on in our lives. He was in the throes of a painful separation from his wife, and I, only six months into abstinence, was just beginning to date again, wanting for once to create a relationship with a man that had clear boundaries, wanting at last to stop confusing intimacy with sex.

Jonas was touched by our mutual honesty. Tears sprang to his eyes.

Instantly I was anxious. "What's wrong?" I asked him, leaning forward across the dining table, a furrow in my brow, alarm in my eyes. "Are you OK?"

Jonas looked at me, grinning through his tears.

"Relax," he said. "I'm just touched by our talk. These are just tears. It's nothing to get upset about."

I sat back in my chair. I thought to myself: I could fall in love with this man.

As I look back now, I don't know which was the greater miracle: the fact that I was in love, at last and for real, or the fact that I found myself drawn to a man who in key respects was unlike my father. Especially in recent years, I had dated men who reminded me of my father—men with the same biting wit, the same capacity for contempt. I had given up dating when I first came into OA partly because navigating food choices demanded my full attention, but also because I knew I had to learn about intimacy from the ground up. I had to begin again, start afresh, when it came to dealing with men. What did I know about intimacy? My relationships with men were rather like my relationship with food: I was a woman of extremes. Either I veered toward isolation, concealing what I thought and felt, or I gave myself away, leaping into bed with a lover far too soon. I wonder now how much of the hunger that I once assumed was sexual sprang instead from a mixture of loneliness and anxiety.

Abstinence demanded that I pay the same close attention to my relationships with men that I now paid to food. I had to listen to myself, to go more slowly. I had to choose with greater care. I had to learn to love myself well in order to be able to love someone else. I had to learn to bear it when I felt lonely or insecure, to ask for help from a friend or to turn to God in prayer, rather than grabbing for a lover as I once had grabbed for food. Learning to be intimate is no easy task, especially for those of us who have been running from ourselves for years. But what I discovered, as I got to know my friend Jonas, was exactly what I discovered with food: mysteriously enough, the arduous and humble path of paying attention can lead to joy.

On that Labor Day weekend of brilliant sunshine and dancing waves, the three of us go sailing together: my father, Jonas, and me. Daddy has changed in less than two months, his hair gone thin and white. It's the first time that Jonas has been out sailing with us, and this trip may well be my father's last, though no one speaks of it. I've never seen my father as reflective as he is this morning, as mellow. I wonder if the prospect of death has softened something in his core.

As we prepare to leave the harbor, I fiddle nervously with the sail cover. To forestall his criticism, I ask, "Can you tell me again the special way of fastening the knot?" I know that to him there is always a right way and a wrong way to do every task—or, more accurately, just one right way, his way, and a host of wrong ones.

This time, though, my father just laughs a little.

"However you do it is the special way," he says.

We make our way out of the harbor. My father seems content simply to watch the sea, the shore, the play of light on the water. When he invites me to take the wheel for a while, I actually accept. Usually my father finds nothing but errors in how I steer the boat, but today he seems comfortable letting me handle the job. Following his instructions, I track the black buoy on the right, dodging the lobster pots. There are times when he steps too close to me, his voice suddenly urgent and sharp, crying out to me through his strained and muffled throat to stop the boat from falling away or pinching; but each time he catches himself, lets go a little, looks away, laughs, pats my knee, tells me to watch the sails not the compass, tells me that I'm doing fine.

We go out in search of bluefish, but today the hooks bring up nothing but seaweed. I can see that my father is disappointed.

"Last year I went fishing with your older sister," he tells me. "We went out for bluefish, and we caught bluefish. It was magic."

This time, there are none.

As the day passes, we unwrap our sandwiches and talk—small talk mostly, nothing big or philosophical, but today each word seems to carry special resonance. We know that death is close, and suddenly the most ordinary moment seems ringed with light—precious, particular, exact, never to be seen again.

Although my father downs several beers, his mood remains quiet, and for once I feel no urge to flee. When he invites Jonas to take the wheel, Jonas immediately accepts. For a while I watch the two of them standing side by side at the stern, facing into the wind as my father points out one landmark after another, his hands ready to grab the wheel in case Jonas's judgment or reflexes falter. There's an art to guiding a boat as it races through the waves, especially when the often-critical father of the woman you're dating is standing at your elbow. Jonas's face is serious, absorbed, but when he sees me looking at him, he grins and throws me a wink.

As the afternoon unfolds, I lie down on the boat's starboard side and look up at the sky. There is nothing to hold on to here, not the sea spray that moistens my face, nor the wind that fills the taut sail, nor the sensation of the boat beneath my back, lifting and sinking in the waves. None of this will last, I know. None of this will endure, these moments that fly by quickly and then vanish, like foam in a sailboat's wake.

I look back at my father and my friend at the wheel; I love these two men, the faces of these two men. This moment suddenly contains everything, nothing is left out, all of it is present, everything is here.

My father relinquishes the steering to Jonas and stretches out on the port side of the boat. We travel for a while in silence, Jonas standing at the wheel, my father and I turning our faces toward the late-summer sun, enjoying the warmth.

Are there words for such a moment? Are there any words to describe it?

"The world is charged with the grandeur of God," I murmur to myself—a line from a poem, one of my favorites by Gerard Manley Hopkins. I suddenly realize that what I've just whispered represents my own deepest conviction. My voice gains strength as I go on: "It will flame out, like shining from shook foil."

A croaking voice beside me adds the next line: "It gathers to a greatness, like the ooze of oil / Crushed."

I turn my head, delighted, as my father speaks from across the boat, gazing at the sky.

We take the next line together.

Slowly we make our way to the end of the poem, stumbling sometimes, correcting each other when one of us misses a word, until we reach the end: "Because the Holy Ghost over the bent / World broods with warm breast and with ah! bright wings."

There's a brief silence.

"Hey," I say to my father, "I didn't know you liked Gerard Manley Hopkins."

"I do," he tells me. "My favorite is 'The Windhover.' Let's see, how does it begin? 'I caught this morning morning's minion . . .' Do you know that one? No? Pity. It's a beauty."

"How about this one," I say. "A little Keats. 'Season of mists and mellow fruitfulness . . .'" I start off, full of myself, ready to impress my father by singing the praises of autumn, all abundance and fecundity before the winter comes.

But my memory fails me. I draw a blank and burst out laughing. I haven't a clue what line comes next.

Neither, it seems, does my father. He tries out a phrase or two, then throws up his hands. We're having a good time, though—this dying, loving father, this professor of English, and the daughter who loves him, adores him in spite of herself, and wants to spout poetry with him.

"So much for a Harvard education," my father says, grinning.

"Well, you always hated the Romantics," I tease. How many times we've argued over the years, each conversation more absurd than the last, more obviously beside the point, as we debated which century was better—the eighteenth or the nineteenth, the Age of Reason or the Age of Sensibility—as if intellectual sparring could settle the real issue between us: whether or not feelings had any value in our family.

Jonas listens quietly, intently, as my father and I spend the rest of the afternoon sharing poems, sometimes reciting them with easy familiarity, sometimes struggling to recall the words, laughing when one of us gets it wrong, finding ourselves caught up in something larger than the two of us, looking for words to love each other.

Late in the day, as we sail toward home, I suddenly want to be physically close to my father. I want to touch him. I know we never touch in our family, except for a perfunctory kiss on the cheek, a quick hug in which two people briefly take each other by the shoulders and lean forward, forming the letter A for a moment in the air.

"A is for Absent," I would secretly comment to myself after such a hug. Once I dared say to my mother, "No, give me a *real* hug." And she did. She did. I ate it up.

I've never dared ask my father for a real hug, and I'm not sure I want to. I've heard him joke about sex, about women's bodies. I've kept my distance when he's had too much to drink. But I do know I want more today than words, even the most beautiful words of poetry.

I go stand for a while beside my father. Side by side, as the boat advances through the waves, we watch the shore approach. I reach out to pat my father's shoulder, and for a moment or two my hand rests against his back.

"I like you a lot," I tell him. That's the best I can do today— try to be jocular, to underplay the mood, to make things more casual than I feel them.

"The feeling is mutual," he says to me.

Have we just said we love each other? It's the nearest we can come. We could connect in the language of poetry. It's harder for us to find our own words. "Tell all the Truth but tell it slant—" says Emily Dickinson. We're good at that in this family, telling the slanted truth. It will have to be enough.

In the harbor, my father starts to pant as we tie up at the mooring.

"I get so short of breath now," he admits. "It's happened so fast, just a matter of weeks."

I can't help glancing at the ragged red line that cuts across his upper chest, the scar left by the biopsy that was taken just a week ago. I'm remembering how the hospital attendants wheeled him away, how he said, "I'm off now to the big battle," waving farewell to me, whispering, "Bye-bye, my dear."

Today, without a trace of self-consciousness, he's wearing a shirt that is open at the throat. Who knows what will come next for him, what suffering lies ahead. All I know is that I am grateful for this day, a day with its own magic, when I found some words in common with my father, when I put my hand on his back, when we came as close as we could to saying "I love you."

When I get home that night, I look up "The Windhover," my father's favorite Hopkins, and am surprised to read its sub-title: "To Christ Our Lord." My father is not a religious man. I know he wouldn't understand my growing interest in wanting to find something genuinely religious. He would be shocked, I'm sure, if I told him I slipped into the back pew of a church whenever I got the chance. I want desperately to have some faith. I want my father to have some too. Suddenly I feel there's no anchor to hold us and the tides are turning, running hard. There's got to be something. Or Someone.

September faded into October. For all the anxiety about my father's health, there were moments of grace. One night I slept lightly, hearing what I thought was rain falling gently on the roof overhead. I got up at dawn, looked out the door, and discovered to my amazement that the ground was dry and covered with gold. Cascades of leaves had been dropping all night from the ash tree beside my house. Everywhere I looked, the earth was gold, the autumn light was gold. The hungry Israelites who awoke to find the desert covered with manna couldn't have marveled more than I did that morning as I stepped outside in bare feet. I breathed it all in. Then I pulled on my clothes and went out for a run around Fresh Pond. Mist was rising over the water. I fairly sang for joy.

On another October night, I came home dull and vacant. I had been visiting my father in the hospital for his second round of chemotherapy and was shocked to see that his beard was gone, his hair was gone, his beautiful hair all gone. My father had been a young sixty-three, a man who always looked a rugged ten years younger than his age. In a matter of weeks, he had become an old man.

Alone in my house that night, I paced restlessly from room to room. Drifting into the kitchen, I found myself standing before the open door of the refrigerator, caught in its baleful light. I wonder sometimes if addiction isn't a desperate effort to hold on to the moment, to stop time, stop change, to grab something solid when the fragility of life seems too difficult to bear. Maybe it's an attempt to stave off death, but of course it ends up killing you.

Somehow I made it safely into bed without eating compulsively. Alone under the blankets, I let time take its toll, and I cried myself to sleep.

As the months went by, I looked back on that Labor Day sailing trip as a peaceful interlude, the period of closest contact with my father that I would experience before he died, the calm before the storm.

Then it was Thanksgiving. An assortment of family members gathered at my house: my father, the woman who would become his third wife six weeks later, one of her daughters from a previous marriage, my father's young son from his second marriage, my friend Jonas, his daughter from his recently ended marriage, and me. We were a motley crew, as miscellaneous as mismatched cutlery, but all of us were concerned about my father. All of us shuttled between worry and hope.

My father was almost relentlessly talkative and critical, finding fault, heaping blame. For some reason I'd decided to suspend the rule that he do no drinking in my house; and as he grew increasingly irritable and intoxicated, the rest of us worked hard to manage his mood, redirect his energy, contain the damage, by turns ignoring him, cracking a joke, telling him to lay off, changing the subject. I can't say we were particularly successful in making it a pleasant afternoon. Whenever my father was drunk, he had more power to set a party's mood and tone than a platoon of sober guests, no matter how finely honed their social skills.

There was chaos in the kitchen when we discovered that the crown roast of pork was undercooked. I'd misjudged the timing, which meant we'd have to wait at least half an hour more for the meal.

My father sat at the kitchen table, imperious as a king, demanding to know who'd made such a stupid mistake. I rolled my eyes. The comment hardly seemed worth a response.

"I did it," I announced anyway, fed up. "It's my fault. It's not ready. It's one of those moments in life when we're not ready for what's to come. What can I say?"

Talking with my father seemed much less useful right then than attending to the tasks at hand. Where was the water pitcher? Could someone find the flour and a pitcher for making gravy? Who would carve the meat? Get the plates onto the table? Find some hot pads and the serving spoons?

Behind it all loomed the unasked questions, the ones no one wanted to ask: Was my father going to die? Would it be soon? How soon? Would we be able to bear it?

All of us were frightened. Grim. I just kept moving, counting out plates, filling water glasses, wiping off the counters, trying to create order where there was none. I probably didn't stop smiling for a moment, something I'd always done as a kid—what Jonas called my attempt to make the world happy with one sweet smile.

At last the pork was done. We sat down to dinner with my father at the head of the table, gulping Scotch. Not once did he stop talking, as if he'd been commanded to put on a show, to perform for us, to fill up every space, every gap, leaving nothing to silence, no space to say anything important. Though my father's voice was muted by the cancer, husky and faint, it still held sway. Here he was, dying, yet still drowning us all with his words.

We ate in silence, staring into our plates, our heads bowed. I finally decided to look up. Only Jonas was sitting upright, his head erect, looking around the table, wondering at all of us as we hunkered down over our plates.

Suddenly my father thundered to his young son, "You're a failure in life even before you've begun to live." He leaned over to clap the boy heartily on the shoulder.

I was stunned.

"Daddy!" I cried. "That's an awful thing to say!"

My father snorted crossly, reaching for the squash. "Oh, for God's sake, Margaret, where's your sense of humor?"

I drew a long angry breath, threw Jonas a look (Can you believe this?), and shook my head sympathetically at my half-brother. I don't know whether the boy saw my smile, or whether it would have helped him much if he had. I do wish I'd noticed when, sometime later during the meal, as the adults continued to spar with my father, fending him off, trying in vain to coax him out of the boxing ring, the child slid quietly out of his chair and slipped out the door to walk home alone, saying nothing to anyone, not even good-bye.

My father seemed startled when he looked up from his pumpkin pie and realized that his youngest child was gone. He seemed taken aback, even hurt. I'm sure he had no idea what had happened, what he'd done.

Was it fear that was driving my father that day, a hurricane of helplessness, rage, and fear? I wouldn't be surprised if the whirlwind of confusion, the maelstrom of hurt that he created around himself that day, was only a reflection of the storm tearing around inside him. I will never know. It was only as we were clearing away the dessert plates that I finally asked my father what it was like to be about to receive radiation treatment. I'd hesitated even to mention this, much less ask him any questions. Everyone seemed so determined that day to say nothing about the cancer.

For the first time, my father spoke openly of how frightened he was, how fearful of having the radiation directed at his brain, how experimental the treatment was, how risky its effects.

"I don't want to forget my name or forget the date," he declared. "If I couldn't recognize the people around me, I'd put a bullet through my brain. Five years ago, with this cancer, I'd have been dead by now. The doctor says I've got maybe two years from the day of diagnosis. But these last months have been hell. I'm not living. I'm surviving. All I want is to go out and sail."

My father's angry, frightened words pierced the afternoon's long pretense that this was a cheerful family get-together. We weren't sharing a routine family holiday. We weren't even in a boxing ring. We were staring at a loaded gun pointed directly at my father. It was time now to retire the costumes, pull down the stage set, pack away the props. Time to be straight with each other. But I fumbled for speech. I had no lines, no words, only an agony of longing.

"Daddy, this is really scary," I told him. "I hate what's happening to you. It breaks my heart to see what you're going through. I want you to sail again too. I'd love to go sailing with you again."

I knew my words were flimsy. I'd tossed a thread across the chasm when what my father needed was a strong rope. But if all your life you've been mouthing your lines, acting a part, chances are that when the critical moment arrives, what comes out of your mouth is going to fall short.

My father shrugged enigmatically, nodded, put up his hand

as if to say, "Enough," took a sip from his glass. There seemed nothing left to say.

I stood up, carried an armload of dishes to the sink, and began scrubbing pots and pans. The group dispersed, some to clear plates, others to wield a sponge or grab a dish towel. Conversation resumed. I could see my father sitting alone at the kitchen table, nursing a last glass of whisky. Now that he'd spoken directly of his fear, his barrage of talk had stopped. His face looked sad. Among a crowd of people, there he sat alone.

As usual with my father, I didn't know what to do, what to say. He was his customary self, drinking, pushing people away. But at the same time, he was frightened, angry, sad. I couldn't tell which my father wanted—to be left alone or to have some company. What could I give him? What was the best way to be with him? I had no idea. I put the saucepan down, walked over to his chair, put my hand on his shoulder. Words so often got us into trouble and made things worse, but maybe he would let me stand there for a while, saying nothing, sending him love with every breath.

Sometimes when two people can't communicate, when everything between them comes up thorns and thistles, when the smallest gesture of reconciliation meets only with silence— a shrug, a wall—and nothing more seems possible, dreams can heal.

Just months before my father died, I had a dream. In the dream I am filled with an evil power. I beg everyone to lock me in a room alone so I won't hurt anyone. It's up to me to transform the evil, to purify it. No one can do it but me. In the dream I begin to pray, repeating over and over, "Lord Jesus Christ, have mercy on me, a sinner." Gradually the evil in me begins to dissolve.

Then Gary appears in the dream. Gary was the sickest of all the men I worked with in the mental hospital, the client most disabled by schizophrenia, the one I found most chaotic, scary, unpredictable. Gary sometimes smeared the walls with his feces. His clothes were dirty, often smelly. His conversations were full of sexual innuendo and lewd jokes based on the latest episode of the TV sitcom *The Love Boat*.

In the dream, this Gary that I find so frightening, even repulsive, is knocking at my door. I have the feeling that if I let him in, it will be the end of me. But then I see that he is holding a piece of paper, a note written in big childish handwriting that consists of just one word: "Pardon." The note is for me, but what does it mean? Is he asking for my forgiveness? Or is he offering to forgive me? I don't know. But I take the risk, open the door. I accept the note he hands me, saying, "Thanks, Gary." He smiles shyly, like a child. And the dream is over.

I woke up happy, as if during the night someone had given me a gift, the gift of knowing that I must close the door to blaming anyone else and get on with my own healing. And the gift of knowing that there was something outside the door that I needed to let in, some childish part of myself perhaps, some underground self. My aggression maybe, or my longing. Everything in me that was messy, unruly. Some part of myself that had been shut out for too long, or some part of my father that I'd been unwilling to accept. And now it was all there in me, the good and the bad, the beautiful and the ugly. Could I take the whole catastrophe, or not?

Whatever reconciliation my father and I found before he died happened mostly in dreams. Sometimes I prayed. Whatever I called it, I was trying to stay open. I wanted to allow into my mind and heart all the pain, rage, guilt, and grief that was arising in me as my father died. Was there a way to embrace this suffering, to meet all of it with love?

I told my mother how much I hungered for contact with my father as he moved toward death. How I mourned what I was losing, mourned what I'd never had.

"Your father's way into death has to be through the way he lived," she said to me, her smile kind.

But how I struggled. And in fact failed, in my effort to let my father die as he wanted to—alone. Near the end, as he lay in his hospital bed straining to draw air into his choking lungs, I wished I could hold his hand, wished I could draw close.

When I finally asked if I could move nearer, maybe sit on the edge of his bed, my father yanked the oxygen mask off his face and whispered as loudly as he could, his eyes fierce with rage, "I want you to be quiet. You have a lesson to learn here. Learn it."

I felt as if I'd been socked in the stomach. I walked to the far side of the room, stood by the window, tried to catch my breath. My father was still glaring at me. Then he closed his eyes, exhausted, and with fumbling hands replaced the oxygen mask.

I saw him open his eyes once more. He blew me a silent kiss. Then he shut his eyes. He wasn't dead yet, but I knew the end was near. We were in the final days.

The hospital room fell silent except for the hiss and pulse of the machines by his bed, the sound of his labored breath. I said nothing, remained silent as a tomb. I was angry, confused. What was the lesson I was supposed to learn? What was the meaning of this terrible riddle he'd thrown at me like a stone? That I should bite my tongue? Stay away? Keep my distance? Did he think that the closeness I wanted would kill him? It looked that way. It looked as if he needed so badly to be free of me that he was willing to risk his life by tearing off his source of oxygen, just to order me away.

But then the silent kiss. Did he mean it? I hoped so, but I found it so hard to accept, so hard to take in, coming as it did on the heels of his announcement—as I heard it anyway—of his right to die by himself. Observed, maybe. In the company of a loving daughter, maybe. But I knew he wanted me on the sidelines, that he still needed to keep me at a distance, away.

That night I wept. Furious. Grief-stricken. Jonas listened carefully, quietly, just sitting at my side, but he urged me to keep my eyes on my father, on what it was he needed now, in these, his final days.

"Your father has to give birth to his own death," he said. "He has to be his own midwife. This is his passage, even though it may be painful to you. He has a right to insist on it. This isn't your death. It's his."

There are memories we go back to again and again, pondering their meaning, fearing that their taste in our mouth will always sting, like a bitter lozenge. The memory of this encounter with my dying father lingered for years. Even a decade later, it was still potent enough to release in me a sharp tang of anger and sorrow.

Only now do I see, looking back, that the meaning I gave this moment is only one of its possible meanings. Perhaps the "lesson" my father wanted me to learn as he died was something quite different from the one I imagined. Maybe he was saying to me, "Look long and carefully at the wreck I've become, the wreck I've made of so much of my life. Don't let your sorrow for me overwhelm your realization of what I've done to myself." In the last hours of his life, was my father facing up to the consequences of the choices he'd made, offering them to me as a kind of cautionary tale? Was that the lesson that he hoped I'd learn? Did his angry words arise from self-hatred, from the guilt and melancholy of a drinker and heavy smoker who considered addiction a sign of moral failure? Here at the brink of death, was he taking a first step in trying to come to terms with his life?

Or perhaps it was none of this. Perhaps, in the confusion and intensity of his struggle for every breath, even he didn't know what he meant when he hurled those words at me.

The facts of the case will never change, but their meaning is in my hands. The lesson I take from my father's life—and from my own—is for me to create. So I sound every possible interpretation. Like someone searching for crystal, I hold up each glass to the light, strike it gently, and bend my ear close as I listen for the ring of truth.

I went with my younger sister to find our father a poster, something to tack on the bulletin board at the foot of his hospital bed. My father had nothing to look at but the clock, its hands going endlessly round and round, his eyes glued to their slow circuit as if they held some long-awaited answer, the clue to a puzzle he needed desperately to solve. The bulletin board was only empty space and a handful of cards, nothing much to hold the eye.

A few days before, my father had gathered up enough energy to point at the scattered thumbtacks and whisper, "If you rearranged them just a bit, they'd look like the Big Dipper."

I laughed at the little joke, touched by my father's capacity to find something funny even in these dreadful days when modern medicine was unleashing all its armaments upon him, as the cancer relentlessly took him down.

With a sigh of frustration, a glance of longing, his gaze turned briefly to the window. My father murmured, "I wish I could sail out of here."

My sister and I knew what we were looking for—a picture

of the ocean and a picture of his beloved Greece, the site of so many diving trips. We found a picture of Greece right away—a large photograph of the whitewashed walls of a sunny village street, a man on a donkey, with blue waves dancing in the distance. We had more trouble finding an ocean scene. We flipped through all the bins, shaking our heads over the choices, most of which were either maudlin or macabre.

Where was the perfect picture of the sea? What was it we were looking for anyway? Was this for our father? Were we looking for a picture for him—or for ourselves? Were we trying to say what was happening to us? Or were we trying to give him something to ride out on? What were we up to?

"How's this? Do you think this is violent enough?" I said wryly, holding up a poster of warships, their guns blazing, while a warplane streaked overhead, going down in flames.

"How about this one?" My sister held up someone's version of the *Titanic* beginning its slide into the sea.

We started to laugh. Too close to the nerve. We ourselves were somewhere between crashing and burning, and busily rearranging the deck chairs as we slipped into the waves.

We started looking through the stacks of smaller pictures on the chance we'd find the one we sought.

"Here's one," my sister said suddenly. She pointed to a picture of a single sailboat out on the ocean alone, heading someplace far away, no land in sight, no company but the open sea. Underneath was written, "Sail on to the end of your dream."

That did it. It may not have worked as a piece of art, but it certainly said what we felt. Both of us were stopped in our tracks by the tears.

Sometimes a simple picture with the most placid of clichés can capture what needs to be said, what needs to be seen. We knew we had to let our father go. It was going to happen any-way, no matter what we or anyone else might feel about it. As far as I could tell, my father was completely alone. He had a lonely core that no one could touch, no one see, as he lay awake at three or four o'clock in the morning. Alone in the hospital at night, every minute ticked slowly by. He endured many long hours, he told me, when anxiety would creep in, sometimes overwhelming him with more fear than he could bear. The night was so dark, and he wondered when death would come. Even so, whenever I asked him if he wanted my company, he said no, finally whispering forcefully, "When I say no, I mean no."

In the end, all we could give him was a picture, a poster of intention, wishing him well on his sail. A hard lot for a daughter who wanted to say so much more. A hard lot for a father who in the end had to rig and sail his own ship, stand alone at the wheel, trim his sail, pinch the wind, and go.

Near the end, time seemed to slow to a crawl. The winds that would take my father out to sea died down, leaving him stranded. He fought for every breath. Restless, almost con-stantly in motion as he struggled for air, he would adjust his pillow, lean forward to grab his ankles, bending his head, then lean back against the pillow, exhausted. His face was haggard, weary. He could eat no longer and hardly slept. He wanted no talking near him, no commotion, no interference. Again and again he would stare up at the clock. Three minutes might have passed. Maybe five.

Once he asked the nurse, "Am I dying?"

"No," she told him. "All your signs are stable."

I couldn't tell if he was relieved or discouraged by the news. "Do you *feel* like you're dying?" she asked him.

"I don't know," he whispered irritably. "I've never died before."

The nurse smiled faintly and apologized. "Ask a stupid question . . ."

My father's new wife, my younger sister, and I took turns beside my father's bed. I was learning the importance of vigil, of keeping watch. We kept our voices low, speaking gentle words to my father and to each other as the long hours passed in this room full of suffering, as we waited for the end.

In August, just over a year after being diagnosed with cancer, my father slipped into a coma. I asked my stepmother for some time alone with him. After she left the room, I sat down beside my father on the bed. Was I intruding on him again? Coming too close? Taking advantage of his helplessness? I hoped, I prayed even, that somehow, now that speech had left him, now that consciousness had gone, something deep inside him had changed as well. I longed to believe that some part of him would be receptive to my presence and forgive my need to draw close, maybe even welcome my company.

My father's head was thrown back against the pillow, his mouth open behind the oxygen mask, his eyes closed. When I touched his hands, I was shocked to feel the stiffness of his fingers, the coolness of his skin. After all the restlessness of the last few days, his body was quiet now, though he still labored to breathe.

I tried to say everything I knew, to name all the truth between us, the anger we'd felt with each other, the disappointment, our long hard struggle to communicate. How much I hoped he would forgive me for the ways I'd failed him, how eagerly I forgave him now, how much I loved him still.

"I'm sad you're dying," I told him. "But it's OK. It's OK

between us, Daddy. I know you're going. This is Margaret, Daddy, wishing you a smooth sail, the best sail every day, wishing you the best sail ever.

"I love you, Daddy."

The call from my stepmother came late that night. Hastily I pulled on my clothes. Jonas and I drove into Boston. The streets were deserted, the night dark. I was more afraid than I had expected. The mysterious, small hours of the night. This was the time when my father had so often lain awake in his hospital bed, full of fear. Now *I* was afraid as we drove through the silent streets.

The elevator took us straight from the parking garage to the hospital's main floor. The corridors were empty. Silently I began signing in, filling in the visitor's name and the patient's name, as I had done so many times before.

"Are you visiting your father *now?*" the receptionist asked, looking surprised, even amused.

"Yes," I said grimly, wanting no words just now, no talk.

"Does he know you're coming?" she pressed me, as if this were some kind of hilarious joke I was playing on him.

I paused to look at her, unsmiling. "He just died," I told her.

"Oh," she said, startled. It was obvious she didn't know he had died. For me, it was a shock to hear myself pronounce the words.

Jonas and I made our way to the familiar room on the fourteenth floor. There he lay, stretched out on the bed as I had left him, the oxygen mask gone, the room strangely silent. I listened in vain for the sound of his straining breath. Sometimes it takes the mind a while to catch up.

My father's wife had been with him when he died. Now she was stroking his face, his legs, his body. She pointed out to me how young he looked, as if thirty years of suffering had dropped from his face.

As I looked at him, I saw that she was right, it was true. His face looked calm now, relaxed, the face of a much younger man. The ease with which she touched his body and spoke her love slowly relieved my numbing fear. I felt my love again and began to weep. I stroked his arm, the freckles I loved, the sun-bleached hair.

I was fixated on my need to see the obituary. I couldn't wait to see it, to get my hands on it. I'm not sure why. It was as if my father could not really die until I'd seen his death in print. Was the printed word more real to me than real life? Or was it the familiar anxiety of someone who grew up in an alcoholic family and didn't trust her own experience, what she saw with her own eyes and touched with her own hands? I didn't trust my memory. What if I was only imagining what I thought I'd seen? The printed words made my father's death real in a way that touching his dead body did not. This scrap of paper with these words on it—I could hold on to this, believe in this. The words nailed it down, made it final, made it true. My father was dead.

After the funeral, everyone gathered at my house for a reception—the whole complicated collection of people who at one time or another had been part of my father's life. I found myself smiling as I looked around at all of us, remembering how my father had laughed from his hospital bed, whispering that he had shocked the nurses when he explained who his visitors were: two ex-wives, his present wife, five children, two grandchildren. Even in his sickest moments, he wanted to preserve his identity—the rapscallion, the charmer, the rogue.

So here we were, after the funeral, together in one place for the first time, along with my father's stepchildren, his former in-laws, his current colleagues and friends, introducing ourselves to each other, talking about my father, sharing stories of affection and pain.

For all my sorrow, as I looked around at the men and women standing in clusters on the lawn, telling stories, sharing memories and plates of food, as I watched the children running around us and laughing, I felt as if for one shining moment all the parts of my father's fractured life had come together. It astonished me to see enemies embrace and outcasts welcomed. To see mercy and truth share a kiss.

Sometime later a smaller group of family members assembled at my father's home in Marblehead. We stood on the beach, opened the urn, and cast his ashes into the waves.

As I look back over our lives—my father's, my mother's, my own—I can see plainly that this is a story of desire: desire sometimes gone awry, sometimes stifled and repressed, sometimes fulfilled, sometimes set free. It's no easy business, learning to befriend our desires, to get past our lesser appetites in order to find what we really long for. It's hard to set a course and sail straight in the face of distraction, frustration, and defeat; in the face of high winds, heavy storms, and rough seas. And no one can chart the course for us. Sure, we sail together; we crew for one another; and in real trouble, we summon all hands on deck, every hand we know that will reach out to help us. And well we should. But we're not so different from the ancients when it comes to the business of life and death, and the meaning of the journey. In my case, I hungered, I yearned for something—or Someone—that would really fill me, fill up my life, give me something to live for, something larger than the ordinary of everyday but found there, nevertheless, in the turning of the days and the seasons, the rising and the setting of the sun, in the sheer gift of being alive.

By the time my father died, I knew I was on my way. I had set my course. I knew that whatever my life was about, it was about desire, the desire beyond all desire, the desire for God. It was about learning to listen to my deepest hunger and to let this hunger guide me, as a ship steers at night by the stars.

Holy Hunger

E very time I look back to that Outward Bound summer when I got lost in the Minnesota woods, I see something new. What I notice now, as this book draws to a close, is the fact that it took four days for one of us to remember that she knew how to start a fire with wet wood. Four days to realize she had the wherewithal to get herself—and all of us—out. I don't know what jostled that memory loose for her, what sent it up to the surface. Maybe we have to be starving before we can reach deep inside ourselves to find the resources we had all along. For me, at least, it wasn't until my eating disorder was grave that I began searching in earnest for the outer guidance and inner wisdom that would set me free. When it came to healing, I had to be not only outward but also inward bound.

Sometimes, to find our way home, there are facts and memories we need to salvage, feelings we need to reclaim. I know that in my search for my self, my mother, and my father, I needed more information. About my parents, my family—and about me. But information in itself does not always heal. Sometimes it's not what we know—or think we know—that makes the difference, but how we use it.

I am a compulsive overeater. I grew up with a father who was alcoholic, a mother who was emotionally reclusive. These are facts, yet the recognition of these facts was hard-won, indeed. It came at a price. It took years of inner work before I could perceive the truth, years before anyone could break through my denial about my addiction to food, my father's drinking, my mother's depression. It was essential to my healing that I know these things, but knowing them was only the beginning. Maybe it's not what happened to me, or what happens to any of us, that really matters, but rather what we make of these things. How I string the facts together, the meaning I give them, how I tell them and for what purpose—these are the real questions, the questions on which the degree of my healing, or anyone else's, depends.

One of the reasons I ate so much was that I lived with the emptiness of not knowing my own story. I wasn't able to gather up the fragments of my life and put them together in a way that made sense for me. I felt numb during those years of overeating, shut down and silenced, my voice eclipsed. There was no one to tell the tale and no tale I knew to tell, except for a half-hearted litany of confusion and complaint, punctuated by frantic episodes of eating. What saved me? Putting down the food. Finding a story. Speaking the story. Feeling the anger and the pain, picking up a pen and beginning to write. Finding people to listen, people who wouldn't let me settle for overeating but who wanted to hear from me, wanted to know the story. My story.

But it's not just any story that will save us. I grew up thinking that the only story I should tell, could tell, could even know about, was the family story, the story we told the world, the one about our being happy, normal, even perfect. The official story, the one for public consumption. That story was eventually toxic to me. In fact, it almost killed me. I swallowed everything when I lived with that story—the pain, the sadness, the rage.

But if the official story doesn't always heal, what about the hidden stories behind it—the underbelly of loneliness and sorrow, abuse and pain? Is it healing to tell these stories, to unburden ourselves of our secrets and shame? The answer is simple: It depends. Depends on whom we tell our stories to, and for what purpose, in what spirit.

I know the temptation to blurt everything out willy-nilly, bingeing with words as I once binged with food. I know the lure of tell-all talk shows where strangers confess everything to everybody and eagerly "tell it like it is." But does that kind of storytelling lead to healing, for either teller or listener? Can these stories saturated with blame and steeped in resentment ever heal? Or are they only the prelude to healing, the sign that the true work of meaning-making has yet to begin? Telling or listening to such stories can become as compulsive as bingeing on food. And neither kind of binge ever leads me to life.

Learning to face and speak my pain was a critical step in finding my path out of the woods. It was the starting place for healing. It marked the first step—but only the first—in my search to find a life narrative that could really feed me and speak to my desires. What kind of story heals? A story that is both loving and true. True, because nothing essential is left out, neither the pain nor the joy. Loving, because everyone in the story—narrator, protagonist, and characters alike—is seen with compassionate eyes.

It takes a long time to find and tell such a story, lots of practice, lots of listening for false notes, grandstanding, hedging. It took me years before I could begin to tell a story of my life that was both loving and true, years before I became a person even remotely capable of telling such a story. I'm tempted every day to slip into telling stories in which I'm the hero or victim while the others are the villains and fools; stories in which I can shore up my sagging self-esteem by boasting or finding fault, by puffing myself up and putting someone else down. If such stories are "true," they're only partially true. And they certainly aren't loving at all.

I know I still have a long way to go. I'm not there yet. There always seems to be a bit more pain to face, a bit more denial to undo, as I look squarely at the pain in my own life, in my family's life, in the world around me. There always seems to be more love to learn, as I try to grow a heart big enough to encompass all of it with tenderness.

Here is the story I would like to tell about my life: The story of a woman growing up confused about her desires, uncertain whether it was even acceptable to have desires, uncertain about what to do with the ones she had. A woman persistently looking outside herself for what she was hungry for. A woman growing up in a culture that was all too ready to tell her what she wanted and to create a climate of craving. A card-carrying member of a culture that urges all of us to eat, shop, buy, acquire; for there in the material goods around us, in possessions and commodities, prizes and grades, accomplishments and lovers, doughnuts and ice cream, surely we'll find what we're looking for, our heart's desire. The story of a woman who was perpetually restless, afraid of her own emptiness, afraid to listen to her longing.

Like my mother during my childhood, I tried to quell my desires. Eradicate them. Transcend them. And like my father, I eventually went to the other extreme, spinning in a whirlwind of cravings that I couldn't control. My infinite longing devolved into insatiable craving. I had to have food, more and more of it, an endless supply to stave off the hunger that refused to go away.

I couldn't speak my story, could find neither words nor silence that helped me connect. So I choked off my words. Filled up the silence. And ate. At last I reached a crisis, a crossroad. I had to choose between life and death. As starkly as that. And it was life that I chose, life that chose me. A day at a time, I learned to stop overeating, I learned to stop killing myself with food.

You might think that the story ends there, that healing from an eating disorder is complete when the addict puts down the extra food and stops overeating. But for me that was only the turning point, the story's pivotal, crucial chapter. The rest of the journey, this story of desire, had yet to unfold, as I continued to search for myself and my own true story, as I continued to make peace with my parents. Even though my parents had divorced, I still needed to marry within myself the parts of them that I loved most.

My mother. This woman I spent a childhood searching for, trying to read her silence. Did I find her? Did the lively little girl who loved horses ever find the mother she hungered for? Yes, she did. Yes, I have. That little girl has changed. I've grown up and learned a thing or two about living inside my own skin, about being separate from my mother, so that she can love me as distinct from herself, and I her. And my mother has changed as well. Her depression has vanished, cleared up, healed, and along with it the enigmatic silence that made me so anxious as a child. That silence I once tried so hard to interpret in every nuance of its meaning, that silence no longer stands between us.

Is our relationship perfect? What would that mean? I've learned I don't need perfection in my mother or in myself. And in truth, my mother and I share our feelings more openly than ever before. When silences come, they're usually filled with love and meaning and a depth of communication that I simply didn't know as a child. There's a hospitable silence, one that breathes joy, in the company of my mother.

A few years ago my mother went to New Mexico on a meditation retreat. Every day she went hiking alone up a path through the woods, until she came to a clearing at the top of the mountain. Then she sat down to pray, with the valley spread out below her and the mountains beyond. She knew there was a wild horse nearby. She'd heard its whinny, seen the droppings it had left behind. But she had never seen it.

One day, after praying silently for several hours, she became aware that an animal was standing not ten feet away from her. My mother slowly rose to her feet. The horse, she says, seemed enormous. Chestnut brown. It stood in silence, looking at her. She tells me that she felt no fear, only peace. Slowly she sat down again, and after a while the horse approached. With its great muzzle, it prodded her face, her neck, her chest. My mother did not move. Said not a word. Just kept breathing, peaceful. The horse walked all around her in one slow circle and began nuzzling her back. And then the horse stood behind her, lowered its head, and rested its muzzle against her shoulder for a long, long time. For a time out of time.

"It was one of the most wonderful experiences of my life," my mother says.

I marvel over the power to soothe and tame a wild beast that her presence had. Perhaps, in her attentive presence, a barrier between humans and other beings fell away, as if a door had opened between two worlds.

My mind goes back to the picture book she gave me more than forty years ago. In *Play With Me*, the little girl makes silent contact with the creatures around her. That's how it is, sometimes, with my mother. You know you're in the presence of someone exquisitely sensitive, someone in whose presence you can rest in loving silence, because here it is safe, here you'll find love. Giving me *Play With Me* was perhaps my mother's way of telling me something about herself, but as I look back on it now, that book seems also to foreshadow what was to come, what would one day be realized in her. And perhaps in myself as well. The silences that used to frighten me—my mother's silence when she was depressed, the empty spaces inside myself that I feared to explore—these silences have been transformed. They've been redeemed.

My mother and I can talk now too. There's lots of talk on every subject under the sun; talk that is substantive, juicy, satisfying. Talk that feeds us both. I can be lively now in my mother's presence without fearing that she'll slip away.

But of all the gifts that my mother has given me, it is the passion for God that I treasure most. Somewhere along the line, maybe at the very beginning, she passed on to me an ineradicable longing to connect with the Holy. I used to imagine that my mother alone had access to God, that she was the custodian of spiritual treasures that I myself would never reach, try as I might. I've since learned that neither my mother nor God is as stingy as that belief would suggest. I have found my own way now to God, one that is different from hers. Somehow she's given me permission to do this, and delights in what I've come to understand, even when my insights differ from hers. It is my mother who sparked—and who shares—my quest for the Light that I find at my center when I'm silent in prayer and that sometimes radiates through me as I speak. How do I thank her for this great gift?

As for my father, we have made our peace. Mourning his death was one of the most tumultuous passages I've ever had to navigate, like a rowboat plunging through riotous waves. Was I sad that he was gone? Relieved? Angry at the things he'd done and said? Was I longing to see him again, to have one more encounter with this man I dearly loved, one more word? All of these feelings roared through me, sometimes sequentially, sometimes all at once, in a hurricane of emotion.

I was grateful for all the friends who listened to the truth of that experience, for those who gathered together after the funeral in a little community united by love and pain. How different my father's funeral was from the one for my friend Alice, when everyone had been so constrained by the need to keep up appearances, even at the cost of intimacy with each other, even at the cost of the truth.

Tell a story about my father that was both loving and true? That would take me years. It's a slow process sometimes, learning to see with a wider vision, a more generous heart.

The turning point in my relationship with my father came many years after he'd died. I was alone in prayer. In my mind's eye, one person after another was quietly coming to me, bearing gifts of love. I was weeping with joy to see them all again, all the people I loved, some who were living and some who'd died, close friends, family members, my grandparents, who were now all deceased—DeeDee, Granny, Grandfather. And then my father. He came too. I heard him say my name, the affectionate nickname he had for me when I was young and that he alone would use: Maggoty Mag.

It was always an ambiguous name to me, for it reminded me of a walk we had taken together along the ocean shore when I was very small. We came upon a severed head of some creature, washed up on the beach. I don't remember what kind of head it was, whether of a dog or a horse, but it was a grisly sight in any case, something straight out of *The Godfather*. I bent down to look more closely. Horrified. Fascinated. Inside the tangle of seaweed, the skull was crawling with maggots.

My father's teasing nickname for me always spoke to me of love and death both. I didn't quite know, when I heard that name, whether I wanted to draw close or pull away. Loving him always seemed to open me to pain.

But here in my prayer was that name again, my father's name for me, and a voice filled with love, my father's voice, as if death could not separate us, nothing could separate us from the love we shared. There was no disgust in me when I heard him call my name, no horror or fear. Only love. It was the first time that my father's voice and presence had ever spoken to me so clearly of love. Why hadn't I heard it before? Was it I who had changed? Was it he? Through the healing of memory, the alchemy of grace, something had been transformed. Nothing would ever be the same. Love and death, beauty and ugliness—all of them, I now saw, were part of the cycle of things. Death seemed not so fearsome anymore. And it was love that had the last word.

I can't think of my father now without remembering that prayer, my discovery that afternoon of the love within my father's words. That moment marked the beginning of a new way of knowing and telling the story of my father's life.

The gift my father gave me was the gift of language, of using words. He never was able to redeem his words, at least not in this lifetime, just as he never found a way to quit drinking and connect his life with a stream of desire deeper than his craving for booze. But he passed on to me a passion for life and a pleasure in words, a desire to give voice to the life that flows through me, to mourn and to dance on the page.

I give thanks for him, for this father of mine.

The faith that now upholds my life springs from whatever it was that led me into abstinence, urging me to face life as it is, to seek what is really real. If I told my story all over again, I might tell it differently this time. It would be a story laced with grace. The story of a woman who ran from God for a good chunk of her life but who finally consented to being sought by the Lover of her soul.

Never imagine when you put down your drug, your food, your alcohol, your credit cards that everything will be peaceful, everything will be calm. Never think for a minute that stopping an addiction means that your desires will fall obediently to sleep. On the contrary. For me, at least, it was only when I stopped attaching all my desires to food that a larger, deeper desire could flow freely through me. It was a desire for something infinite, something I could neither name precisely with words nor fully intuit in silence. A Someone who was elusive yet intimately present, mysterious yet charged with love. A Someone I wanted fiercely to know, to adore, to serve, and whose living presence I longed to make visible in the world around me.

When I put down the extra food and stopped overeating, I had no idea where this decision would lead me, no clue as to how deeply or how quickly the desire released in me would eventually change everything in my life, the friends I chose, the values I lived by, the vocation to which I felt drawn.

Early in 1983, less than a year after entering OA, I renewed my baptismal vows. In a ceremony that touched me with wonder, a small group of us stood before the bishop. One by one we knelt before him. Placing his gentle hands on our heads, he prayed that the Holy Spirit would direct and uphold our lives.

I marveled at the prayer. And feared it, too. What if it came true? If the winds of the Holy Spirit continued to blow through me, where might I be sent? What might I feel called to do and to become? Already so much life was erupting within me. Horses had come back to visit me in my dreams. Once I dreamed of riding bareback. It was exciting. Sensual. Scary. I felt contact with the horse through my thighs and my mind, an embrace at once erotic, intellectual, and spiritual. Wrapping my arms around its neck, I knew that, if I dared, I could canter. It was all a matter of courage. Did I dare?

In another dream, I was preparing for an expedition on horseback, led by my godmother. I was sitting down, but suddenly to my astonishment found myself lifted up and astride an enormous horse. I hadn't realized that I'd been sitting on a sleeping horse. Would it be too powerful for me? Maybe.

Would it stay under my control? Probably not. In the dream I already had a little horse of my own which I was able to manage, but it didn't look likely that I could manage this one. It was too big for me. Too big to control.

"Let go and let God," says the twelve-step program. And then, I might add, look out. When the desire for God awakens, when the God who sleeps within you wakes, who knows where the journey will take you?

It was fear that drove me into recovery, but it is love that keeps me there. And there's no going back. I used to think that a saint was someone who had no desires. Now I know otherwise. A saint is someone who knows what he or she most deeply desires and, if need be, can let everything else go. By either definition, I'm no saint. Often I lose touch with what I really long for. I find myself kidnapped again by lesser desires, smaller wants. But at least I can trust now that listening to my deepest desires is a worthy enterprise, even a holy one.

In the years since coming into OA, I have gradually come to know a Power that welcomes my passions, my hunger, and my body; a Power that neither eliminates nor extinguishes desires, but rather transforms them. I have come to know a Power that arouses my desire and brings a subtle and restful order to my life. In my better moments, I simply feel at home. I know I belong here, in this life, that my life is a gift that has been given back to me. Now it's up to me to live it.

Notes

Chapter 2: Angels, Ghosts, and Knives

pages 38–40   Quotes from *Play With Me*: Marie Hall Ets, *Play With Me* (New York: Puffin Books, 1984).

page 55   "During his college years . . .": "Memorial Minute," adopted by the Faculty of Arts and Sciences, Harvard University, April 8, 1986, and printed in *Harvard University Gazette* 81, no. 43 (July 25, 1986), 8.

Chapter 3: Body Language

page 63   "with no expression . . .": Robert Frost, "Desert Places," in *The Poetry of Robert Frost: The Collected Poems*, ed. Edward Connery Lathem (New York: Holt, Rinehart and Winston, 1975), 296.

Chapter 5: Clearing a Space

page 150   "I would prefer not to": Herman Melville, "Bartleby the Scrivener," in *Great Short Works of Herman Melville*, ed. Warner Berthoff (New York: Harper & Row, 1966), 47.

page 156   Quotes from *King Lear*: William Shakespeare, *The Tragedy of King Lear*, ed. Tucker Brooke and William Lyon Phelps (New Haven: Yale University Press, 1967), 80, 73, 73, 71.

page 160   Miller: Alice Miller, *Prisoners of Childhood*, trans. Ruth Ward (New York: Basic Books, 1981).

Chapter 7: Telling Stories

page 181   "The heart's necessity . . .": Archibald MacLeish, "Reasons for Music," in *The Mentor Book of Major American Poets*, ed. Oscar Williams and Edwin Honig (New York: New American Library, 1962), 445.

page 181 ff   Herzen: Alexander Herzen, *My Past and Thoughts: The Memoirs of Alexander Herzen*, 4 vols., trans. Constance Garnett, rev. trans. Humphrey Higgins (New York: Knopf, 1968), 1:17.

Chapter 8: At Sea

page 220   "The world is charged . . .": Gerard Manley Hopkins, "God's Grandeur," in *Modern Poetry*, 2nd ed., ed. Maynard Mack, Leonard Dean, and William Frost, vol. 7 of *English Masterpieces: An Anthology of Imaginative Literature from Chaucer to T. S. Eliot*, gen. ed. Maynard Mack (Englewood Cliffs, N.J.: Prentice Hall, 1961), 31.

page 221   "I caught this morning . . .": Gerard Manley Hopkins, "The Windhover," in ibid., 32.

page 221   "Season of mists . . .": John Keats, "To Autumn," in *Romantic and Victorian Poetry*, 2nd ed., ed. William Frost, vol. 6 of *English Masterpieces: An Anthology of Imaginative Literature from Chaucer to T. S. Eliot*, gen. ed. Maynard Mack (Englewood Cliffs, N.J.: Prentice Hall, 1961), 242.

page 222   "Tell all the Truth . . .": Emily Dickinson, "Tell all the Truth," in *The Poems of Emily Dickinson*, ed. Thomas H. Johnson (Cambridge, Mass.: The Belknap Press of Harvard University Press, 1983).